BREAKING FREE OF NEHRU

BREAKING FREE OF NEHRU
Lets Unleash India!

Sanjeev Sabhlok

ANTHEM PRESS
LONDON • NEW YORK • DELHI

ANTHEM PRESS
An imprint of Wimbledon Publishing Company
www.anthempress.com

This edition first published in India 2008
by ANTHEM PRESS
C-49 Kalkaji, New Delhi 110019, India
75–76 Blackfriars Road, London SE1 8HA, UK
or PO Box 9779, London SW19 7ZG, UK
244 Madison Ave. #116, New York, NY 10016, USA

1 3 5 7 9 10 8 6 4 2

ISBN-13: 978 81 905835 8 9

Printed at Sadhana Press Pvt. Ltd.
200 B B Ganguly Street, Kolkata - 700 012, W B, India

Dedication

This book is dedicated to:

- *your* success;
- your *family's* success;
- your *country's* success; and
- the success of *everyone on Earth.*

Dedicated most importantly,
to your freedom to *think* and to *be.*

Contents

Acknowledgements

> So long as the millions live in hunger and ignorance, I hold every man a traitor, who having been educated at their expense, pays not the least heed to them.
>
> Vivekananda[1]

I would like to acknowledge and thank the following people, listed in no particular order, for their influence or role either in shaping my thought or in helping me with this book.

First, I want to thank my family including my parents (Prem Kumar Sabhlok and Adarsh Sabhlok) and siblings (Rashmi Mehta and Rajeev Sabhlok), my arguments and debates with whom have shaped my world view. Without these discussions and the ready availability of a range of books at home, the principles of ethical liberalism may not have found fertile ground in my mind. I am also grateful to my wife Smita for suffering me for well over two decades and not going insane despite my temperamental excesses, and my children Sukrit and Prateeti for suffering (quite happily, if I may add) my neglect of their studies while writing this book.

Second, I am greatly indebted to my fellow thinkers and 'believers' including eminent liberals whose work in bringing the ideas of freedom to the people of India has been an inspiration; among them, I would like to mention Gurcharan Das, Dr Parth Shah, Bibek Debroy, Barun Mitra, Madhu Kishwar, Dr Nirvikar Singh, Sharad Joshi, Dr Jayaprakash Narayan, Sauvik Chakraverti and S V Raju, in no particular order. Among them, I'd like to thank Gurcharan Das and Parth Shah, in particular, for their encouragement and support during the writing of this book. I'd also like to thank those Indians or people of Indian origin from across the world who have supported a range of my policy or political enterprises since 1998. I trust they found at least some value in engaging in our common activities while these lasted. I take the lion's share of responsibility for the failure to continue my initial spurt of work, largely on account of my developing an extremely painful condition (Repetitive Strain Injury or RSI) from typing for up to 16 hours a day without appropriate care or precaution in late 1998 – a problem that is still with me despite years of intensive treatment.

Third, I want to acknowledge my critics and helpers. I would particularly like to thank Suresh Anand, a retired senior public servant from Hong Kong and also my cousin and mentor, for supporting my activities over the years and guiding me in many ways. Drafts prior to 15 April 2007 were informed by extensive comments from Suresh. Gavan O'Farrell and Manish Jaggi also commented. From 15 April 2007, I made the draft manuscript available on the internet. Subsequent drafts were informed by comments from a wide range of people from across the world. I'd particularly like to thank Suresh for his invaluable comments and also Capt. Surya Pullat, Sriram Natarajan, Dr Anil Chawla, Vandana Jaggi and Smita. Chapter 5 has particularly benefited from the comments of Professor Alasdair Roberts of the Maxwell School of Citizenship and Public Affairs at Syracuse University and Professor John Halligan of the School of Business and Government at the University of Canberra.

Fourth, I am indebted to my teachers and colleagues, in particular Professor Michael Magill of the University of Southern California for bringing home to me during his lectures the simplicity and beauty of the price system. He also introduced me (as part of his class) to Hayek's paper of 1945,[2] a paper that summarizes, to my mind, the entire useful information in the discipline of economics. I'd like to thank Gokul Patnaik and Dr Atindra Sen, civil servants, for being exemplars and role models through their dedication to knowledge, openness of mind and personal character.

Fifth, I express my gratitude to my therapists and injury managers – in particular, the technical geniuses behind the development of *Dragon Naturally Speaking* software (hat's off to them!) which, since early 2002, brought a ray of hope into my life and by now has become the mainstay of my 'writing' (dictating) both at work and at home. This book was almost entirely dictated using this software. I also acknowledge my extreme debt of gratitude to Peter Prskalo, my myotherapist. Had someone told me during my particularly bleak days of 2000–2 that I might be able to actually write a book in a few years' time, I wouldn't have believed it, being unable at that stage even to type or even write with a pen a short paragraph, or sign my name, or lift a small bag of groceries, without experiencing excruciating pain and numbness. To Peter's work must also go most of the credit for reviving me from what, in retrospect, was surely a depressive state of mind. I have supplemented Peter's therapy with Pilates, Yoga and swimming. I have been fortunate to learn about Yoga from teachers like Adrianne Cook who is sprightly fit at 80 plus, and Chitra Stern.

There are many others naming whom individually would convert this book into a telephone directory. They also include those who have exercised great influence on me without ever having known me, namely writers, both living and dead, of books written across the ages. I'd like to mention just three names to keep this brief – Ayn Rand, Milton Friedman and Julian Simon.

I take full responsibility for all errors found in this book, particularly given that this has been produced in bits and moments snatched from a busy full-time job. Finally, a disclaimer: my views are not to be taken as *in any way* representing the views of organizations I have worked for either in India or in Australia. Finally, given my intention to revise this book in the future, I seek your questions, suggestions and comments at sabhlok@yahoo.com.

Sanjeev Sabhlok[3]
Melbourne, Australia

1 May 2008

Preface

> Nehru was the best leader we have had in independent India's government. It has been an even more downhill journey ever since.
>
> Chapter 3 of this book.

This is a book about changing India. About setting us free. This is a book about restoring our values and our national character. A book about making India a great place to bring up our children. More a pamphlet than a book, this is a conversation between one Indian and another, an attempt to discuss what we have lost by letting socialists trample on our country's ancient genius and moral character for 60 years; and to explore what it will take to bring back India to the right path – of freedom – and then take it to a tryst with true greatness.

Despite progress made by India over the past six decades, Pranab Bardhan has argued that India is now effectively a failed state. One can't agree fully with such a characterization, for India won't implode – even if Indian governments can't seem to provide the fundamental services for which they are elected: things like law and order, justice, and infrastructure. But the underlying concern repeatedly raised by many commentators is quite legitimate. India's future success will hinge critically on whether it takes such concerns on board.

The message is thus clear: India's governance must be reformed. This book illuminates a path to such a reformed and much better India. It uses proven ways of thinking and analysis to suggest solutions that will make India tremendously more prosperous even as it will lead the world in ethical values.

While this book's message is very important, I must hasten to add at the outset that I have absolutely nothing new to say. I am promoting old, well tried out but very successful ideas. Even though these ideas are old, they do enable everything new and innovative to arise. Nothing else comes even close to fostering innovation as these old ideas of liberty and freedom do. Evidence of the success of the ideas I will promote in this work abounds in hundreds of books and thousands of research studies. The truth of these ideas is evident in the easily observable difference between the performance of India and any free nation on virtually any indicator of well-being. Scores of major thinkers have already said, over hundreds of years, what I will say in this book. If you know and understand what Socrates, Voltaire, Adam Smith, J S Mill, Frédéric Bastiat, Ayn Rand, Milton Friedman, Friedrich Hayek, Julian Simon, Rajaji, Minoo Masani and Gurcharan Das have said; and if you understand the details of how governance systems function in free countries, then you know exactly what I am going to say. In that case you should go straight to the final comments of this book and start upon a different journey; you don't need to read this book.

But despite these old ideas being widely known I felt there was a really urgent need for me to write this book to integrate and clarify some of these ancient arguments, but most importantly, to tailor these ideas to our times. Ideas do not exist in the ether. They have to be meaningful in a real context – they must be things we can relate to. This book gives freedom a foundation in India.

The main news I have for you is that freedom works. The functioning of successful Western nations such as USA, Australia and UK, and of successful eastern nations such as Japan, Singapore, Hong Kong, South Korea and Taiwan is informed by the simple model of freedom: *Let the government provide justice, infrastructure and security, and let people do their own thing.*

On the other hand, the other headline I have for you is that India chose the failed and disastrous model of socialism, a model that *only* failed countries have followed so far, such as the erstwhile USSR and its satellite states, North Korea and Cuba. We are no longer obliged to follow the worst ideas of mankind, just because Nehru and his followers advocated them.

The real choice before us today is between the two western models of governance – socialism or capitalism; between the life-denying concept of *equality* and the life-sustaining concept of *freedom*. Even if we don't care about the philosophy of freedom, pragmatism would lead us to the more successful model. Capitalism is dramatically successful, just as socialism is dramatically unsuccessful.

But there are far more important and compelling reasons to follow the path of freedom. Of these, delivering a society based on ethics and morality ranks the highest. Despite the noble intentions of its practitioners, socialism is immoral and destroys the moral fabric of entire societies. Freedom, on the other hand, delivers the highest ethical values and creates for each individual a level playing field by providing *equality of opportunity* through which the individual is enabled to discover his or her talents and achieve his or her highest potential. While the *individual* is the moral centre of a free society, the *society* is the immoral centre of a socialist one. Freedom is about far more important things than economic success, although a poor country like India should welcome its merits on that ground alone.

Before I get started with my project to change India, let me pause for a moment to tell you a few things pertaining to the background of the book, such as about its title and its style. About its style first.

STYLE AND STANCE

One of my friends who read parts of an earlier draft of this book suggested I should try to be less strident about changing India and be a bit more hospitable towards my readers. He said that I must recognize that they are investing their valuable time in reading this book expecting to find something of genuine value. They will not be persuaded merely by my enthusiasm and excitement about India's great future. I must invite them into this book and sketch out first what they can expect to find here.

That was sound advice. In the early drafts of this book I was so intent on getting my message across that I almost forgot that the message was meant for you! I had to get this book off my chest first; to that extent, I had no choice but to just write it! But I was obviously trying to communicate something to someone, somewhere. I just needed to pause and review what I was doing, like an artist must sometimes pause and step back from his painting.

In my mind's eye I had no doubt that you and I would ultimately find each other. I was then going to spend my time in persuading *you – and you alone* – to think like me! My wise friend's advice was that I should recognize your existence as the *only* reason for this book. The most beautiful mountain cannot exist without a beholder. No book can exist without a reader; books are not written for stones and plants. I have written this book to move *you* into action!

Yes … that's right! This book is purely meant for *you.* And so, hello and welcome to a journey across India's rugged political, economic and social landscape. In this book I will show you how we are badly underperforming today, and then show you how we, *together*, can take India to the plane of freedom and greatness it has never visualized before.

As I thought more about my friends' advice, it became clearer to me that I couldn't really follow it completely. If I were to implement my friend's suggestion to become less strident, I would have to literally throw away this book. I would either have to write a technical academic book summarizing the key mathematical theorems and proofs that underpin the arguments of this book – in which case most of my intended audience wouldn't touch it with a barge pole. Or I could try to be more hospitable throughout the book by telling you lots of interesting anecdotes. But then this book would go into double its number of pages, for hospitality takes time; chatting takes pages. Most problematically, if I were not to be strident, this book would lose its urgency and I would lose all motivation for writing it. I want to see change. I want you to do something after reading this book. Else I have no reason to write it at all and should rather go and lie down in the sun.

And so I stepped back from the second recommendation. I said to myself that while this book is undoubtedly very strident, what else should a book be which has set as its *sole* mission the goal to change India? This book, as I said, is less of a book and more like a political pamphlet of times gone by. It doesn't have an ordinary book's ambition to enchant and dazzle, to intrigue and mystify or to otherwise lose its reader in a make-believe world of fairies or of lovers eloping through the window at night using a rolled-up bed sheet as rope under the full moon, with misty and dreamy clouds glistening in the sky. Mystery, romance, action – none of these is on offer. This is actually non-fiction! But I also believe that this non-fiction is *far* more important for everyone in India to read than the next great novel on the exploits of the British officers in the early years of the Raj. My message, I was convinced, is *too important* to be said in either a technical or a chatty manner. I decided I would probably have to remain strident!

I also then realized that I had a massive challenge ahead of me, an almost impossible task, of somehow first making you read this preface and then the book. But I consoled myself that if I can at least find just one other reader (other than myself!) I would be benefited. That would set up a chain reaction and everyone in India would then read this book. After all, everyone else is only *one* other reader – if you know what I mean! I argued that the best way I could find one more reader was to be myself, to be true to myself, to speak my mind. To be strident if necessary, even annoying; to be exciting in the way that only I can be exciting; to paint a picture of the lovely free India of tomorrow in the way that only I can. And to lay bare my soul for you to see into it, so you can build some trust in what I am saying.

And having thus mulled over the practicability and implications of my friend's suggestions, I have decided on two things: one, that I will definitely try to be a little bit more hospitable in this book, and to engage with you a bit more than I would have otherwise done. Two, I will also get my stridency down by one notch. For instance, I had called Marx a devil in an early draft; I had called politicians murderers, not just thugs; I had said our bureaucracy is third-rate. I have toned that kind of flowery language down a notch. You can already sense the great effort I have put in to reach out to you. I'm trying my best to be refined, even polished, not like that angry young man in *Deewar*.[2] As a result, politicians have now morphed into ordinary bad buys; Marx has reverted into a terribly mistaken thinker – a confused man with a big beard. Nevertheless, I retain my urgent approach and speak what I think I must. India's problems do not allow me the scope for anything less.

Simultaneously, I decided I'd ask you to indulge me a bit – I mean, in my stridency. Permit yourself some initial bemusement about me since you and I have not met before so you don't know me. Rest assured that none of my stridency is without cause. Give me a chance to be heard, and who knows, you may become strident yourself! In fact, if I could explode a bomb of freedom deep inside your head, my job would be done.

And so I trust that with this mutually agreed position, where you understand that this is not a leisurely love story or exciting melodrama and I understand that I must keep you good company, we are now ready to pack our bags and sandwiches for the journey. Do call out to me loudly by my first name if you need to find me in the thickets as I rush headlong at top hiking speed. Don't worry if you have to skip some dense portions of this book. You can always return to them later. By the end of this journey I hope to have your commitment to undertake yet another, longer journey that you will probably have to undertake on your own. It is that second journey that will transform India.

I'd like to add a couple of other brief notes related to style at this stage. This book was started in February 2005 when I was still an Indian citizen. Since then, things have changed and I am now merely what is called an *overseas Indian citizen*, a lifelong visa holder for Indian residency without voting rights. While writing this book I have therefore managed to bridge two tribal identities, one Indian, the other Australian. This raises a question I often wonder about – how much does one's identity change merely by virtue of holding a different passport? Fortunately I don't watch cricket too much; I would perhaps get confused about which tribal badge to wear in an India–Australia match. But tribal identities take time to mature; even generations. I therefore feel that I am entitled to continue in the same tone I started this book with, namely, as an Indian citizen; even as I grapple with existential debates about identity.

The idea of actually packing up and leaving India permanently never struck me as a *real* possibility till well into 1999, after I had resumed work as a secretary to the Government of Meghalaya upon returning from USA after a doctorate in economics. Even then I tried my best to avoid having to leave India. And as recently as in 2005, four years after my leaving India for Australia, I retained the fond hope that *India* would rise to my expectations. I was not going to lower my standards, I had decided, for the privilege of returning to my country of birth. I said to myself that India had *no choice* but to reform itself and rise to my standards if it wanted me back. But of course India did not care for puny little me! Nothing happened, nothing changed despite my many protests and efforts. The mammoth wheels of corruption continued to grind and crush my motherland's soul while I stood by like an ant in a corner of the globe demanding loudly (with my squeaky voice) that our leaders stop their corruption.

Today, once again, I ask the same question: if India can't let go of its addiction to corruption and shoddy governance, why would any of its children who have abandoned its shores want to return? Does India think it can get its people back for nothing? We who have left in sheer frustration have a soul that deeply cares for India; but it cares for its own integrity even more. We ordinary diaspora want only a few simple things: our dreams are modest – we want a good place to bring up our children.

We do not want to bring up our children in a society obsessed with caste and religion, a society that breathes hatred towards other communities, that engages in corruption first thing in the morning, and that is constantly at war with itself. How hard can it really be to create a free and peaceful country for our children, I ask you?!

This book, which as I said started in February 2005, has been written during seven weeks taken off work and on tens of weekends. It is not as if weekends in Australia are designed for writing. Since only the fabulously rich can afford servants here, activities like cooking, ironing, cleaning, gardening, and so on, leave barely a moment's respite. Why I say this is because if I had kept going at this pathetic rate for ten years, this book may have ultimately become something I may have been pleased with. It would have been clearer and have sparkled with wit. (Yes, even I aim to become a witty person some day.) But delaying its publication for ten years would have made its message potentially obsolete.

In the battle against Evil you sometimes have to enter in a hastily assembled suit of armour not yet polished with Brasso. *Speed is of the essence when the battle is on*! This book, being my one-man assault on Evil found in India, is therefore being launched without my having had time to polish it to my (never achievable, I'm sure) standards. But even if my armour is not shiny and only glints patchily when the sunlight catches it, I do ride an invincible horse. My steed of freedom is sturdy and strong.

The point is, I would really appreciate it if you focus on *what* I have to say, not *how* I say it. In addition, to keep this book down to a manageable size, I have lopped out large chunks of detail from the original draft and consolidated these chunks into *Online Notes to Supplement 'Breaking Free of Nehru'* (referred to henceforth as *Online Notes*). I will cite relevant sections from these notes at appropriate places in the book. These notes are like the extra scenes you get when you buy a DVD. You can download and print these notes freely from the internet.[3]

BIG VERSUS SMALL

I want to change the entire Indian governance system and make it the world's greatest, ever. That is my goal. But surely that's a ridiculous goal to have for a mere individual! I must surely have the common sense to realize that this idea of changing the whole system is silly. People have therefore asked me: 'Shouldn't we all do the right thing in our lives, do our little bit well, do our duty; and the rest will take care of itself? Why should we think so big when we have so many small things to attend to in our daily lives?'

Well, this is it! I'm stopping my banter now, as our journey of discovery has now begun in earnest. I am now going to become all worked up and red-faced while I try to demonstrate to you why, at times, big things must take precedence over the small ones.

But just before I do that, let me tell you a little bit about myself, for that will also tell you why I am so disenchanted. My formative beliefs were made through readings in philosophy during school days in the early 1970s. That led me to rationalism and the scientific attitude as the primary means of inquiring into the truth. I was very young at that time, but I concluded that the behaviour of Indira Gandhi and Sanjay Gandhi during the early 1970s wasn't what we should expect from our leaders. I wasn't into things like socialism and capitalism, but I knew their behaviour wasn't right. On observing the state of the nation preceding the Emergency in 1975, I made a painting[4] to depict my sense of concern with continuing poverty in India despite the *Garibi Hatao* slogan. I was not convinced about the merits of the family planning programme either which led to incursions into people's personal lives by Sanjay Gandhi.

In 1976, after passing out from school, I decided to serve India through the civil service, to which I was recruited in 1982. Unhappy with hordes of officials around me who were corrupt in many ways and also misappropriated money meant for the poor, I developed systems of administration to minimize their opportunities of corruption and diligently investigated the records of projects to confirm that things were being done in the correct manner. I 'trapped' individual corrupt officers wherever possible. I caught (and got jailed) one officer in Dhubri district and a 'revenue' assistant in Barpeta district for taking bribes. Similarly I pursued cases of corruption against Inspectors of Schools while I was Secretary in the Education Department of Assam.

But in all these cases, and in many others too numerous to mention that I came across in my later roles such as Assam's State Enquiry Officer, corrupt officials – even those caught taking bribes red-handed – were quickly reinstated by their corrupt senior officers at the behest of corrupt political bosses or released by corrupt courts. I later also spent a lot of my energy in trying to prevent corrupt ministers from misusing public funds. But in each case they triumphed by replacing me with a more malleable officer, or by otherwise bypassing me.

In the meantime, I also discovered that the poverty alleviation and education policies in place in India were not delivering their intended results at all. I found subsequently, upon reflection, and after considering extensive academic literature as part of my studies in Australia and USA, that our policies were bad policies to begin with. They could never have succeeded. My reflections were not biased by working in, say, badly governed states alone. I have worked in three states: Haryana, Assam and Meghalaya and travelled extensively to other states, and the same things happen everywhere. And at the National Academy of Administration, where I have taught for a while, one gets an overview of administration from all parts of the country. Nothing I had concluded was repudiated by experiences in any part of India. I was confident that my conclusions were valid and well-founded. They applied to the entire country.

Anyway, after 15 years of doing 'small' things on a daily basis, I finally had enough of it. My analysis showed that the problem was clearly systemic. I had to stop wasting my time with individual corrupt officers and ministers who are found below every stone in India. The corruption was being fuelled by ideology which had led to significant misallocation of resources and systemic misgovernance. This fuel had to be choked off, else the fires of corruption would rage endlessly across the country for ever, no matter how many of them I tried to put out. I hope you'll agree that there is no point in fighting a fire while someone is pouring petrol all over it from behind. The smart thing is to shut the petrol off, first. A doctor doesn't waste time on fixing each boil or rash separately, but focuses on analysing just one of them through the microscope to find the cause of all of them. Then he treats the underlying factors and banishes the disease. Killing one mosquito at a time won't fix the problem of malaria. The swamp has to be drained.

I concluded, almost simultaneously, that my role in the Indian Administrative Service (IAS) was indirectly supporting the abysmal poverty and endemic corruption of India. One fine day in mid-1997, while I was pursing my doctorate in Los Angeles, I decided I needed to stop wasting further time on small things and look for ways to fix the big things. My analysis under the microscope showed me millions of socialist bacteria swarming in the brains of Indian leaders and bureaucrats. These were causing the national disease of corruption and poverty.

I'll tell you briefly about what I did at that point – so you understand that I am not an arm-chair intellectual. Book writing of this sort is the last thing on my mind. At first, I didn't plan to be a political leader. Now! Please don't laugh! I'm not a political leader today and won't ever be one now by the looks of things; nor do I have any of the attributes of a charismatic leader. But it is worth reminding ourselves that each one of us has the obligation to train himself to become one, *should that be the need of the hour.* Initially, I actually thought that writing a book may help. So I began in mid-1997 to furiously write a little book during my night shifts as a part-time computer operator at the University of Southern California. The book was on the causes of South Asia's grim failures, but it never got finished.[5]

While I was still working on that book, it dawned upon me in February of 1998 after a conversation with a South Korean fellow student that I really had no choice but to reform India from the top – through political reform. Whether or not I would be successful was immaterial; this was the only way forward. I had no other choice. I resolved to either form or join a political party that would implement the changes I wanted to see in India.[6] I began by designing a little website called *Victory of India Party.*[7] That led in stages to about 200 people coming together on the internet, which led to the establishment of the India Policy Institute[8] in Hyderabad in late 1998. We wrote a *People's Manifesto* – about what an ideal party in India should do. I tried to sell this idea – of starting a new *values and capitalism-based* party in India – at a dinner meeting in mid-1999 of *The Indus Entrepreneurs* to senior executives, mostly of Indian origin, from the IT industry in Silicon Valley. But no support was forthcoming. Indeed, people at that dinner had the weirdest ideas about what was wrong with India.

Next, in 2000 I organized a meeting of five people in Delhi to discuss potential steps to form a liberal political party in India; nothing came of it. I therefore left India, disheartened, aware that things weren't going to be easy at all. Also, I had by then lost the capacity to type (write) due to severe repetitive strain injury. As it turned out, leaving India was one of the best decisions in my life. My consequent exposure to the inner workings of a first rate governance system in Australia has been absolutely invaluable. No PhD or reading any amount of books can possibly substitute for the real feel and understanding of what actually happens inside a world-class government, and particularly, how dramatically it differs from India's system of misgovernance. Both are Westminster style democracies, but goodness me! What a difference in their performance.

Despite severe physical limitations, I tried to keep things moving. In January 2004 I organized and led discussions in a one-week workshop in Delhi of about 20 eminent people from all over India to consider a liberal political strategy for India. That led to my joining the Swatantra Bharat Party (SBP) of Sharad Joshi. We got one MP elected to the Rajya Sabha – Mr Joshi himself. This book was started in Feburary 2005 to support that effort. However, my involvement in that effort ended in a little after a year of my joining the SBP for reasons I'll elaborate some day.[9] After I left the SBP in May 2005, I started the Liberal Party of India, which I see as my third political attempt.[10] A handful of people signed up. I needed at least fifty people. On failing to raise fifty supporters of freedom, I decided to stop further political work but to finish this book, nevertheless. The original book has split into two books now, this one being the first of the two. I'm still working on its sister volume tentatively entitled, *The Discovery of Freedom.*

This book therefore stands loose from its original moorings and ambitions. I have failed. I have failed to change India. I have failed to persuade enough people to come together on a values and freedom-based platform. I have nevertheless learnt a lot from these failures, and this book, written after my initial experiments were completed, reflects some of those learnings. Much wiser now, I don't expect much, but I must nevertheless pass on my key message.

As you will note, I am not into politics, but into greatness – I mean India's greatness, not mine! While politics is said to be the art of the possible, a country's greatness must surely be the art of the impossible. I have set my eyes only on that task. Nothing less than a truly great India will meet my expectations. Even if this vision is not delivered in my lifetime, or not delivered at all, I cannot aspire for anything less. We do not serve our nation or our future generations well if we do not steadfastly uphold the highest possible aspirations. Living with rubbish heaps, corrupt politicians and potholed roads is not an option; not, at least, for me.

A stalemate now prevails in my relationship with my country of birth: the country that brought me up and educated me. I am a stubborn Indian, unwilling to sign off my soul to my corruption-infested and shackled motherland. I am not a paragon of virtue by any means – simply a person of normal prudence with a clean conscience. Neither do I demand to live only amongst angels. But India is so abysmally unethical that it is impossible to live there now.

In the *Ramayana*, there is this very ethical and loyal gentleman, Hanuman, who carried the entire mountain of Dronagiri along with its s*anjivani buti* to revive Ram's brother, Lakshman. Today (metaphorically and melodramatically speaking!), I bring this very same *buti* – the life saving herb after which I get my name 'Sanjeev' – through this book, to save India. If Hanuman could move mountains, then surely we mortals can uproot India's 'mountains' of corruption and throw them far into the sea! What a splash they'll make as they sink to the bottom of *Patal*.[11]

Even if we fail, we must try. I don't see any point in wasting our time trying to clean one dirty pebble at a time by fighting each individual corrupt officer or minister. Let us hose the whole lot at one go with the River of Freedom. I am not concerned about my past failures; after all, changing human systems is not renowned to be an easy thing to do. But I am more convinced than ever before that this reform is needed in India, and that it *can* be done. This book will show you how to do it.

BUT WHY BRING NEHRU INTO THE PICTURE?

This book's title implicates Nehru. It asks us to break free of Nehru. If the title of this book has piqued your curiosity, or if you are vehemently opposed to the title, then, if nothing else, this book will provide you with some food for thought. I haven't given this book its title casually or without thought. I know about the hallowed place that Nehru commands in the Indian pantheon of heroes, and I too hold him in high esteem in many ways.

So why have I felt it necessary to set him up as the leitmotif of this book around which it finds a coherent story? Surely I could have avoided alienating a large part of India's populace by not choosing such a divisive title. Half of India's population might not read this book simply because of its title. In fact, a friend told me that Indian Government libraries probably won't buy this book because of its title either. My labours would therefore have been in vain, losing large chunks of my audience.

But we must speak the Truth. Obfuscation is not my style. To my mind, this title speaks best for my message. In fact, this book had started with a harmless title, *A Short History of Freedom*, but once I clarified my thoughts and split the original book into two, this title emerged inevitably. I must therefore retain this title no matter how divisive, for it best represents the fact that Nehru played the key role in designing India's system of socialist governance. Nehru was, at times, a severely mistaken genius, whose errors of judgement have cost us very dearly. The facts must be allowed to speak. Let me summarize my arguments.

To start with, a quick clarification: this is not a book about Nehru. I have only a modest interest in historical meanderings or biographies. If I have time, I prefer to dig up my garden or go for a walk among the trees rather than read, let alone write, biographies.

Next, this book does not pick on Nehru for the sake of picking on him. This book is by no means an irreverent and rabid attempt to undermine the enormous contributions of Jawaharlal Nehru and the goodness he represented. However, I attribute our country's poor performance in large measure to him. While Nehru should be honoured and be given immense credit for things he did well, equally, he is also accountable for his failures and misjudgements.

I mentioned earlier that it is impossible to fight corruption when the system is pouring huge quantities of petrol to fuel the fires of corruption. Nehru was without doubt an exceptionally fine person. However, the system of governance he designed, his socialism, created disastrous consequences all around for 60 years, consequences that cannot, unfortunately, be wished away. His was a great personal misjudgement; we must recognize that misjudgement, note that we should break free of it and then change direction to the right path.

Two views exist on Nehru: one, which finds Nehru completely redundant to us today; the other, which regards him very highly and finds him extremely relevant. This book's title will appear outdated to those among you who have long 'broken free' of Nehru's socialist legacy. You may wonder why a book has to be written on a historical curiosity as this. I do accept that the changes to India's economic policy that have taken place since 1991 have left parts of Nehru's legacy in the dust. But if breaking free of Nehru were merely a matter of economic policy change, I would not have needed to bother with writing this book, leave alone resigning from the IAS or attempting to form a liberal party in India. Economic policy had changed in 1991, well before I decided I could no longer support the Indian system. We make a great mistake if we think India has broken free of Nehru. We have an enormous deficit of freedom that we cannot even begin to fathom. This book is not about copycat IMF-type policies, but about freedom. I believe my message is relevant.

For others, who regard Nehru very highly and do not want to hear one word said against him, let me assure you that this book is not disrespectful of Nehru. One can have a strong difference of opinion with someone without disrespecting him. Many of us feel deep admiration towards Nehru almost verging on veneration; I am almost there myself, holding Nehru in high esteem for a number of things he did. I also agree with some readers of earlier drafts of this book who pointed out that Nehru faced difficult circumstances. There was little support for India across the world in his time, and little faith in India's capacities; racism and political cold wars raged. There is absolutely no doubt that Nehru made outstanding contributions to India.

The greatest of these were his contributions to India's independence. The nine years he spent in jail were a very heavy price to pay for his dreams for India. I applaud and honour Nehru for his sterling role in helping India obtain independence. Secondly, his contributions to Indian democracy were phenomenal. I admire his deep faith in and hope for democracy in this vast, illiterate land; a faith that none else held in the world as strongly as he did. He played a pivotal role in our adoption of democracy. As Raj Mohan Gandhi wrote, 'As Prime Minister for seventeen years he [Nehru] strove hard to coach Chief Ministers, MPs, MLAs and the masses in the norms of democracy. The letters he wrote to the Chief Ministers almost every fortnight are for the most part lessons in democratic procedure'.[12] The roots of the democracy Nehru fostered have spread deep into the far reaches of the Indian psyche. This is something to be very proud of as a nation. As Pranab Bardhan points out, 'democracy [...] has spread out to the remote reaches of this far-flung country in ever-widening circles of political awareness and self-assertion of hitherto subordinate groups'.[13] This awareness among our peoples of their democratic privileges and powers has enabled our governments to acquire an enormous – and historically unprecedented – legitimacy, a legitimacy which provides India with unprecedented stability in comparison to, say, Pakistan. I applaud and honour Nehru for his role in establishing Indian democracy. Finally, Nehru went out of his way to promote science and rationalism, two things extremely dear to my heart. I applaud and honour Nehru for his role in Indian science and his quest for reason.

These contributions would have been sufficient for anyone to be hailed as a national hero; and so Nehru remains one, and will ever remain. For all these things, and many more, Nehru must be admired, praised and remembered.

But we must pause to ask: what could possibly have gone so wrong that despite Nehru's relentless efforts and leadership, India continued to perform miserably on many fronts for decades, and has now gained global notoriety as one of the world's most corrupt nations? For, were not most of our systems and practices put in place during Nehru's time? He had nearly 17 years to kick-start India's march towards freedom and prosperity. That is nearly one-third of all the time we have had since independence, and easily our most crucial years. So why did the system he designed lead to such poor outcomes? Was the system unworkable, or was the implementation of the system bad? Since he had responsibility both for the design as well as for the implementation of our governance system, we can't help surmising that the primary responsibility for things not working out as well as they should have must fall squarely on him and his followers.

And yet, despite incontrovertible evidence that Nehru's ideas on governance proved very bad for us, we do not like someone as respected as Nehru being criticized. Because if someone is a hero he is expected to be perfect. He is not supposed to have any flaws in his thinking. We also believe, as Vivekananda pointed out, that we should 'criticise no one, for all doctrines have some good in them'.[14] In India we put garlands around the necks even of those with whom we fully disagree: every soul must be respected. A reader of an earlier draft of this book made an interesting comment in this regard, in relation to Amartya Sen's recent book entitled, *The Argumentative Indian.* This reader wondered whether Indians are both argumentative and uncritical. I think that is quite plausible. We argue a lot on grounds of caste, religion, place of birth, and race; or on the basis of our 'gut feel' for issues; and then we suddenly bow our heads before everyone who is dead, irrespective of what they said or did. We do not undertake the concept of critical thinking and analysis. We do not talk dispassionately about the facts. We are obsequious towards our leaders, not wanting to question them.

Be that as it may, I have taken the time to critically enquire into the paradox of India's corruption and poverty despite Nehru's unquestionably good intentions, and I must necessarily give my book the title it has.

Some of us would prefer to attribute India's failures to Nehru's daughter Indira Gandhi, or maybe to someone other than Nehru. But I have clearly traced India's failures in governance to the roots. I find Nehru is the source; others merely followed what he established. I will clearly show in this book how the systems Nehru designed for us were unworkable and could never have delivered their intended outcomes.

Further, Nehru is particularly important to this book because it is his policies which, to a great extent, encumbered the progression trajectory of our country. At a fundamental level this is a book about India's freedom. It says that we need to break free of Nehru in order to restore our freedoms. To become free. To be unleashed. Not because we dislike Nehru in any way. Freedom in the abstract may not sound important enough, or even relevant, as we spend our daily energies fuming over the chronic problems of misgovernance, corruption, poverty and a seemingly excessive population. But it is this freedom that we need more than anything else today in India. This intangible but crucial dimension, not commonly factored into our decisions and discussions, is the missing ingredient that will deliver the final blows of death to poverty and corruption, and create an unprecedented equality of opportunity in India. To acquire an understanding of this missing ingredient in our policy we must first find out where we stand in relation to freedom today, and having done that, determine where we should go next. And each time we analyse the facts we discover that Nehru deliberately and consciously blocked our freedom.

The primary requirement of freedom is that people should be left free to do whatever they wish to do, or can do, on their own initiative. A government should intervene only when it is essential that it do so, as in the provision of security, law and order, justice, some infrastructure and equality of opportunity. Going beyond this minimal support, and using people's hard earned money, namely taxes, to set up bread or shirt businesses to be operated by the government, which will invariably be inefficient and non-competitive – thus destroying both our wealth and opportunities – is not the way of freedom. Seizing people's lands and property in order to redistribute them, *à la* Robin Hood; preventing people from establishing their own businesses; laying down barriers to people's creative power and free movement and commerce, is not the way of freedom. But all these are among the things that Nehru's own regime did. He set up processes to systematically block our freedoms. Preserving our freedoms was never his priority.

Nehru's eminently laudable goal was to bring about rapid economic growth in India. But his chosen method was to directly take this task upon his government. He stopped people from undertaking their livelihood so that he could use our money to drive buses, to bake bread and to stitch shirts. He thought that if the government became the entrepreneur, and achieved commanding heights of the economy, then he could push India's growth to the zenith. We citizens were apparently fools who could not run our businesses by ourselves. We needed arrogant IAS officers who had never touched a screwdriver in their lives or sold a banana to run them for us.

After that, his system would apparently produce all the wealth India needed which he could then redistribute and spoon-feed us (having tied our hands behind our backs), setting everything right! Whether anyone became less free as part of his frantic ambition did not matter. Freedom, the means, the very reason for our independence, could be sacrificed if the ends of growth and poverty alleviation were somehow achieved.

Nehru's intentions were surely good in the sense that he wanted India to become a more prosperous country. Growth and poverty alleviation are good things to aspire for. Where Nehru was totally wrong, though, was in his approach to achieving these goals. And yet, in the final reckoning, the means must surely be at least as important as the ends. Destroying our freedom on the pretext of speeding our journey to prosperity is wrong. We would rather be poor but free, than rich but shackled.

But most ironically, Nehru simply could never have achieved his ends by destroying our freedoms. Wealth isn't created but destroyed when governments become entrepreneurs. Such an ambition is in stark opposition to the logic that drives the creation of the wealth of nations. Wealth creation depends on our voluntary choice and independent action as elaborated in 1776 by Adam Smith.[15] It is only freedom that leads to prosperity, not being shackled.

And therefore, the very opposite of Nehru's ambitions came to pass: India's productivity plummeted; production fell; infrastructure bottlenecks became chronic; we never managed to get even basic things like electricity continuously for an hour on hot summer nights. Our population remained illiterate and poor. It also kept growing in size – for poverty breeds desperation, and desperation breeds children.[16] Millions of innocent lives were created and blighted in our so-called 'free' India. Millions of innocents were forced to live and to die in hunger, poverty, squalor and disease: all because of Nehru's policies. Sriram Natarajan, a reader, suggested that we could compute these virtual lives lost in some manner. That would be an interesting area for future research. Large but well-educated populations are never a problem. However, ours is a large and illiterate population now. There are good reasons for seeing this as a problem even though one can never think of any other human being as a problem except when issues of individual accountability arise with a particular person.

Since Nehru's path led to economic stagnation rather than to wealth, we are compelled to critique some of Nehru's contributions and, where necessary, break free of his legacy. Only to that extent, no more than that.

The decline started when Nehru failed to abide by Gandhi's fundamental message – *if we pay importance to the means, the ends will take care of themselves.* Nehru's should have said, 'Let Indian citizens follow the path of freedom and truth; let our natural genius blossom and create hitherto unseen value'. He could have seen himself as a facilitator and enabler, encouraging people to achieve their highest potential and providing everyone with security, infrastructure and equality of opportunity.

I have a nagging sense that a possible failure of character explains Nehru's propensity to curtail the freedoms of the Indian people. Is it possible that his style arises from an arrogant belief that only he knew about the needs and capacities of the so-called 'common man' in India, more than what the common man knew for himself? I ask this because Indian elites, many of whom have achieved world-class standards of arrogance, have similar beliefs. For apparently, the Indian voter, the person who somehow manages to survive in conditions that would kill an ordinary member of the Indian 'elite' within a week, and who manages to raise his or her children despite extreme privation, is 'not mature enough', and 'doesn't know what is good for himself or herself'. We middle and upper class people who have shown ourselves to be intellectually bankrupt and incapable of providing competent governance, arrogate to ourselves a paternalistic ability to make our poorer fellow citizens' day-to-day decisions on their behalf. This is a common failure of character of Indian elites – was Nehru also privy to that?

As Nehru was the single most powerful source of socialism in India since the 1930s, with his emotionally charged glorification of its alleged successes and relentless implementation of its principles, to him must go the credit of being the Messiah of Indian Socialism. Nehru influenced an entire epoch, one that is still under way. All things that have happened in India under socialist design since independence are Nehruvian, therefore Nehru is the most apt symbol of India's first 60 years since independence.

In fact, there never was a significant political discourse on freedom in India. But whatever little discussion started with Rajaji's Swatantra Party was nipped in the bud by Nehru and remains nipped till today. Indeed, by the time Nehru left the scene, we had forgotten why we wanted to be independent in the first place! So much so, that if today I were to state the obvious, that freedom stands for the subordination of the state to the individual, implying that the state (government) is our servant whom we pay to protect us and to provide us with justice, I am likely to be met by an astonished sense of surprise, even bewilderment.

Nehru made the government so important and so large in our lives that it has now become our (modern) God. So how could I – a mere nobody – argue in favour of its getting demoted to becoming our servant? Nehru's legacy undoubtedly lives on long after his death. His socialist way of thought flourishes today as never before, weak-kneed Indian liberalization notwithstanding. And so, wherever Nehru himself did not create socialist policies, his successors stepped in and made his policies 'sharper'.

We must classify Nehru's followers as his socialist godchildren. They include not only his daughter and his grandchildren but also his political contemporaries (except for the Swatantra Party) and his political successors like the Bharatiya Janata Party (BJP), Congress (I) and, of course, communists of various shades; all Nehruvians, every single one of them. We can hear the echoes of Nehru's voice in all their conversations and actions. They talk of self-sufficiency, of the mixed economy (whatever that mixture produces[17]), and 'liberalization with a human face' (what did *that* ever mean; does freedom not *always* have the most beautiful human face?). Senior members of Nehru's own political party, such as the staunch defender of socialism, Mr P Chidambaram, continue to allude to the relevance of socialist goals while even pointing out the serious failures of their own Congress Party over the past 60 years.[18] And, of course, the BJP (and its predecessor Jana Sangha) and the communists have invariably followed or supported most of Nehru's policies.

You'll never ever hear even one of his godchildren talking about freedom. That never strikes them as the most fundamental issue in a society. Barring exceptional voices like Rajaji and Masani, no one ever spoke of freedom in our Parliament. Freedom was already lost in the wilderness well before independence. No one went out in its search after the British left India. No leader tells us today that their policies are designed purely to preserve our freedoms. That is the nub of the problem that India faces today – that Nehru's victory over our minds is so total and complete that we only think of trivial, second order issues such as economic development. We have never cared to go back to the basics to look for the main reason why we wished to be independent; or even why we wish to live at all!

Little do Nehru's godchildren realize that freedom, with equality of opportunity which includes the elimination of poverty and provision of school education, is the *finest human face*, being both just and justly compassionate. Only societies that are underpinned by freedom and hence by justice have the capacity, through wealth generation, of displaying compassion and providing everyone with equal opportunity. All the socialism in the world cannot bring about even the most basic outcomes – of justice, of education for all, and of the elimination of poverty.

I suspect that we are so 'well-tutored' now, and cast so well into a collectivist and socialist mould, that apart from the Indian flag, cricket and Bollywood, the only other thing that binds us together is socialism. And so, if I were to question the 'good' feeling most of us get by chanting the mantra of socialism in our sleep, would that not destroy India? That is the kind of burden placed on my fragile shoulders as I attempt to pierce the veil of Nehru's legacy and restore us to the path of freedom that we never got to step on till today.

But of this I have no doubt that India desperately needs to break free of Nehru's socialist legacy. Nothing can override our freedom to determine our life for ourselves and to engage in voluntary transactions and agreements with each other. Our government must step in only to assist us in securing justice when we fail to work things out to our mutual satisfaction. Getting on to the straight and narrow path of freedom is the only way to achieving greatness for India. Only then will we be able to genuinely say, *Mera Bharat Mahaan*!

Please note once again that nowhere in this book do I ask to abandon Nehru as a person; all I ask is that we discard his ideas of socialism which were seriously problematic. By no stretch of the imagination was Nehru a Lenin or Stalin that we should 'topple' him from the iconic position he holds. He was truly an honourable man; of that let none have any doubt – the greatest Prime Minister of India so far. We must retain his statues and everything named after him, honour him for the good he did and follow the democratic traditions he established. We should celebrate his birthday as Children's Day and adopt his path of scientific rationalism. But even honourable men can make profound errors of judgement. We must therefore break free of Nehru not by casting Nehru aside, but by casting out the socialism he preached.

Interestingly, there is some evidence that Nehru may have chosen to do things differently had he acquired some more personal knowledge.

There seemed to be moments in his life when he seemed amenable to considering a more pragmatic view; pragmatism perhaps of the sort shown by Deng Xiaoping who said, 'Whether a cat is black or white makes no difference. As long as it catches mice, it is a good cat'. While pragmatism is never the way of freedom, at least it has the merit of demonstrating open-mindedness. Dr V K R V Rao reported on one such instance in his *A Study of Nehru.* According to him, Nehru once said: 'It is not a question of the theory of communism, or socialism or capitalism. It is a question of hard fact. In India, if we do not ultimately solve the basic problems of our country [...] it will not matter whether we call ourselves capitalists, socialists, communists or anything else'. Regrettably, Nehru never found the time to examine the hard facts and to arrive at the correct conclusions regarding the methods by which to solve India's many problems.

In any event, what has happened is water under the bridge. It is now time to learn and to move on. And so this book is not focused on Nehru but on India's future. That is what excites me. That is what makes me dictate and type this book through incessant physical pain.

THE DEBATE OUR GENERATION NEEDS TO HAVE

Enough of this post mortem now. Could we fix our country, please, and give socialism a public burial? Getting rid of the word 'socialist' from our Constitution's Preamble would be a good start, despite the convoluted logic offered by the Supreme Court on 8 January 2008 in response to a recent public interest petition. In allowing this word to continue in the Preamble, a three-judge Bench headed by Chief Justice K G Balakrishnan ruled on 8 January 2008 that 'In broader sense, it [socialism] means welfare measures for the citizens.'[19] This is bizarre. It would seem that the Court either did not consider the issue adequately, or is too timid to upset the apple cart. For nowhere in the literature of the world is socialism used in such a general sense. Indeed, in 1976, when Indira Gandhi introduced this word in the Preamble, she meant it purely in the ideological sense that Nehru had spoken about it all his life and based all his policies upon. It was explicitly meant in the sense that Marx and Lenin intended it; even the Fabian use of this word completely opposes liberty as it gives the state primacy over the individual. This word is an interloper and yet the Court couldn't recognize it! This, unfortunately, is not atypical of the Court's performance in the past 60 years when it has allowed numerous actions opposed to freedom to pass through its gaze.

In the end, freedom is too important an issue to be left to economists or political thinkers, or even the Supreme Court. We need to start thinking about it, each of us, and ask that if we were once again in 1947 what would we have done differently to become truly free and successful? Fresh thinking of this sort is going to be hard. Bombarded for decades by socialistic sermons and statist[20] perspectives that inform most of the writings in our press and media, millions of neurons have now been laid inside our head in a 'socialist pattern'. It will be very hard for us to allow new patterns of thought to compete with our hardwired negative emotional response to capitalism. But we should try, if for nothing else but to rekindle our tryst with destiny that Nehru so eloquently promised us but failed to deliver.

The good thing is we have already left parts of Nehru's legacy behind us. Rajiv Gandhi started this process in 1984. He was a middle-of-the-road thinker – not believing in, nor committed to anything. That did help a bit (though being without deep-rooted beliefs is not a trait to be recommended in our Prime Ministers). He allowed new technology to reach India almost as quickly as it was being invented elsewhere in the world, even as customs duties remained sky high. Under that semi-open environment, some of the IT companies which are hugely successful today were able to get their first foothold in India. But his openness was not based on an aspiration for the freedom of citizens. The trickle of freedom we experienced was entirely incidental, or rather accidental. For the rest of Rajiv's government still firmly controlled our freedoms and manipulated the economic vitals of our country in a manner that only socialists know about.

In the end, economic reform, the reform of governance, and the maximization of freedom in a society are a closely integrated whole. We cannot compartmentalize freedom into economic reform on the one hand and political or governance reform on the other. We need the complete 'works' of freedom. That is where Rajiv Gandhi's half-baked 'reforms' completely failed. I won't discuss post-1991 liberalization, which has been more of the same.

Nehru's shadow of socialism still hangs like a low black cloud over India and blocks out our sun of freedom. After two generations have lived in shackled independence, the time has now come to blow away this cloud and let the sunshine of freedom light up our lives. The time has come for the country to engage in a debate to review our history and to improve our future. The best ideas presented in this debate should shape our future.

For such a debate to occur, each of us must throw open our best ideas to the test of democratic debate. Hiding our thoughts behind esoteric tones of academic jargon or being cynical and not participating in debate because we think others are inferior to us or won't understand us or being dismissive of others who present their ideas is not the way forward. We should trust the judgement of present and future generations to select whatever they find to be useful from among the ideas that are presented to them. I am therefore throwing open this book to debate. No self-censorship or self-consciousness restricts my proposals. I am not afraid of criticism or failure, having failed sufficiently in life. Besides I don't have an ego that will be pricked if you toss this book into the bin. You are indeed the sole judge of my proposals. I trust in the market.

The ideas in this book will show how an entirely different India has always been hidden behind what we see. 'Many fail to grasp what is right in the palm of their hand' (Heraclitus, 500 BC). This new India, which is resplendent, clean, beautiful, healthy, wealthy and innovative, sits right below our nose, waiting to be uncovered by our minds and hands, by getting rid of the chaff of socialism and removing barriers to our freedom. The magic wand of freedom will unveil a truly Shining India like Aladdin's lamp unveiled the cave containing unimaginable treasures.

Let me suggest at the outset that while some of the ideas I have proposed may appear far-fetched, each of them is based on the inexorable logic of freedom. I therefore trust that my suggestions will make sense upon reflection, if not at first glance. Second, most of 'my' ideas are *road tested*, many of them being things I have seen and experienced first-hand as practical working solutions to the problems of governance in the USA and Australia. Some of my ideas, of course, go well beyond the levels of freedom experienced by citizens of these countries; for I assure you that even these countries could do with more freedom.

I aspire, as I am sure all of us so aspire, to one overarching achievement for India – namely, that India becomes the world's greatest country *ever*, as measured not only through wealth, which we must necessarily acquire, but through the respect we demonstrate for life and humanity; a country so great that it would ultimately influence the entire world into breaking down all existing barriers to human freedom, including national boundaries – till the world can finally live in peace without reference to geographical, religious or nationalist affiliations. We need a peace which brings out the best in each member of the human species; a peace, particularly, which is in harmony with nature.

I have faith that the new generation of Indians today will be able to critically assess the merits of the arguments made in this book. If these ideas make sense to them, I trust they will take the steps to make India change. Just a quick last word before the real book begins. I am not preaching consumerism or materialism even though capitalism has that common connation. I am not preaching that Indians should pursue wealth by ignoring other goals. What I am 'preaching' is freedom, which also calls for self-realization and an ethical (not perfect) life. To that extent this book is about restoring India's lost values.

Chapter 1

Freedom in Indian Life

Government that is ideal governs the least.

Gandhi[1]

Our independence was a blessing on many counts. Even with the rudimentary democratic accountability that our system allows for, we have been able to put an end to the chronic famines we once faced. No matter how inefficient a government is, allowing a famine to develop is guaranteed to lose it the next election, no matter how hard the politicians may thereafter try to buy our votes or stuff ballot boxes.

Independence also meant that our economic growth rates were able to wake up from their fitful slumber of the British period[2] and canter at the so-called Hindu growth rate of 3.5 per cent for the first thirty years, before being spurred to a five per cent trot by the erratic liberalization of the 1980s,[3] and finally to a eight per cent gallop by the semi-capitalist medicine forced down our 'socialist throat' by the IMF after June 1991. (Socialist politicians had made India almost bankrupt in 1991; almost brought us down to our knees and forced us to fly our gold reserves to the Bank of England as collateral for an emergency loan of $5 billion from IMF.)

Montek Singh Ahluwalia argues[4] that most of the post-1991 medicine was self-administered, something that is widely known as being only partially true. Yes, reformers in India did get an upper hand for a while during the financial crisis of 1991. But even if that were entirely true, no one from the current socialist regime wants to publicly admit that: firstly, this was blatantly capitalist, not socialist medicine; secondly, it was the right medicine; and thirdly, such medicine had been freely available in virtually every library of the world since Adam Smith first discovered it in 1776 and put it out for the benefit of the world. Our socialists had to first plunge us into high fever before some of them agreed to take this medicine. Why eat contaminated food (socialist policy) in the first place?

Recent economic growth has helped to reduce poverty and has made a few people very rich, but all this has not translated into a significant improvement in the quality of life of the vast majority of Indians, who continue to be illiterate and poor. That is primarily because our governance is still driven by socialist and other antiquated principles. For India to aspire to much higher growth rates, to eradicate poverty and corruption, and to preserve its environment, we now have to internalize the requirements of freedom which call for individual responsibility and accountability. *India has not yet, as a nation, understood what it means to be free.* That being a key message of this book, it will be useful to start with a bird's-eye view of freedom in Indian life.

HOW FREE WERE WE IN THE PAST?

This section provides a stylized overview of the history of our freedom. Broadly speaking, there have been three phases in India's freedom: pre-1757, between 1757 and 1947, and post-1947.

Phase 1 – Pre-Plassey (1757)

We can combine the entire period prior to the battle of Plassey into a single phase. While the India of the past was not a cohesive political entity, there being hundreds of kingdoms with fluid borders covering this 'country', yet most of what is called India today was even then a single, recognizable nation. It had a cultural unity based on Hinduism. As Vincent Smith noted in 1958, 'Indian unity rests upon the fact that [...] India primarily is a Hindu country'.[5] Hinduism has therefore had a significant influence in India on the concepts associated with freedom.

During this period, the people of India were steadily moving away from their collectivist tribal roots. Individual actions were beginning to be recognized; like other emerging civilizations, the people of India were developing their initial understandings of individual accountability, the principle that underpins freedom. Interactions in agricultural and commercial societies tend towards individual accountability and rewards; tribal societies tend to act as a single mass. A thief was now individually distinguished from non-thieves; a savant from a peasant. And yet, the individual still didn't count for much, being merged into collectivist identities such as caste. Very rarely do we find an individual artist's name acknowledged in an Indian painting or sculpture. Our handicrafts industry displays that lack of individuality even today: beautiful paintings are sold without individual signature.

Freedom also depends on dignity, or the regard shown towards the individual. Incipient concepts of individual dignity within rigidly prescribed caste structures evolved in India during this phase. These included the practice of *jajmani*[6] which gives every member of the community at least some recognition, if not prestige, provided that person performs his caste duties 'well'. However, these concepts were strongly rooted in group identity. Entire groups, such as *sudras* were completely denied individual dignity.

Individual accountability is not merely about individual identity and dignity but about holding individuals to account. This process of holding them to account takes a considerable time to evolve. Without such a process, though, there can be no freedom, for freedom must necessarily be limited by individual accountability. Historically there have been two processes to hold individuals to account:

- The religious process, which holds people to account through an after-life mechanism based on the judgement of an extra-terrestrial entity such as angels or God. The *karma* theory and the concepts of heaven and hell are significant developments in this field. These ideas tend to keep individuals in check as they worry about future accountability in their after life.
- The political process, which seeks to uphold and deliver accountability in this life itself, through a man-made system of justice. The more systemic the rule of law, the more free the society can become, as individuals are able to operate within clearly defined boundaries. Aristotle's initial explorations in justice are an example of this kind of thinking.

There is no counterpart in India's history to the theories of justice commonly discussed in the West. In India, far more emphasis was placed on the religious process of accountability. This perspective, which meant that justice was not a matter for this life but the next one, led to the caste system being strengthened. Caste became the means of justice, if we can call it that. If someone behaved well and worked diligently within his 'allotted' sphere in his lifetime, he could hope to rise to the next caste 'level' upon rebirth; and vice versa – you could fall down the scale in your next birth.

In terms of developing political processes of accountability, the struggle to create man-made laws of accountability has gone through the following stylized stages in mankind's history:

- minimizing the tyranny of autocrats;
- reducing the links between the church, or religion, and the state;
- disbanding the 'divine right' of kings;
- reducing inherited powers;
- creating parliaments with limited representation, noting that in the early stages of democratic representation, weaker sections of the society, such as indigent white men, women and blacks, were not represented;
- creating democracies with universal franchise, i.e. where all adults are able to vote; and, finally,
- preventing democracies from degenerating into majority-rule mobocracies through a comprehensive network of checks and balances supported by vigilant citizens.

Against this broader picture, no advance in political theory or in the practice of freedom of the kind that took place in England with its Magna Carta took place in India. Virtually no argument to advance justice or freedom was articulated in ancient India. Indian rulers generally adopted norms of voluntary accountability for their own actions, largely driven by the fear of religious accountability, and oppression of the masses was a relatively infrequent phenomenon.[7] A few feeble attempts were made to argue why kings should be just and not tyrannical. For example, Kautilya tried to persuade kings to be good in their own self-interest through his *Arthashastra*,[8] written in the fourth century BC. Further, governance through a formal system of democracy, or asking kings to abandon their 'divine rights', remained alien to us, although there were a few assemblies or *gana-sanghas* that could have advanced such thought, but did not really expand their initial experiments or record their merits.

A long stalemate was therefore established, in which kings were passively acknowledged as a natural part of the society, and their excesses, though infrequent, were taken to be a normal part of life and accepted without retaliation. As Harish Khare notes, 'From Manu onwards, the King was an indispensable, integral part of a sanctioned social order and was not subject to competitive challenge […] All this led, naturally, to religious sanction for royal absolutism and passive obedience to the King became a highly valued prerogative of a commoner'.[9] This obedience to royalty became deeply embedded in the Indian psyche – a uniquely Indian trait of obsequiousness that continues till today in many ways. It is amazing how obsequious we are towards 'seniors' in India. Calling people by their first name and talking to each other as equals may perhaps need to be recognized as an important cultural marker of freedom as well, so distant we are from recognizing individuals as persons worthy of regard in their own right. In brief, the pre-1757 Indian was severely constrained both in freedom of thought and of action.

Freedom requires a stance of openness of mind and of curiosity. The thinking of other civilizations must be welcomed and chewed slowly, as a cow may, as food for thought. Without such openness no society can aspire either to reach the truth or to obtain freedom. But India displayed a singularly high level of insularity towards other civilizations. Despite being a major trading power in the world with extensive commercial relationships, India did not care to find out what was happening in other parts of the world. No analysis took place of the changes taking place in England and elsewhere in the world since the Magna Carta of 1215. The English language had come to India in 1603 in Akbar's time. But no one showed curiosity about these traders or their society. No one asked them the 'latest news' in England. No one hitched a ride to England to investigate and report back in the manner of a Huen Tsang. There was no urgent economic reason for Indians to learn English before 1757 either. And so English remained, for India's first 150 years of association with the British, merely one of the many foreign languages along with Portuguese, Dutch and French. The Indian world was decidedly self-centred.

This insularity can only partly be explained by difficulties in travelling to different parts of the world in those times. One of the reasons was the focus on the problems arising from incursions by foreign powers (Islamic in the West, and Southern Chinese, Ahoms, in the East). High levels of illiteracy also did not permit most people to use their minds intelligently. Most importantly, perhaps, it was due to a great haughtiness among the Indian elites who believed they needed to learn nothing from others. I say this because this trait continues in India even today. I have often suggested to my erstwhile civil service colleagues to ask me questions about how things work in Australia so they can consider improving things in India, but I have always received a stunned silence in response. For how dare I even suggest that people other than Indians know something better? This all-knowing Indian mind strikes me as a uniquely Indian trait.

There came a time when even crossing the oceans was forbidden to members of the higher castes and could hurt their social status. Frogs in the well – that is what our ancestors were for most of our history prior to 1757. This is not to deny that many uniquely wonderful things happened in India in that period. But while Europeans explored new ideas and sent exploratory expeditions to all parts of the world, while they discovered new continents as far away as Australia and America and populated them, India put on blinkers around its eyes and turned inwards to save its soul. Not only was individual freedom not on the agenda of pre-1757 India, there was no ambition even to conquer the world. Great ambition is a great driver of progress but India displayed none; it still perhaps has none. Arrogance without ambition – a combination destined to guarantee mediocrity.

Phase 2 – 1757 to 1947

British influence in Bengal arose from Clive's victory in the 1757 battle of Plassey. That period also coincided roughly with significant developments of political thought in England (e.g. John Locke in the 1680s, Edmund Burke who became influential from the mid 1700s and Adam Smith a little later) and in the USA (e.g. Thomas Jefferson, John Adams, Alexander Hamilton).

After the consolidation of Bengal by Robert Clive, the economic advantages of learning English started becoming increasingly obvious. As a result Indians started to show interest in learning the English language and its literature. By 1835, Indians were paying good money to be taught English. T B Macaulay noted in his famous 'Minute' that 'the natives' had become 'desirous to be taught English' and were no longer 'desirous to be taught Sanscrit or Arabic'. Indians picked up English very well. '[I]t is unusual to find, even in the literary circles of the Continent, any foreigner who can express himself in English with so much facility and correctness as we find in many Hindoos.'[10]

While the British may have wanted to teach English only so that Indians could become their clerks, once the Pandora's Box of knowledge is opened, its consequences are unstoppable. Indians quickly became aware of the enormous leaps made by Western political thought over the centuries. This awareness laid the seeds for subsequent demands for self-rule. But India faced a steep learning curve first. It had not paid the slightest heed to what had been going on elsewhere for centuries, if not millennia. But in the meantime the world had completely changed. People's power was on the rise as never before in Britain. While British kings still existed, their powers had been dramatically truncated. In 1757, a young man of 24 years in Scotland by the name of Adam Smith was thinking about the entire world and examining how the wealth of nations was created. His ideas would convert the tiny island of England into the world's most powerful nation by the mid-1800s.

It was not possible for Indians to advance straight to the forefront of the theory and philosophy of freedom given their late start. While people like Raja Ram Mohan Roy (1772–1833) started to internalize the political arguments of freedom, no one could yet articulate new insights. All that the Indians did in this period, and could have reasonably done, was to catch up with liberal ideas and start demanding self-governance in India. Lest we blame these Indians for lack of creative insight, we must remember that things like 'independence', 'representation of the people', and even 'nationhood' were completely new concepts for most parts of the world then. England had a head-start in freedom which would take many countries a long time to catch up with. Apart from Raja Ram Mohan Roy, other contributors to the political discourse on freedom in nineteenth century India included Dadabhai Naoroji (1825–1917), Mahadeo Govind Ranade (1842–1901), Gopal Krishna Gokhale (1866–1915) and Pherozeshah Mehta (1845–1915).

By the time the Indian mind finally caught up with the West by 1850, Western thought had moved even further on its journey. But also by now, a battle against liberty was under way in the West. A competing theory to the theory of freedom had arisen in the dying years of feudalism – the theory of socialism (or communism). Both liberalism and socialism agreed that kings were no longer needed. But on what would come next, they differed completely. These radically opposed Western world views, one founded on freedom, the other on equality, had begun a battle for the minds and hearts of people.

Socialism wanted us to revert to our tribal state without the aristocratic overlay of feudalism. It did not want anyone to become exceptionally wealthy or powerful. Its approach had to be implemented, where necessary, by chopping the heads of the rich. The socialist model did not agree with Adam Smith who saw wealth as an unlimited product of the human mind, a mere consequence of innovation. It saw life as a zero-sum game where people had to fight for a *share* of the fixed pie: capital versus labour. In the model of socialism individual effort, merit or enterprise was irrelevant, for the total wealth was fixed. Therefore redistribution of wealth was the primary purpose of life.

The vision of socialism held hypnotic sway amongst untutored minds. It was on the upswing by the mid-1800s. In a brave bid to foil socialism, Frédéric Bastiat wrote *The Law* in 1850 and John Stuart Mill his essay *On Liberty* in 1859. Thinkers of the Austrian school advanced further explorations on the economic impacts of freedom and created the science of economics. In the early twentieth century Friedrich Hayek, Ayn Rand and Julian Simon advanced these ideas even further. While socialism overpowered parts of Europe by the late nineteenth century, England and USA remained the bastions of freedom and kept trying to improve their political and democratic institutions of governance. The greatest advances in freedom therefore took place only in the West, not in India. The Indian intelligentsia remained focused on its challenge of independence.

The Indian mind was distracted by another thing as well. Indians had suddenly come down from being supremely haughty and disinterested in the rest of the world to becoming ruled first by the Mughals and then by the British. A doubt arose in their minds that they were potentially racially inferior. The British encouraged this doubt through their own haughty behaviour, for when one is powerfully placed it is easy to be arrogant. British racism left little breathing space for Indians to focus on the broader global issues of justice and liberty. But British arrogance was clearly misplaced on two grounds:

- First, the rapidly growing technological prowess of the British was not a product of racial superiority but the natural consequence of the *freedom* that its philosophers had propounded and its people fought for over many centuries. It was this freedom of thought which had enabled its society to become increasingly more creative and flexible, and thus technologically superior to other societies. Before the ideas of freedom improved the life of the common man in England, the British 'race' was actually quite 'inferior', being short-statured with mediocre intelligence. Normally, soldiers are the tallest and strongest representatives of any society, but British soldiers were very short till 1814, averaging only 5 feet 6 inches.[11] But even these tiny fellows managed to conquer India because they rode the steed of freedom which gave them self-confidence and allowed them to innovate at each step. The rapidly developing sciences in Britain arising from this culture of freedom led to higher survival rates of its infants and consequently to rapid population growth. This excess population also fed into England's international exploits. The virtuous cycles of freedom kept reinforcing themselves. Their superiority for 150 years or so had nothing to do with race.
- Second, it was a great mistake for the British to think that there was nothing for the West to learn from India. That learning is a two-way street became apparent to them when some intrepid

European scholars discovered the many-splendoured Indian past using methods of research and analysis hitherto not applied in India.

Such findings about glorious achievements in historical India brought some comfort, even a sense of renewed confidence, to English-educated Indians. Unfortunately, with the advent of European scholarship of Indian history, a lot of navel gazing started among Indians. The Indian mind, both Hindu and Muslim, began to spend most of its time looking backwards, in reconciling its multi-faceted and possibly exciting past with its unhappy present. A few Indians did raise broader issues in relation to freedom, such as Rabindranath Tagore (1861–1941) and M K Gandhi (1869–1948). However, that was incidental to the focus on self-rule and opposing racism.

This great mental energy led to the most awe-inspiring independence movement the world has ever seen. It was an exemplary movement – far ahead of its times in its principle-based standards of political protest. In addition, the British were gently taught a very important lesson in freedom by Gandhi. His exposition of the equality among peoples and of non-violent protest were significant contributions to the freedom of mankind as a whole. Through humane and dignified protest he demonstrated that all humans were equally worthy of regard. This was of course helped by allegiance of the British to their rule of law. It is unlikely that Gandhi would have made a difference with Japanese or German 'masters' of that era. His methods also reminded the people of Britain that they should not lower their *own* principles of liberty by diminishing the liberty of others. As a result of Gandhi's actions the age of racial discrimination officially came to an end in many parts of the world. Oppressed peoples of the past, such as the blacks of the USA and South Africa, acknowledge the contributions of Gandhi. Gandhi has therefore brought about a fundamental shift in the world's landscape of freedom. In that sense, Gandhi was without doubt the most influential proponent of individual liberty (and thus, indirectly, of classical liberalism) in India in the first half of the twentieth century.

Of course, the age of racial discrimination is not yet completely over. While the West seems to have largely moved on, based on what I have experienced in USA and Australia, ethnic and caste discrimination continues within India in a big way. Colour consciousness and focus on outward looks is rife in the Indian marriage market. Also, it is Indians living abroad who raise the matter of colour in their social dealings. In USA, many Indians I knew used to refer to the Blacks in a derogatory manner ('*kallu*'). In Australia, many Indians here draw attention to '*goras*' as a group, not referring to individuals on their own merit. I can therefore assure you that the average Indian is perhaps the most colour conscious and racially aware person on the planet.

Self-inflicted racism is also reflected by Indians needing a constant pat on the back by the West. The Indian beats his chest and howls like Tarzan each time an Indian company purchases a foreign company, or each time an Indian author wins a foreign award. Even today, an Indian must have been recognized by the West first or else that Indian doesn't count. Lurching from one extreme to the other, the Indian mind struggles to find balance. The transition to a confident, plain vanilla human being, curious and willing to learn, willing to contribute to mankind's development without drum beating, may take a while to happen. I flag this issue as a matter of concern for potential social reformers to look into.

Given the impact of Nehru's ideas on India, it is worthwhile contrasting them with Gandhi's.

Gandhi and Nehru – key differences

Gandhi's philosophy was the most compatible with the ideas of freedom among Indian thinkers of his period. He placed great importance on individual freedom and independent action. In his mind, the individual remained the maker of his own destiny, with the state having only a very limited role in an individual's affairs. His views were based on a combination of his interpretation of Hindu ideas mixed largely with the ideas of the liberal American philosopher Henry David Thoreau (1817–62). Thoreau had said, 'That government is best which governs least'. Gandhi repeated that like a mantra on many occasions. In fact, Gandhi merged the concepts of accountability from classical liberalism with those of the *karma* theory of Hinduism. His can be said to have been an eclectic synthesis of Hinduism and liberalism. Despite its indifferent contribution to liberty in the past, once an effort is made, it appears that just as Christianity can get along with liberalism, Hinduism can also get along with liberalism quite well, arguably even more so. I have little doubt that Islam can also be interpreted likewise given a broader understanding of its message. Turkey shows us that it is possible to do so.

Gandhi opposed the collectivist and centralized approaches of communism not on intellectual grounds but because of his 'intuitive' grasp over the concepts of accountability and justice. Quotations from Gandhi in the table below tell us about his liberal credentials. The page numbers at the end of these quotations are from Fisher.[12] My comments on Gandhi's views are in the second column.

'Government that is ideal governs the least. It is no self-government that leaves nothing for the people to do' (p.196).	The government has a minimal role in a free society – a key message of classical liberalism.
'I look upon an increase of the power of the State with the greatest fear because, although while apparently doing good by minimising exploitation, it does the greatest harm to mankind by destroying individuality which lies at the root of all progress' (p.304).	Here Gandhi is reiterating the most fundamental principles of a free society. The individual is the hub of the society; the individual must be allowed to develop self-knowledge, self-respect and become responsible and accountable.
'Submission [...] to a state wholly or largely unjust is an immoral barter for liberty [...] Civil resistance is a most powerful expression of a soul's anguish and an eloquent protest against the continuance of an evil state' (p.165).	Liberalism resists tyranny, and nothing is generally more tyrannical than a state that barters liberty for immorality, as socialist governments have, in India. Gandhi's chosen method of protest was supremely ethical and persuasive. There was no secrecy involved, no deception. Attacking people, as terrorists do, never changes the beliefs that people hold.
'[The] means to me are just as important as the goal, and in a sense more important in that we have some control over them, whereas we have none over the goal if we lose control over the means' (p.305).	Liberalism focuses almost entirely on the process, or the means. The ends are seen as a natural consequence of the means. There is no coercion, only persuasion.
'I hope to demonstrate that real Swaraj will come not by the acquisition of authority by a few but by the acquisition of the capacity by all to resist authority when abused. In other words, Swaraj is to be attained by educating the masses to a sense of their capacity to regulate and control authority' (p.202).	Liberalism requires the active participation of each citizen in the regulation and control of their government. In a free society the best of its citizens come forward as representatives. There is no better way to prevent the abuse of authority than for freedom loving people to form the government.

Let me add that Gandhi was not a 'full-fledged' liberal given his lack of intellectual rigour about why he advocated what he did. He had strong liberal inclinations and intuition but no vision for human freedom as a whole (at least not one in which the proper mechanisms of freedom were fully defined). He was clearly not a Hayek and did not even understand the great moral character of capitalism. This is evident from his theory of trusteeship through which he sought (in his mind) a 'compromise' between freedom and economic equality. Gandhi did not grasp that these objectives are mutually contradictory. And so he needlessly hit out against capitalism. He wrote, 'I desire to end capitalism, almost, if not quite, as much as the most advanced Socialist or even Communist. But our methods differ, our languages differ',[13] his difference being that he did not like using coercion. He also diluted his concept of equality somewhat by saying, 'Economic equality of my conception does not mean that everyone would literally have the same amount. It simply means that everybody should have enough for his or her needs'.[14] He then proposed a via-media of sorts – the theory of trusteeship, whereby the rich ('capitalists') would use their 'wealth [...] for the welfare of the community'.[15]

Unfortunately, this view seriously misrepresents the foundations of liberty and capitalism. For Gandhi to even imply tangentially that capitalists were not using their wealth for the welfare of the community was wrong. Businesses contribute to the welfare of society in many ways:

- First, they do so through the services they provide. By applying their mental energy to combine natural and human resources with capital, they generate products and services that would not have existed without their efforts. These products and services increase our knowledge and improve our health and longevity. That is their most important contribution.
- Second, businesses generate employment for thousands, if not millions, of families, taking each such person employed out of the quagmire poverty. This is their second most important contribution.

In this manner, those who achieve wealth through their own initiative have already contributed so disproportionately in comparison to ordinary people that we should be ashamed of asking them to further look after the 'welfare' of society. Are we beggars that we can't stand on our own feet? In the second chapter I will show how a free society readily delivers on things like the removal of poverty without requiring charity from anyone. Anyway, whether or not trusteeship was a good concept, it did not go anywhere. Nehru ignored it and no one else cared to pick it up.

Also, Gandhi was not a 'systems' thinker and was unable to elaborate the design of institutions by which governments of free India would be held accountable. It is not enough to say that a 'government is best which governs the least'. It is important to specify how this will happen. This inability to think at the systems level, i.e. by building from the level of individual incentives right up to the social level, is perhaps a cultural trait of most Indians. We prefer to tinker with things at the margin or to appeal to the good intentions of people, rather than think about systemic incentives which will give us the results we want. On the other hand, the West has been very competent in this area. And so, given Gandhi's rather limited understanding of systemic processes, we still need to look to the advances of Western economic theory such as the theory of public choice for a more complete picture of governance.

Nehru, who was far more aware of the history of liberalism than Gandhi seems to have been, had surprisingly little faith in an individual's ability to think for himself and to take personal responsibility. He did not ask us to undertake self-reflection and to choose ethically at each step. He believed, instead, that the government should make our choices for us. In his model, all decision-making powers were to be concentrated in the government. Decentralization, where power and freedom are vested in the people at the lowest practicable level, was anathema to him. His aristocratic background perhaps played a major role in defining his thinking. Whatever the reasons, he clearly veered towards statist thinking.

Nehru's choice of socialism was a conscious and deliberate decision. His analysis of the Indian Liberal Party in his autobiography shows that he knew quite well about the alternative to socialism, i.e. of freedom. He wrote:

> One is apt to be misled by the name 'Liberal Party'. The word elsewhere, and especially in England, stood for a certain economic policy – free trade and laisser-faire – and a certain ideology of individual freedom and civil liberties. The English Liberal tradition was based on economic foundations. The desire for freedom in trade and to be rid of the King's monopolies and arbitrary taxation, led to the desire for political liberty. The Indian Liberals have no such background. They do not believe in free trade, being almost all protectionists, and they attach little importance to civil liberties.[16]

Upon reading this observation, we may be forgiven if, for a fleeting moment, we form the impression that Nehru was a fiery liberal, condemning the weak-kneed liberalism of the Indian Liberal Party; wanting to forge ahead with civil liberties and free trade on his own! But Nehru had nothing of this sort in mind, in his Presidential Address at the 1936 Lukhnow Congress, he reiterated his 'faith' in socialism, remarking, 'socialism is thus for me not merely an economic doctrine which I favour; it is a vital creed which I hold with all my head and heart'.[17]

Further in his autobiography, Nehru outlined his preference for the Russian form of socialism despite unremitting evidence of state-based violence that accompanied it. His Russian influence later came through by his adopting five-year plans and his vigorous opposition to property rights. Nehru argued lamely that the Russian violence was mitigated by the even greater violence that he allegedly found in capitalist societies. He wrote, 'I had long been drawn to socialism and communism, and Russia had appealed to me. Much in Soviet Russia I dislike – the ruthless suppression of all contrary opinion, the wholesale regimentation, the unnecessary violence (as I thought) in carrying out various policies. But there was no lack of violence and suppression in the capitalist world, and I realised more and more how the very basis and foundation of our acquisitive society and property was violence'.[18]

Nehru prevaricated here; possibly lied. In continuing his comments, he not only denied the causal link between the ideology of socialism and the violence he saw in Russia, but also argued, 'Violence was common in both places, but the violence of the capitalist order seemed inherent in it; whilst the violence of Russia, bad though it was, aimed at a new order based on peace and co-operation and *real freedom for the masses.* With all her blunders, Soviet Russia had triumphed over enormous difficulties and taken *great strides* towards this new order'. [Emphasis mine. Perhaps I should have added quite a few exclamation marks of disbelief!]

There are at least three objections to this statement:

- We can't make out which capitalist societies he was referring to. I don't know where such capitalist societies ever existed – not the USA, UK or Australia, for sure. No mass detentions and killings of the sort that routinely took place in the erstwhile USSR ever took place in these societies. Given that he lived for many years in the UK himself, where did he experience violence in the UK, apart from possibly (?) an occasional taunt for being a black student at Harrow.

- Second, even if we were to accept that there was racial discrimination in Western societies, and disregard for the poor among the *nouveau riche* who are ill-grounded in the logic of freedom anyway, how can one compare verbal rudeness of this sort with the Russian system where life could be taken at the whim of any petty communist party functionary? Capitalist societies had, by Nehru's time, developed a great many protections of freedom such as the rule of law and democratic accountability of governments. Most communist leaders were, on the other hand, serial killers who revelled in the opportunity to use Marx's socially acceptable arguments to justify their psychopathic urges. If violence was inherent in either of the two systems, it was clearly so in the Russian communist system.
- Third, in this manner of interpretation of the facts, he completely glossed over the great advances to mankind's freedom made by capitalist societies – advances won through furious resistance to feudalism and mercantilism. No capitalist society has ever (even today) achieved complete freedom. Each generation has to work hard to stretch the boundaries of freedom by removing residual kinks. Freedom is a journey which mankind has only recently started to undertake. It is hard to explain why Nehru expected perfection from capitalist societies but was oblivious to the most blatant imperfections of socialist societies.

Statements of this sort that Nehru made from time to time don't inspire confidence in his wisdom. And yet, the fact that the violence of the Russian system was right 'in his face' annoyed him. Given that the 'disturbing reports of violent purges in the Soviet Union [...] repelled Nehru', he tried to moderate his enthusiasm for Russian socialism by moving towards what is called a 'pragmatic' but very similarly highly centralized form of socialism,[19] namely, Fabian socialism.[20] This type of socialism is neither fish nor fowl for Fabians imagine they can bring about socialism gradually. They can't explain how people will be made equal and property rights abolished without coercion.

It was not only Nehru who turned a blind eye towards the violent killing fields of socialism. There was a malaise generally found in the air at that time. Professor Harold Laski taught *against* freedom even as he enjoyed the freedom of expression accorded by the academic portals of capitalist England. The early twentieth century consensus against capitalism seems to have been a Hobbesean consensus which claimed that our freedoms are not an end in themselves, and that the state was the pinnacle of human achievement.[21] It also saw a constant 'struggle for the control of economic power'[22] in society, instead of delighting in the vast amounts of freedom available to the West through which people took responsibility for themselves and created ever-increasing levels of wealth. Marxian language clouded the eyes of the beholder.

Further, some economists falsely implicated capitalism as a cause of the Great Depression. The Depression was, however, in large part caused by the monopolistic control over banking brought about in USA by its 1913 Federal Reserve Act.[23] In this manner, the Federal Reserve made significant errors in the management of the supply of money, errors which in the multiple private banking system that prevailed earlier would at worst have caused a few bank collapses here or there. As it so happened, these errors were magnified by centralization and led to an almost wholesale collapse of banking in USA. This centralization was surely influenced by socialist ideas in USA, for centralization is always the disease of socialism, not freedom. Given false attributions of economic failures to capitalism, Keynesianism and big government were on a further upswing by the 1930s. It was in that sense a time for dirigisme – the direction of our activities by central authorities. Even our industrialists, with the centralized approach recommended by their Bombay Plan,[24] sided with Nehru.

This confluence of the interests of big business with ideologies that support big government is not really surprising. Barring a few exceptions, big business never likes the competition that freedom and capitalism engender. It prefers to distort markets by colluding with governments to create monopolies. Its activities make capitalism the object of mockery not because capitalism is bad but because politicians love to mingle with big business and give them special privileges. I will show in the second chapter how long-term monopolies are always created by governments. It is mostly the smaller businesses, farmers and independent thinkers – the 'small fish' in the pond – who promote capitalism and freedom.[25] (Just to keep the record straight, I am not glorifying small business at the expense of big business. Many small businesses are unethical too, and fail to declare their incomes and pay taxes. We therefore need strong systems to check unethical short-cuts taken by business, both big and small.)

Through this period of centralist approaches, Nehru continued to hold the erstwhile USSR, more particularly Stalin, in great esteem.[26] Later, speaking on Stalin's death, Nehru told the Parliament on 6 March 1953: '[L]ooking back at these 35 years [...] many figures stand out, but perhaps no single figure has moulded and affected and influenced the history of these years more than Marshal Stalin'. It is astonishing to find that Nehru did not pick Gandhi as the most influential person in the world between 1918 and 1953, but Stalin! Such glorification is a telling commentary on the way Nehru saw the world, and thus himself. Our role models speak for us. They tell the world what we would like to be but haven't yet become. Similarly, Nehru warmed instantly towards Mao – who arose on the world stage in 1949 as yet another communist butcher. That Nehru's ardour for communist China cooled soon had to do with *realpolitik* – about the question of which of them would occupy greater prominence on the world stage, as well as to the events leading to the 1962 India–China war – than to his principled disagreement with Mao's ideas and methods.

Once it was clear that Nehru was determined to impose the Red Socialism on India, his close colleagues like Jayaprakash Narayan tried to temper his misplaced enthusiasm. Narayan, who had started his career as a Marxist, but later concluded he had been on the wrong path, declared prophetically:

> History will soon prove that Communism, instead of being the final flowering of human civilisation, was a temporary aberration of the human mind, a brief nightmare to be soon forgotten. Communism, as it grew up in Russia and is growing up in China now, represented the darkness of the soul and imprisonment of the mind, colossal violence and injustice. Whoever thinks of the future of the human race in these terms is condemning man to eternal perdition.[27]

But Nehru's colleagues failed to change his mind. Nehru was also possibly getting too old, being around 60 by then, and was not inclined to be receptive to new ideas.

Fortunately, despite this environment in which socialist ideas flourished, India did get to enjoy at least a few liberties. These included things like the right of assembly under reasonable circumstances, a modestly framed right to property, some freedom of expression including a relatively free press. These became part of the Indian landscape even before independence through British India's laws. The fact that powerful people like Robert Clive could be impeached (he was acquitted) must have sent strong signals in early British India about the supremacy of the rule of law – a concept that until then was completely foreign to India. Later advances made in British political institutions were also largely transferred and embedded into Indian governance arrangements by its British rulers, at times in response to the demand for self-rule.

These experiences of the rule of law premised in freedom led to India producing a strangely confused *quasi-liberal intelligentsia.* This group saw the benefits of liberal institutions such as democracy, but advanced a socialist agenda; some focused entirely on religious matters, mixing religion and politics. A very confused landscape indeed. We thus ended up in 1947 with somewhat liberal structures but with predominantly illiberal socialist ideas. Our Constitution is a by-product of this amazingly incompatible mix of confused ideas.

Phase 3 – Post independence

I will touch upon some of India's experience of post-independence freedom in subsequent chapters, but an overview now will help to set the scene. As noted above, our 1949 Constitution allowed us a few of the freedoms that the British and Americans had come to routinely expect by then. India also extended franchise to all adults – this was actually more than what many developed countries had at that time. For example, even though Australia gave its white women voting rights in 1902, it wasn't till 1962 that members of its Aboriginal (tribal) community were granted franchise.

However, given the huge confusion about various ideas prevailing in the minds of Indian leaders at the time of independence, an almost stunned silence descended on the subject of our freedoms. It was also perhaps erroneously assumed by most that independence and freedom were the same things. On 15 August 1947, India's Nightingale, Sarojini Naidu, declared that 'The battle of freedom is over'.[28] Sorry, Ms Naidu! Not over – just started!

Freedom doesn't enter into a close relationship with a society that easily. It has to be wooed, begged, cajoled. The right conditions have to be created for it to feel welcome. Independence is at best a minimum condition. It is very poorly related to the level of freedom prevailing in a society. Monarchies in the past were independent; USSR was independent; so also Mugabe's Zimbabwe. Even a cursory acquaintance with history proves that freedom needs constant attention, even fawning, and at times ferocious battle to protect it against the enemies of freedom. Very reclusive, reluctant, but the most beautiful and graceful lady of all, is freedom. We failed to realize that merely replacing white sahibs by brown sahibs would not make freedom welcome into our country. There had to be a change in our feudal and socialist mindset, which never took place. And so we let down our guard; and socialists who hate freedom with all their heart promptly threw a left hook and smashed the lovely face of freedom out of shape. And there she lies, bleeding for six decades, hiding in the dense jungles of the upper Himalayas, waiting to be rescued.

I believe the Indian community was also possibly quite weary of the travails of independence and had lost its appetite for further change or discussion. The communal rioting, the daily tensions of living, were just too much. There was no time to think back about the poem Tagore had sung decades ago. I cite this beautiful poem below ('Heaven of Freedom', *Gitanjali*, 1912) noting that nowhere did Tagore talk about independence. For without independence we can't be free, but independence is not the end of our life. Freedom is.

Where the mind is without fear and the head is held high;
Where knowledge is free;
Where the world has not been broken up into fragments by
narrow domestic walls;
Where words come out from the depth of truth;
Where tireless striving stretches its arms towards perfection;
Where the clear stream of reason has not lost its way into the
dreary desert sand of dead habit;
Where the mind is led forward by thee into ever-widening thought
and action –
Into that heaven of freedom, my Father, let my country awake.

Tagore's poem is truly embarrassing, for socialists. Each of Tagore's lines resists socialism. Tagore doesn't sing poetically about how our government will do things for us when we become free. He doesn't sing praises to public sector undertakings; doesn't sing praises to equality; doesn't aspire for commanding heights of the economy; doesn't aspire for planning. He is asking, instead, for each *individual* to achieve this 'heaven of freedom'. Tagore's poem points to an enabling role for government, not an organization that closely monitors our religion, caste and tribe, and bakes our bread. Nehru never reminded us of this embarrassing poem. If he had a modern shredder, he would have shredded it. And so the most important task of all for independent India, namely, of creating mechanisms to defend our freedom, was ignored.

There was one exception – Rajaji. I'll talk about him separately, a little later. This grand old man advocated freedom irrespective of his advancing age. But other notables of the independence struggle sat tight, twiddling their thumbs, pretending to be busy. Given this great indifference towards freedom, India slipped without ado into the socialist mould that Nehru had created for us; one in which our governance is still fully moulded.

* * *

Oblivious to the extreme dangers of socialism, confident in their ability to solve other people's problems, our leaders who had been catapulted to the leadership of the world's second largest nation itched to apply their untested experiments on 300 million captive Indians eagerly waiting in line to be experimented upon.

The first thing they did was to significantly increase government intervention in our lives. We even lost some of the freedoms that had been assured in our Constitution – property rights were truncated, and we were soon enough constitutionally declared to be a socialist country, just to make sure that no one could possibly misunderstand what was happening.

I suspect that our feudal past – which never faced a serious challenge, particularly after independence – had a lot to do with this absence of critical discussion on the role of government. Over many centuries, our village folk had gotten used to the idea of living in a small corner in a tiny crevice below a small rock at the bottom of the power structure. It was 'programmed' into them that in the overall scheme of things they were beasts of burden tasked with working for – even carrying literally on their backs – their aristocrat masters: the landlords, kings and king's cronies. Their job was to grow their masters' food, to pay for their masters' luxuries through punitive rates of tax, to get beaten and humiliated and their daughters raped, at the end of the day. Their spirit had been completely thrashed out of them; they barely stood. 'Stooped' is the right word. Some of them, the untouchables and tribals, were shunted to the village fringe or jungle.

Under such circumstances, if a relatively benevolent aristocrat or bureaucrat chanced to come their way it was natural for villagers to be so beholden to his little mercies that they called such functionaries their '*mai-baap*', revering them as we would our parents. Pure subservience, not just obsequiousness, was the order of the day for the vast majority of 300 million Indians. The idea of freedom had never occurred to them even remotely, and their powerful overlords weren't about to put it into their heads. Our village folk therefore could not have been expected to be at the vanguard of freedom. They did graciously support Gandhi's marches, but to say that they had a plan of how things would look after independence, or that they expected in any way to become equals of others, let alone becoming the masters of their governments, would be an exaggeration.

On the other side of the coin, as a result of the paternalistic attitudes deeply entrenched in the Indian aristocratic mind, it did not seem incongruous to them that their governmental 'rulers' were directing every aspect of our business, trade and life, and demanding 'baksheesh' for this completely unsolicited favour. Aristocrats (most Indian journalists, not just politicians and bureaucrats, are in this group too) lived in their ivory towers and spoke of, and wrote about, the rest of us dusty and smelly people as 'the masses'. But we did not even know that we were being insulted, lumped together as someone might a mass of termites seething in their freshly uncovered nest. To know that we were being insulted, we first had to understand and realize that in free India we were the natural equal even of the President of India, in dignity. But Nehru kept that information from us. He continued the imperial pageantry and paraphernalia; in fact he created even grander celebrations of the power of the state. We therefore never got to know that we had been released from bondage, for it all looked and felt the same as before.

It is only now, many decades after these smelly 'masses' have participated in elections and learnt a few basic lessons of democracy, that the hold of feudalism has begun to weaken, to some extent. Today, a good number of villagers are prepared to say to our politicians: 'We, dear politician, are not "masses" of voters waiting for your mercies. We are your *employer* and you had better learn to listen to us and think of us as your equal. We ask you therefore to let us live our lives and make our decisions for ourselves. Leave us free. *Hamein Rahne Do. Laissez faire*!' This awareness has definitely been helped by organizations such as Shetkari Sangathan, as well as political parties of all forms and colours.

But in 1947, our paternalistic ethos of feudalism simply blended very smoothly, and seamlessly, into the dogmatic statist framework of Nehruvian socialism. The vehicles of government chosen after independence remained the same as before, being re-labelled for instance from ICS to IAS. The 'imperial' offices of the Deputy Commissioners or Collectors, where no functionary had ever been accountable to the people of that district, flourished. Elected politicians now added to the local feudal structures while the ever powerful Patwaris or Lot Mandals (junior level revenue officers) continued to misuse their powers, abetted by the same local feudal establishment as before.[29]

In this netherworld, between an ancient feudal culture and a hoping-to-be-modern one, three social forces – of feudalism, of industry seeking monopolistic favours from government, and the all-powerful Nehruvian government machinery – merged into a behemoth, generating an unprecedented level of nepotism, corruption, and, at places, even violence against the weak. Thus began the onslaught of government heavy-handedness on our freedoms – an onslaught that no one has been able to contain till today. It has become fully institutionalized by now: institutionalized corruption; institutionalized linkages between politicians, business and the mafia. There is no British Parliament any longer to impeach our Robert Clives. Nehru shrewdly damaged the only internal opposition to his socialism, the Swatantra Party. Some examples of his strategies are cited by H R Pasricha in his book *The Swatantra Party – Victory in Defeat.*[30] And so, corruption is now king.

Nehru's government soon declared in the Parliament that what it really wanted to do when it 'grew up' was to be a successful *Businessman.* Nehru had no interest in the hard grind of governing, or providing the rule of law and security. He was excited at the prospect of the government becoming a *Businessman* and achieving commanding heights of the economy. Government functionaries would fly aeroplanes, drive buses and generally zoom about acting busy. All this would apparently make us all very rich.

Nehru's government *did* reach dizzying heights of incompetence. It dumped two-thirds of the country's investable funds into the public sector. By 1978 the paid-up capital of public sector firms comprised 71 per cent of the entire paid-up capital in India.[31] Government factories sprung up overnight and churned out shoddy watches, fridges, scooters, bicycles, milk, cheese. You name it. And oh yes! Bread. The government did also produce a few capital-intensive things like cement and steel – but these were things the private sector in India had already been able to produce in British India, so it merely prevented private enterprise even in these areas. The decision to start these factories was taken not on the basis of a sound business case but by politicians whose objective was to provide jobs to their relatives and cronies, and to get some easy (corrupt) money. Therefore these factories immediately racked up huge losses[32] and never got into the habit that good businessmen tend to develop early in their lives, namely, of making profits. This meant that public money was literally burnt up. There was no money left to provide justice or to educate our millions of children. For a while Nehruvians languidly churned out more money from the money printing shop that the British had bequeathed to them, but that led to inflation. After some time,

Nehruvians stopped paying even lip service to the concept of the rule of law and good economic management.

There was no incentive to build an effective system of justice or police, either. An efficient police force would backfire quite badly on politicians. It is inconvenient to be corrupt if Mr Sherlock Holmes breathes down your neck each time you dip your snout into public funds. Therefore the police and the courts were deliberately allowed to go to seed. Astronomical backlogs soon built up in the courts. And so in socialist India you were – even today, are! – allowed to murder at will, then pay bribes all around and get away from the very slippery 'grasp' of justice. On the other hand, you could as easily be falsely charged with murder by a local policeman whom you didn't give a suitable bribe and be locked up for ten years without trial.

Despite the terrible consequences of Nehru's socialist legacy, his development of infrastructure was not as bad for India as his 'commanding heights' aspiration. But we received the short straw even on this, since scare resources were drained off by failed public businesses. For each successful Bhakra Nangal Dam we got a Modern Bakery that made a bonfire of our wealth, easily halving our infrastructure capability.

Nehru's socialist Frankenstein, which now stood large on India's murky horizon, grew unchecked and ran amuck, stomping over everybody after Nehru's death in 1964. Indeed, this monster gained a truly fierce bite with his daughter Indira Gandhi's ascension to India's 'throne' in 1966. Claiming Nehru's socialist legacy, she embarked on a frontal assault on freedom. Property rights were diluted even further. She dismantled large private organizations by nationalizing almost everything in sight including banks and cloth manufacturing mills. This is a good time to emphasize that in the lexicon of freedom, 'private' means us – the citizens. 'Private' is not a derogatory word; it is the word of freedom, acknowledging our individual existence and effort. Organizations run privately are run by *us*, individuals. What could be a thing to be more proud of than to produce our livelihood through our own, individual, *private* effort?

Mrs Gandhi also drew an iron curtain over the Indian economy by blocking off trade with the rest of the world. Our share of world trade plummeted to a mere quarter of what it had been at the time of independence – which in any case was an insignificant shadow of what it was before the Industrial Revolution began when about 25 per cent of global trade originated in India. Our freedom should have released us completely, and made us open our economy to the world's best technology. Instead, we blocked everything from abroad. Kicking out IBM with a flourish that would have done David Beckham proud, Indira Gandhi choked off the vital lifeblood of new technology to India. She then promoted the absurdly futile paradigm of self-sufficiency. It is futile and contrary to all common sense to expect that any country can ever become, or should try to become, self-sufficient, leave alone a largely illiterate and poverty stricken country like ours was then. Huge shortages of consumables and ordinary gadgets became the norm. People could not get things like a few cement bags to repair the walls of their homes. Obtaining 'luxuries' like electricity and water or public sewage became out of the question. I remember doing my school homework using kerosene lamps on many nights, sweat pouring out of my brow and hands sticking to the notebooks.

By 1975, the government was emboldened by the absence of any fight-back from citizens to enter our bedrooms. One of Nehru's grandchildren, Sanjay Gandhi, a small-time feudal dictator with a pea-sized brain, led a crusade to sterilize us by force, as we may sterilize unwanted dogs. Rajaji had by then died, his efforts having been in vain. At that point there was really no one left in India to protect our freedoms.

And there is none today. Parents of the dozens of innocent children slaughtered during 2005 and 2006 by Moninder Singh Pandher, the Butcher of Noida, surely ask each day before they go, distraught, to bed whether there is any protector of our children's freedom and innocence left in this *Mahaan*, 'free', India. Innumerable complaints of missing children to the Police from these parents were trashed into the bin by our law and order machinery which simultaneously deploys thousands of expensive guards to protect our totally corrupt political leaders. A child only matters in India today if its parents have big money or big power. Bootlicking journalists run around with cameras and create a ruckus if a big name is involved. But if you don't have money, simply jump off the cliff. Be fully aware that neither you nor your children matter.

Socialists make sure to give us a hallucinatory pill periodically. We are periodically lulled by a frenzy of celebrations on Independence Day to believe that we are free, even great! Long speeches are made, none of which talks about fixing the total corruption we find in government. We never find any political leader protesting against our freedoms being trampled upon. No Dandi marches; no fasts to death to protest the absence of the rule of law or against corruption. Instead, if only we care to strain our ears hard enough, we will hear the distant echoes of the following words of wisdom of our politicians and police reverberating in each corner of India: 'You've lost your land? Not a problem! Enjoy the footpath!'; 'You've lost your trade? We couldn't care less!'; 'And what, you have been put behind bars without trial, and beaten black and blue? Too bad. Wasn't it your responsibility to pay the necessary bribe?! Didn't you know this is *free* India?? Ha Ha.' We may have been the land of the Buddha and Krishna, but today it is everyone for himself and the Devil take the hindmost! We have to learn to live by the rules of 'free', anarchic India, or to leave. Quit India, calls out the morning bird.

* * *

And yet, for decades we have kept voting our corrupt socialist leaders back into power, perhaps eager to obtain some of the 'spoils' of self-rule for ourselves and for our families. From early days of independence, many of us jumped straight into the bandwagon of corruption to make merry, thinking possibly, that 'if you can't beat them, join them'. In any event, for a while at least, everyone seemed to have a gala time. Everyone had at least something to celebrate. Even the poor.

Jobs were being created in the government at an amazing rate! All you needed to do get one was to bribe the local politician and a handful of bureaucrats and clerks, for which you could borrow money. Once you had landed the job you could take life real easy; relax for life! There was never any expectation of work in any government job. If you were so inclined, you could also 'mint' money on the side without the fear of being punished. If ever that crazy Sanjeev Sabhlok managed to catch you while taking a bribe, you could run to your corrupt MLA or MP for protection and shunt such a ridiculously out-of-touch-with-reality officer into cold storage.

To top up this good life, there were these election festivals. Zamindars, rajahs, rich urban folk and the political aristocracy; even movie stars – fat, oily skinned people you'd normally only see photos of in the newspapers – attended these festivals in which they spoke theatrically with forceful release of significant lung energy. Their histrionics were well worth the tedious effort involved in listening to their outlandish promises. It was a colourful event as well. Attired as if going to a fancy-dress ball in the garb of ordinary villagers, these 'gentry' would pretend to humbly beg villagers for votes. These festivals enlivened the humdrum existence of villagers considerably and often gave them a brand new excuse, such as of the atrocities committed on the unused building called Babri Masjid or some such thing that happened five thousand years ago, to end up the day of theatrics by going out with a sharp knife to spill the blood of that neighbour whom they never liked in the first place. Large cut-outs of politicians in truly obsequious postures, if not yet fully sprawled on their knees, dotted the country's otherwise barren landscape. The British surely had no clue how much fun democracy could be – if only it was properly organized!

In due course, villagers found themselves being given good money, free food and transported (free of cost, of course) to big cities for so-called election 'rallies' where journalists did a headcount and declared one leader or the other the new God. These rallies were an enhancement over the ordinary election festivals – the villagers could now get to see the big city and also meet their urban relatives, for free. Until these dramas started, not everyone in the Indian villages had known that the British had left; some probably didn't know they had ever come to India in the first place. The good thing is that this theatre told them that something had changed. It made them think about issues of governance, for the first time ever.

* * *

But the chickens of socialism soon came home to roost. This initial euphoria evaporated quickly. Getting jobs for relatives who had no capacity for work or chanting *Garibi Hatao* to the accompaniment of cymbals seemed to do no one any good. The existing feudal classes merely got richer, and to this class was now added another, much more venal category – the corrupt politician. Corruption moved straight to the top, much of it in Nehru's time itself.[33] Despite being touted in Nehru's 14-point, Sanjay Gandhi's 5-point, or Indira Gandhi's 20-point programmes, economic development refused to happen. Despite all this hubbub, the results were spectacularly missing.

And thus a kind of *new*, cussed stalemate, reminiscent of the many prior, thousand-year long stalemates seen in Indian history, set in. The 'masses' had no expectation of accountability from their governments. And yet, in the back of their minds they realized that they now had representatives in Parliament who were supposed to work for them. But they found it very hard to obtain even basic answers to their questions. A solution apparently was to upturn each government during elections and to get a new one. Indira Gandhi's losing her family's royal sinecure in 1977 was a watershed event in India. She lost even as she was worshipped in extensive rural quarters as a Modern Goddess. This was a turning point for India, for it demonstrated in no uncertain terms that the Indian voter was finally starting to expect at least some accountability. Freedom needs such events. This was perhaps the greatest event of India's five thousand year old history.

* * *

But the voter soon found that changing governments did not make any difference. New ministers came snorting hungrily to power, desperately sniffing for their 'share' of the socialist loot. While earlier ministers had by now probably somewhat satisfied their hunger for black money, new ministers greedily dipped their dribbling snouts into the trough.[34] The swindle and fraud on public funds, and the accompanying rape of Freedom went on relentlessly; and goes on till today. It perhaps accelerates now with each change in government.

Given this mayhem, the urban upper and middle classes completely switched off. They stopped bothering with democratic participation. India's mammoth corruption haunted them, too; but while some had decided early in the piece to sell their souls, others now 'adjusted' and let the dirty games go on around them while they continued thinking clean by themselves as a lotus in a dirty pond. Whoever could, secured whatever freebies they could through their 'influence'. But beyond that, they switched off entirely. While agreeing to give bribes under 'unavoidable' circumstances, most Indians do continue to retain their moral sense. That is a primary reason why most of them refuse to join in the fray of 'democracy' which has become dependent totally on black money. On the other hand, village folk still continue to participate in democracy in large numbers, particularly the groups that were really badly treated in the past in India. Exercising indirect control on their ministers perhaps gives them at least some solace in the dark recesses of their poverty-stricken lives.

By around the early 1970s, the urban elites started to physically quit India. They groomed their children, initially more by accident than by design, to leave India. *All* of them knew what would happen to their children who went to prestigious institutions such as the IITs or AIIMS – namely, that they would leave for countries that were free and better managed. Arguments of patriotism stopped working when merit was condemned to obscurity, and mediocrity was destined to rule. There is an old saying in Bengal that where a king declares '*taka seer kaju taka seer bhaja*',[35] there people run for their lives! And so our very best children left us just as soon as we trained them at great expense.

* * *

Things were beginning to get quite bad by now. The stalemate was rapidly deteriorating into a lose-lose situation for everyone. Nehru's children and grandchildren were also no longer safe, either. The lack of the guiding message of freedom and compassion, and use of linguistic and other superficial means to divide the country's administration, had meant that hard-nosed approaches were being adopted by the government to deal with potentially violent rebellions. These policies were exacerbated by significant failures of the semi-defunct law and order machinery. These reasons were at least partly to blame for the tragic mix of events leading, separately, to the dastardly assassinations of Nehru's daughter Indira Gandhi in 1984 and his grandson Rajiv Gandhi in 1991.

By the late 1970s, fear and terror had begun to raise its ugly head wherever one looked. Communal rioting kept the country ablaze well into the long darkness of the night. The country started losing its generals, commissioners, deputy commissioners and thousands of soldiers and policemen to the unending rebellions and antinational revolutions festering in all parts of India – revolutions driven by a frustration of which there seemed no end. A pall of despair fell like a dark cloud over India, and settled heavily and uneasily on the land.

My personal grim experiences in the 1980s and 1990s of chronic terrorism in Assam (ULFA and Bodo terrorists); of bodies blown apart by bombs in buses; of having to work with my Superintendent of Police to organize early dawn ambushes and then see the dead bodies of terrorists next morning; of escaping from a bridge set on fire on our path; of moving about with the police in total, pitch darkness at night, revolver in hand – surely mirrored this dark mood.

That dark mood has not lifted. Even now, numerous terrorist organizations are active in India, having developed networks among frustrated Indians in every walk of life; many are linked to wealthy Indians abroad. No one is truly safe anywhere in India today. Law and order is a distant dream, a remote vision. We are a society where everybody has learnt to survive on connections, on moral turpitude, or on sheer luck. We wear golden and brass rings on each finger and ten charms and amulets around our neck, seeking spiritual protection against the devastating uncertainties that besiege us from all sides. The real *Kali Yug*[36] is upon us; the *Kali Yug* wrought by Nehru's false dream of socialism. Most painfully, particularly for many elderly people left behind alone in India, almost every young and educated person in India now wants to get *out*, to simply leave – for places in this world where things like law and order and electricity can be taken for granted.

And these elderly parents have no option but to support this choice even as their personal old-age plans go awry.

The precipitous decline in values in Nehruvian India is of particular concern. Many of India's younger people today have come to accept corruption and moral anarchy as a normal part of their lives. They no longer question why this situation has come to pass, or why corruption should now be our global brand, our national emblem, like a black turban always sitting uneasily on our heads. There is no idealism in the young Indian's soul any longer. Pragmatism rules: this most heinous word 'pragmatism' is now our national motto.

There is, of course, a solution to all of this – namely, seeking out freedom and its counterpart, accountability. The interrelationship between freedom and values was explained by Adam Smith in his *Theory of Moral Sentiments.* Values only exist where merit and quality, as decided in our free interactions with each other, counts. Values are strongest where a government remains focused on delivering freedom and accountability.

The frightening thing is that while feudal serfs rebelled to better their lot, we have become paralysed into inaction; immobilized as if inside a bad dream. As if this country doesn't belong to us.

Some of us rationalize – delude ourselves that ours is the best of all possible worlds 'under the given situation', that our situation is caused by the great size and diversity of our country. We even deny that we have failed by claiming we have succeeded beyond imagination! We invent delusional slogans – the last such was *India Shining* (*India Sinning* would have been more apt). In our more practical moments we hide behind gated communities; travel only in chauffeur driven cars or by air; skip the 'bad' parts our cities and avoid villages and slums altogether. And we read only about stock prices which are wonderfully up! But this problem just won't go away no matter how hard we dig our head into the sand.

Simultaneously, our fear-stricken, besieged governments are in physical retreat. After so many politicians and officials have been killed over the years, governments are now afraid of the citizens who elected them, equally as citizens are afraid of the governments they have elected. While we are a 'free' nation theoretically, almost all the doors and entrances to our government offices are securely locked, including the beautifully carved wooden doors that the British adorned our Central Secretariat with, and which were kept open in the days gone by. Political leaders, escorted by hooded gunmen, live inside sheltered cocoons with Z category security. All people are cleared from the roads before they travel. 'Free' Indians, with the poorest amongst us being the most vulnerable, are stopped at numerous check-posts or watched at zigzag barriers by police with rapid-fire sten guns ready to shoot at the slightest suspicion. We could say that our government is not the world's exemplar of approachability.[37]

With all these distressing outcomes of our failed experiment with socialism we never seem to tire, but like Oliver, ask for more! Surely some of us must wonder sometimes about the purpose of having democratically elected political leaders. Wouldn't a whimsical emperor not have been better? If lucky, we may even have got an Akbar. And, does that blasphemous question not at least sometimes arise at the back of our minds – was *this* why we fought hard for independence?

* * *

There was one key advantage we had in India – our almost instinctive sense of tolerance; a basic requirement of a free society. Unfortunately, in recent times we have not 'walked the talk' even on this. We have killed each other with wild abandon, indiscriminately, on great scale. Bombs, burnings, lynchings. That is India. We no longer demonstrate through our actions that we value human life sufficiently; and that we at least tolerate, if not respect, each other. The decline of tolerance has come along with the decline in morality.

* * *

I would like to suggest that each of these problems is, without exception, the direct or indirect consequence of our inadequate emphasis on freedom. Living in a shackled society can never be the way of *self-respecting* people. Rebellion under such circumstances is the only way out. Even if our rebellion miserably fails, adjusting to this deplorable reality is not acceptable. The rebellion I refer to is, of course, a non-violent rebellion to be delivered by contesting bad policies through elections. How about our using democracy to rebel? Surely a thought! Fight fire with fire! If democracy is so good and we sing its praises day and night, and write long articles about it in global newspapers, why don't we give it a go? Once – in our lifetime – let us each contest the elections. Or is that too rebellious? Have I said something too strong for children to read? Hide this book!! Maybe my book should be banned…

We now need thousands of fighters for freedom to arise and battle socialism. We need thousands of thinkers to show the world the future of freedom. The good thing is that at long last, a growing clamour is now being heard from educated Indians born after independence. We may not yet have found our voice through our Hayeks, Ayn Rands and Jeffersons, but this may be about to change. I hope and believe that we will start seeing our own philosophers of freedom soon, people who will show the entire world, not just India, how human freedom can support all people and their lives on this planet for the next million years.

I feel deeply grieved at the opportunities we have lost in the past 60 years to bequeath to our children the greatest possible country on earth. For, at exactly the same time when India has been reeling under Nehruvian socialism, parts of Asia such as Japan, Singapore, Taiwan, Hong Kong and South Korea have been powering their way to developed-country status using the basic tenets of freedom. These countries threw open their economies, adopted world standards in governance, built outstanding infrastructure and were able to get wealthier at an unprecedented pace – all by following the ancient dictates of freedom that Adam Smith wrote about.

We look back wistfully at what could have been, and what we have become. Had Nehru and his godchildren focused on freedom instead, on breaking barriers to trade, on building institutions of good governance, India's growth rates would have swung into double digits from the early 1950s. With compounding, we would now easily have been six to eight times the economic size of China, with half the population we have today.[38] We had come from such a low base that even a half-baked set of policies based on freedom would have boosted us like a vasopressin and adrenalin shot given to a patient whose heart had stopped beating.

But it is time to move on. Let us write off these 60 years as a very bad dream. So long as common sense finally prevails, India can cope with one very idealistic but very severely misguided Nehru.

REDISCOVERING RAJAJI

In saying that there were very few advocates of freedom in independent India, we must not forget Rajaji's contributions. He formed and led, between 1959 and his death in 1972, a small band of real freedom fighters (as opposed to 'independence fighters') who presented themselves on the battlefield in the war against socialism.

Chakravarthi Rajagopalachari, affectionately known as Rajaji, was the second Governor General of India; a *Bharat Ratna.* He was a close collaborator of Nehru during the independence movement, but after independence he began to view with increasing concern the risks to India of letting Nehru's fervent experiment with socialism go unchallenged. He saw that Nehru was creating a leviathan that would strangle the initiative and creativity of an entire generation and squander our extremely scarce resources. Without regard for his own advanced age (Rajaji was 80 years old then, and being a chaste Hindu would have preferred a quiet retirement), he decided in 1959 to form the Swatantra or Freedom Party to offer us policies compatible with freedom and oppose Nehru's socialism tooth and nail. For the next 13 years until his death in 1972 Rajaji waged a ceaseless battle with Nehru's Congress.

Rajaji, however, was no match for Nehru. Nehru was far more charismatic and popular. He also had populist policies. He jealously guarded his large donations from big business. And finally, he wielded the enormous resources of the government. Rajaji was also just too far ahead of his times. People simply didn't understand what he was saying, and he did not have sufficient time left to explain to them what he wanted to say. And except for a few outstanding followers like Masani, he attracted only a motley bunch that had no clue about freedom. Despite all odds, his party put up a good fight and became the largest opposition party with 44 seats in the Fourth Lok Sabha (1967–71). Rajaji kept up the good fight till his very end. He was a very brave and dutiful man; true to his country till his last breath.

I quote below what he wrote in the early days of his party's existence, in 1960:[39]

> The Swatantra Party stands for the protection of the individual citizen against the *increasing* trespasses of the State. It is an answer to the challenge of the so-called Socialism of the Indian Congress party. It is founded on the conviction that social justice and welfare can be attained through the fostering of individual interest and individual enterprise in all fields better than through State ownership and Government control. It is based on the truth that bureaucratic management leads to loss of incentive and waste of resources. When the State trespasses beyond what is legitimately within its province, it just hands over the management from those who are interested in frugal and efficient management to bureaucracy which is untrained and uninterested except in its own survival. (Italics mine)

> The Swatantra Party is founded on the claim that individual citizens should be free to hold their property and carry on their professions freely and through binding mutual agreements among themselves and that the State should assist and encourage in every possible way the individual in this freedom, but not seek to replace him.

Rajaji's staunch opposition arguably helped minimize some of the excesses of socialism. For example, Swatantra was part of the opposition to the misguided Nath Pai Bill[40] that advocated primacy for the Directive Principles of State Policy over Fundamental Rights. Fortunately Swatantra's votes mattered in consigning this atrocious Bill to the bin. There were surely countless other occasions when Swatantra spoke as the only voice of reason during those very unreasonable times. But Swatantra finally ran out of steam in 1973, after Rajaji's death.[41]

ARE WE READY TO BE FREE?

Have things changed now? Are we ready to be free now? I don't think so. Nehruvian socialism has not been given a burial. Despite China having abandoned the tenets of Marxism in 1979; despite the wall of Berlin having been breached in 1989; despite the Soviet Union having fallen asunder in 1991; we cling on to socialism. We continue to elect an overwhelming majority of socialist and communist parties. Indeed, there is no political party today wedded purely to the high standards of freedom. There is no liberal party. No capitalist party. No freedom party.

Even as we begin to reap the benefits of the IMF's freedom-enhancing capitalist policies of the 1990s, of the sort that Rajaji fought for but never got to see in his lifetime, we find that:

- many progeny of our freedom fighters have left India permanently, settling in these very countries that oppressed India in the past such as England – we ask whether this was what our 'freedom' fighters fought for, the right to settle their grandchildren abroad?;
- our Constitution continues to tout socialism in its Preamble;[42] and
- our Finance Ministers continue to reaffirm India's commitment to socialism.

And there is a lot of hypocrisy in the air. And so our country does not honour Rajaji or reject Nehru's legacy. Fresh winds still seem to be unable to get through to our minds. It is a time for change, and yet India is lost for words. The Indian is confused and can't pick the correct one of the only two options that exist in the world – freedom or equality. Till today very few people have made a clear link in their minds between the socialist policies and imperialist administration adopted by Nehru on the one hand, and the frustration they experience in their daily lives on the other. It is extremely confounding to them to have such a large and impoverished population surrounding them, and so they try to blame the size of the population itself as the cause of this frustration, or say that India is a special case, or blame the unbearable heat. One problem is offered as the cause of the other problem! But who started it?

What distresses me most is that almost all the solutions promoted in India particularly by our socialist journalists and leftist intellectuals still ask the government to do something about 'the problem', which amounts to feeding a Frankenstein even more human heads! How big does our Frankenstein have to grow before we start to pin it down?

Can we now please stop running around helter-skelter, pointing fingers in every direction, and stop for a moment to understand the root cause of our grief? Increasing the role of government is not the way to help ourselves out of this mess. Your role and my role as citizens of a free country are to understand the requirements of freedom, and to advance freedom. That is the only way we will be able to change things, by getting involved. Fixing the country is not the job of our government. It is our job.

Our challenge today is what S P Aiyar said of India's challenge many years ago – to find 'solutions appropriate to given situations but only those compatible with freedom'.[43] The good thing is that while the Indian government is not the best protector of freedom in the world, it does not censor books of this sort. It does not prevent people from talking about their views. Its laws almost fully protect our freedoms. We are almost there! Just a nudge to our systems of governance – including making our government get out of things where it has no business to be in, and rebuilding our political and bureaucratic institutions to make them compatible with the transparency and accountability that are the hallmarks of freedom; and we could soon have the freest country in the world – and thus, ultimately, the greatest. Many other parts of the world like our truly unfortunate and beleaguered neighbour Pakistan have a much longer way to go than us, and one can only wish them luck and offer them genuine wishes for the welfare of their children.

Today, it is imperative that Indian citizens leave aside their 5,000 year old cynicism and actively participate in the democratic and political processes of India. It goes without saying that organizations like the ULFA should lay down their arms as well. Using arms is a guaranteed sign of the weakness of their arguments, apart from being completely violative of their freedoms. Let them come forward and talk in public forums about what they would like to do to improve India and make it more free. The way to freedom is only through persuasion, through discussion, debate and electoral politics. No more violence, please.

* * *

That was a quick review of the history of freedom in India. Having introduced the key issues, the rest of this book is now a discussion of the way out of our mess. I begin by exploring how a free society looks like and how it works. Then I discuss the systemic shortcomings in our political and administrative systems. Finally, I end this book with my recommendations, for whatever these are worth, on how we can become a free nation.

And now, it is time for you, dear reader, to lay down your backpack, get out your sandwich, and take a short rest. Make sure you don't miss the fragrance of those lovely fresh flowers behind that rivulet. Please return in one hour sharp for the rest of the journey. See you soon!

Chapter 2

Overview of a Free Society

> Democracy is not a state in which people act like sheep. Under democracy individual liberty of opinion and action is jealously guarded.
>
> Gandhi[1]

This chapter explores key features of a free society. It first explores what a free society looks like, and then how it works. By exploring what a free society looks like, we will be in a position to recognize when India finally achieves freedom. By studying how a free society works, namely examining its engines such as markets and democratic governance, we will get to know when India is finally fitted with the right means of propulsion. There will remain the challenge of getting the people's mandate to fit these engines of freedom to India's ramshackle machine of governance; but that can be discussed later.

WHAT DOES A FREE SOCIETY LOOK LIKE?

Freedom is a multi-faceted thing, and there is much relativity among the levels of freedom prevailing in different countries. Since freedom cannot be measured at one go, a number of indicators have been developed.[2] But at a certain level freedom is a subjective experience; a way of life more than an end-product; and instead of looking for precise measures, it will perhaps be better to seek its essence. I have therefore tried to summarize a free society in the stylized facts outlined in the following sections. These stylised facts are discussed more fully in the *Online Notes*,[3] should you wish to explore these at greater length. On a matter as important as freedom, I suspect that such an impressionistic outline better represents the ethos we seek for India than a pedantic comparison of surveys or numbers related to freedom.

Free societies are human magnets

Ask of a society what its net balance of migration is and you'll get a sense of its level of freedom. Does the society attract more migrants, or do more of its citizens leave it? In this way, freedom comes closest to being measured objectively through its effect on the physical flow of people from a lower to higher levels of freedom. We can predict this flow with almost the same precision with which we predict the flow of water which flows, instead, from a higher to a lower level.

While economic reasons may impel people to temporarily work in places like Saudi Arabia or Libya, for the most part people do not migrate to or move to countries merely for a better standard of living. What they look for is the opportunity to achieve their own, and even more importantly, their children's highest potential. A consequence of their people-magnetism is that free societies are almost always multi-cultural and multi-ethnic melting pots.

While nowhere in the league of ill-fated North Korea or Afghanistan, India also has net outflows of people. Indians have essentially fled from socialist tyranny and injustice. Despite the lack of welcome in the West till recently (racism is lesser now than it was in the past), many Indians prefer to live in the West than in their own shackled homeland. This exodus has stemmed somewhat with the Indian economy being freed up, though the data indicate an overall accelerating trend.

The following Tables outline some of the trends of emigration from India.

Table 1: Indian Emigrants to the United States[4]

Year	*Number*	*Share of immigrants received by USA*
1998	36,482	5.6%
1999	30,237	4.7%
2000	42,046	4.9%
2001	70,290	6.6%

Table 2: Indian Emigrants to Australia[5]

Year	*Number*
1992–3	3,553
2001–2	5,091
2002–3	5,783

India's corrupt governance and dearth of good educational institutions largely explain this acceleration, despite increasing economic opportunities within the country. Corruption in India is frequently, among the main reasons, cited by people for leaving India. If India does not reform its governance, this exodus will gather pace since it is currently restricted by limited intakes by the West. We know that the more talented people of a society are disproportionately more important to that society than their sheer numbers would indicate.[6] The problem is that it is these more talented people of India who are most likely to leave. 'Indians in the United States are almost 20 times more likely to be college educated than Indians in India.'[7]

The culture of freedom: flexible, connected, relaxed

The second key indicator relates to the culture of a free society. There are numerous traits that come together to form such a culture:

- **Flexibility and mobility:** A free society is socially, economically and geographically mobile. There is a palpable sense of freedom in the actions and motions of its people. Its people move up and down the economic and social ladder routinely; often in a single generation. Its children tend to choose occupations different from their parents', live in cities different to where they were born or grew up, and create new cultural lifestyles for themselves.
- **Shared interest connectedness:** A key cultural feature of free societies is the level of networking among its citizens. Its people are linked to a lot of other people; particularly in areas of shared interest. Also called civil society, the 'value' of these networks is often added up to give us the 'social capital' of a society.
- **Social status is based on actual contributions:** The free society gives everyone an equal opportunity to blossom. There is no caste system, no feudal residue of hereditary titles. Everyone gets an equal chance to display his or her talent.
- **Openness of mind:** No one is forced into a mental straightjacket in a free society. The mind of each individual is completely unleashed; free to think. Through critical examination of its past a free society is able to establish higher standards of freedom and justice with each successive generation.

- **Relaxed, tolerant, happy:** Freedom is a state of relaxed tolerance and appreciation of the diversity of the thousands of types of people around us. This relaxed state of mind leads to a contented, even happy, expression on the free citizen's face – just as a free bird's chirping is more melodious than a caged one's.

Economic mobility, including occupational mobility, has been increasing in India after the 1991 reforms. The same, unfortunately, cannot be necessarily said of social mobility in India, except maybe in pockets. We continue to live in the twilight zone between tribalism, feudalism and socialism. While India's feudal social structures have definitely been impacted by economic reforms, they have a long way to go to unfreeze. India's majority religion, Hinduism, has a deep-rooted foundation of institutional discrimination. It is said that the caste system wasn't so rigid in Vedic times, but today this discriminatory practice is fully embedded in India. Besides, there are numerous other social constraints in India, such as linguistic barriers, which make it socially inflexible.

While Western societies like Australia, each with migrants from 140 countries or more, are engaged in debates on the challenges of becoming multicultural societies, India has not yet overcome basic parochial pressures. We need to robustly challenge the caste system, tribal and language barriers, and the 'son of the soil' policies. Everyone in free India must be made to feel comfortable and welcome when they move to other parts of India.

Free societies do not breed terrorists

The third major indicator of a free society is the absence of violence. Violence is not used as a means of persuasion in free societies, which therefore do not breed political terrorism.[8] Why is a free society *antithetical* to violent political discourse? Because in such societies people are well-educated, prosperous, aware of their obligations and accountabilities, and fully conscious of the vital significance of life and their freedom. Each person in a truly free society can attain his personal goals through hard work, diligence and persuasion, either through the marketplace or by participating in the government. He doesn't have to take recourse to terror to achieve his desired outcomes.

Many people have noted that India has the world's second-largest Muslim population but our Muslim brothers did not participate in the wave of global terrorism that was unleashed by some Muslim fanatics in 2001; something that unfortunately found, and continues to find, support in neighbouring Pakistan.[9] This lack of Indian Muslim support for world terrorism is not a freak accident. Despite its low levels of freedom, India does enjoy a democracy (albeit imperfect) and relatively free press. Even these limited measures have been therapeutic and, so far as terrorism is concerned, largely preventive.

On the other hand, the fact that we lack sufficient freedom is evident from the numerous terrorist outfits our country has spawned such as the ULFA, the Naxalites and militants in Kashmir. We therefore can't be called a free country yet, and we have a lot of work ahead of us to demonstrate that we genuinely value life and the freedom it demands.

Free societies are innovative

The fourth indicator relates to the level of innovation in a society. This indicator, along with the next two I will outline, accompanies free societies but may also accompany societies that are not so free. These three indicators are best seen as 'necessary *but not* sufficient' indicators of freedom, to distinguish them from the first three which are both necessary and, all together, sufficient to characterize free societies.

Innovation depends upon the free and unbounded exercise of our intellect as no other human activity does. It requires completely fresh, new thinking. It requires the mind to be free of 'hangovers', biases and misconceptions that can prevent it from forming new links between disparate concepts. To say that 'necessity is the mother of invention' is only partly true. Primitive tribal societies had the greatest necessity in comparison to us, but were the least inventive. Only free societies respond to necessity with fresh, new thought. Tribal societies merely look in confused amazement at the heavens and dance around a fire with paint smeared on their bodies, hoping that the frenzy so generated, which dulls the brain, will appease the Gods and lead them to their next meal. The rate and level of innovation is therefore predominantly related to the level of freedom in a society. Tribal collectivist societies and socialist societies generally prevent innovation by blocking new ideas. In free societies the mind is allowed to range freely across the entire universe of known and unknown human thought. As a consequence of this different mindset towards life and its opportunities – a mindset that does not resist free exploration – free societies constantly churn up a storm of innovation in every sphere of life.

But innovation also appears to happen sometimes in societies that do not enjoy freedom. It appears, though, that such innovation is largely restricted to the machinery of war. The fanatic nationalism of Nazi Germany and imperial Japan led to a few of their scientists focusing single-mindedly on instruments of warfare. But such focus, or 'evil genius', is not versatile, and theft of intellectual property is the preferred method used by such societies. It would have been impossible for modern Germany or Japan to become as innovative as they are today in their post-World War II *avatars* had they not opened up and freed their economy after the war.

In comparison, Australia, with one-fiftieth of India's population, not only produces more world-class swimmers, cricketers and hockey players than India does, but more research papers than India (Table 3). Its citizens have been awarded nine Nobel prizes[10] with eight of them being in science and one in literature, as against only nine, including only three in science, in India. On the scale of its population, India would have had to have 450 Nobel prizes by now to be comparably inventive.

Table 3: Number of Research Papers Produced

No.	Country	Papers published (2000 SCI CD-ROM)
1	USA	2,62,892
2	Japan	68,056
3	UK	63,972
4	Germany	63,365
5	France	44,990
6	Canada	31,929
7	Italy	31,673
8	Russia	23,041
9	PR China	22,061
10	Spain	20,546
11	Australia	19,067
12	The Netherlands	18,826
13	Sweden	14,278
14	Switzerland	13,828
15	India	12,127
16	South Korea	12,013

Source: 'Is Science in India on the Decline?', *Current Science*, Vol. 83, No. 2, 25 July 2002.

Moving beyond scientific papers and Nobel prizes, we could consider the level of innovativeness in our industry. But given the shelter provided from competition under our mercantilist and socialist regime, our industry cruised well into the 1990s by using Western inventions of the 1950s. For instance, Hindustan Motors continued to produce Ambassador cars – the Morris of the 1950s vintage – well into the 1990s. Industry is only now becoming slightly more innovative than before.

Free societies are wealthy

Free societies are necessarily wealthy. In other words, it is impossible for a free society to remain poor. That doesn't mean that societies which are not free can't be rich. Some shackled societies like Saudi Arabia, Russia and Kuwait have become temporarily rich based on natural resources. Wealth, in the absence of other information, is a necessary *but not sufficient* indicator of a free society.

The main drivers of wealth in a free society are its openness through free trade and openness to new technology, and robust internal competition and innovation. The next section will examine how free societies are able to churn out literally infinite amounts of wealth. Actually that is not very hard, really! Ever since Adam Smith explained it in his 1776 book, it is a well known secret. On the other hand, shackled countries like Saudi Arabia are guaranteed to collapse into poverty after their oil runs out unless they unshackle their society right away; and that includes completely changing their culture.

As far as India is concerned, it is a poor country by international standards. More problematically, it has underperformed in comparison to its South East Asian counterparts like South Korea. Korean per capita income has grown six times faster than India's in the last 40 years. Given that South Korea has 500 lakh (or 50 million) people, it would be wrong to think of it as a small country. South Korea merely followed – mostly imperfectly, at first – the standard text book model of economic and political freedom. It later became a more genuine capitalist democracy. In consequence it is now considered to be one of the most innovative societies of the world.[11] Comparing South Korea with North Korea teaches an even more powerful and obvious lesson!

People in free societies live longer, are taller and smarter

Freedom also drives the vital indicators, namely, things like height and longevity. These are impacted primarily through the effect of freedom on wealth and then on nutrition. Genetic factors obviously play a limiting role.[12] The effects of nutrition on human height are relatively well-documented and quite startling. For example, young Koreans were roughly the same average height across the Korean peninsula before South Korea decided to expand its freedoms while North Korea choose to shut them down. As a result of this difference in freedom, young South Koreans are now 7 cm taller, on average, than their North Korean counterparts – a change brought about in merely two generations. Similarly, wealthier countries are healthier, as measured by longevity; noting that it is possible for shackled countries like Cuba to also do well in healthcare while underperforming in everything else.

Most problematically for India, freedom also impacts intelligence. Despite intelligence quotient (IQ) being only a relatively modest predictor of success, and despite its well-known limitations being a construct, as well as difficulties in measurement, the average IQ of a society's population surely counts for something. While the average IQ of an average Western society is standardized to 100, the average IQ of Indians living in India is around 85, which is very low. This figure is based on measurements conducted in India by a range of different researchers over decades. Despite the methodological issues that the underlying data may raise, I have little doubt that this IQ difference is real (I would be pleased to be proven that this is an error.) We can't simply shrug aside a difference of this magnitude; we should try to explain it. The model in the diagram below explains this difference from the perspective of freedom. For a fuller discussion of the model, with a detailed discussion of the pathways, please see the *Online Notes.*[13]

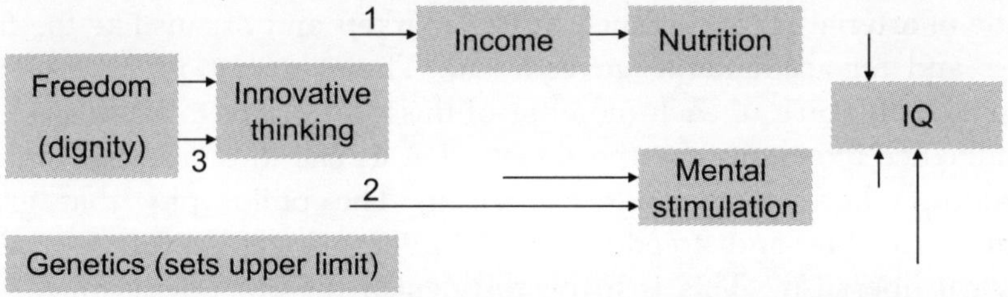

The model is underpinned by a simple argument. India and the West were very similar in income levels till 250 year ago. What has changed in the past 250 years is the way the Western people use their brain; not the genetic makeup of their brain. Free societies have moved from tribalism and coercive restraints on human thought to free thinking, thus significantly increasing their IQs.

This model suggests that it is our lack of freedom as well as our deeply entrenched caste system, through which nearly half of our population suffers from a sense of inferiority, that has made us relatively less intelligent as an entire nation.[14] India therefore underperforms in every way relative to their potential. The good news is that this can be reversed simply by increasing the level of freedom in India, which will also help to break down the caste system. A study reported that the IQ of Indians living in the UK was 96, which is close to the Caucasoid mean, demonstrating that with greater freedom, normal IQs should re-emerge in India.[15]

In concluding this section we note that India has tremendous scope to become far more free. We also note that if India does opt for becoming free, everyone in India will become enormously better off not only in health and wealth, but also in mental capacity.

INNER WORKINGS OF A FREE SOCIETY

Now that we know what a free society looks like, let us explore how a free society works. We seek to find how the energies of millions of people, impelled freely and in the most diverse directions in response to the countless opportunities that are constantly being created, are 'co-ordinated' invisibly for the benefit of society without any central planner. In particular, we will find out how the all-too-human problems of cheating, deception and pollution are minimized or resolved even as the society produces its abundance of wealth and health.

A free society is a fascinating thing. On looking inside it, we find a bustle of arterial processes such as free markets and organs like the free press and an accountable government. These institutions enable the independent voice of each member of the free society to be heard and to influence the choices of the society. Let us call these mechanisms of freedom, taken together, as capitalism. The philosophy that gives primacy to life and freedom, and underpins capitalism, is called classical liberalism. This is to be distinguished from liberalism of the American sort, which is really 'welfare socialism', an unsustainable mix of incompatible ideas. It is through well-designed capitalism that the oxygen of freedom courses strongly through the veins of individuals in a free society.

* * *

Without freedom of expression (this freedom is not unbounded, just as no freedom is), there can be no freedom at all. The battles for a free press have been more or less won in India. Even though some battles are still being waged,[16] I propose to skip discussion of this crucial organ. Societies that are not as fortunate as India in this regard must, of course, establish this organ first. On the other hand, arguments for free markets and an accountable government have not yet been internalized in India; so I'll discuss these in some detail. First the highlights:

Free markets

Nehruvian arguments of socialism have made us afraid of free markets, although that fear is muted now, having seen the positive effects of liberalization. Even then, for someone to advocate 'free markets' almost sounds like advocating corruption and immorality! The busybodies inside the government don't encourage free markets one bit, either. They find the idea of citizens taking risks and learning from their own mistakes very challenging. That free people should be allowed to buy and sell voluntarily, and without supervision, sends a shiver down their spines. But it is crucial that our governments stay away from our natural learning experience, and let us make our own mistakes.

On the other hand, we often don't get support from economists in this regard either. Despite promoting the merits of markets, economists talk in hushed tones about market failure. But there is no such thing as market failure. What people call market failure is primarily individual, ethical failure. It is important to attribute these ethical failures to specific individuals, not to markets in general. Markets are a collective; and there is no such thing as collective ethical failure. Even in Nazi Germany a large part of the population remained good. Occurrences of individual failures ought to result in the justice system being strengthened, not markets being strangled. If a few individuals do wrong things we cannot freeze entire markets or tie up everybody's hands behind their backs.

More problematically, in using the language of market failure, pseudo-economists shut their eyes to the chronic failure of governments in undertaking even their fundamental roles concerning issues such as provision security and justice, leave alone the disastrous attempts some governments make to become businessmen. In India, we see this government failure at each step: almost everything our government has done in independent India has been done very badly. Therefore loud alarm bells should ring in our heads whenever we hear anyone talking of market failure without elaborating upon the huge risks of government failure!

But at times, markets challenge us emotionally as they appear to be heartless. We are not comfortable with the outcomes of a free market which we may reluctantly agree produces great wealth, but which we find also results in increased inequality. We tend to see inequality as fundamentally wrong, even though we know that every individual will actually become much better off in a free market than he or she is today.

I wonder, though, about the hypocrisy behind our alleged preference for equality. Gandhi once asked some socialists who had come to visit him, 'Now tell me how many of you have servants in your homes?' The socialists Gandhi was talking to said they had a servant in each home. Gandhi replied, 'And you call yourself Socialists while you make others slave for you! It is a queer kind of Socialism which, I must say, I cannot understand'.[17] If we genuinely wanted everyone to have exactly the same income, why do we bargain so hard with our poor garbage pickers and maidservants and pay them only the market rate? And if bargains of this sort are good for us (it being a free market for the services of these poor people), why are these negotiations bad for the society as a whole?

But given that these concepts, namely, of equality or its variants such as equity or egalitarianism, play such an important emotional role in our minds when considering capitalism, I will discuss these at length a little later. I will show that not only has equality no real content, but that it is dangerous. On the other hand, I will show that equality of opportunity is a critical requirement for a free society, and helps us to eliminate poverty.

Accountable government

Finding someone to protect our security and provide justice is far more difficult than is commonly understood; far more difficult than creating free markets. We don't like to create Frankensteins, but our protector can easily become a predator if we are not careful enough. The main thing is that good government never arises from our natural tribal state – to get one we have to put in a lot of hard work. India suffers from shoddy governance because we have not invested sufficient thought into our mechanics of governance. In 1947 we rushed to grab the seat vacated on the British Imperial buggy. We then replaced the buggy's horses with bullocks pulling in different directions (e.g. our Directive

Principles of State Policy). Then we added upside-down aeroplane wings (e.g. Nehruvian socialism). And now we expect this contraption to fly. Of course, it won't. In fact good governance needs far more thought than designing a manned-rocket to Mars.

Let me get into some details now, and first examine the mechanics of wealth creation.

WEALTH CREATION THROUGH FREE MARKETS

No society can call itself free without its markets being almost entirely free. The qualification 'almost' is explained later in this section, but let me discuss the main premise first. When we talk of a 'free' press, and advocate more of it, we feel a sense of righteousness, even pride, in our 'forward looking' position. More of this particular 'free' thing is surely better, we assert confidently! Well, it turns out that the same holds for markets.

It is surely reasonable to assume that an average adult is competent enough to determine what is in his or her best interest – unless he or she is seriously challenged intellectually. Such citizens of one or more nations who *voluntarily*[18] exchange legally permitted goods and services, produced or otherwise sourced by them, with each other, and value these goods and services through the unhindered exercise of their personal judgment, can be said to constitute a market. Markets are thus agglomerations of two or more trading peoples, including organizations of people, at a point in time. They cover a big chunk of our interactions with others.

For a market to form there is no requirement that the buyer and seller should be located next to each other. If, living in Australia, I buy a book from Amazon.com which ships it to me from USA, I become part of the online market. In this online market I am interacting ultimately with some human being somewhere in USA; a person whom I don't need to see or to know about at all. A market is thus a fairly general concept. We may also refer to markets by what is traded in them, e.g. the labour market where employees hire their labour for a wage, or a grain futures market where people can buy grain from farmers even before the crop is sown. At other times we apply this concept to the place where people assemble to interact with each other, e.g. a shopping centre, a website, or an auction centre. A market in this broader sense is any interface of voluntarily agreed commercial interaction between trading peoples.[19]

More broadly, even non-commercial interactions can form part of markets. Temples and churches are part of the market for spiritual services, where we receive spiritual services in exchange for our allegiance and monetary contributions. The concept of markets can also be applied within a family, where husbands and wives 'trade' services between themselves. Every sensible husband knows the consequences of not doing his part of the 'bargain' such as trimming the lawn or mending the leaking roof; or even bringing an occasional bunch of flowers for his excellent wife. Wives are known to keep a detailed scorecard. A reader reminded me that consequences also exist for wives who do not keep their share of the bargain! Life's no joke! There are markets, trades and accounts everywhere!

We can reasonably assume under this non-coercive and loosely defined structure called market that people agree to buy something only if they are made better off[20] by the purchase. Similarly, they do not sell unless they are made better off by the sale, even if it is a so-called 'distress' sale. These assumptions are valid only for the particular instant when a trade is agreed upon – both the buyer and seller perceive themselves being better off at that moment. If this were not so, it would mean that one of them has deliberately chosen to make himself worse off – which doesn't make sense. If that happens it may be because the person has been coerced, which means it is no longer part of a market. There is a 'limiting' case when trade is agreed to by someone who remains only as well off as before.[21] This limiting case is only a mathematical curiosity; since why would anyone trade if there was no benefit, either tangible or intangible?

What about people who apparently become better off by choosing to make themselves materially worse off? Charity is a case in point. During a festival at Prayag in the seventh century AD, king Harshavardhan gave away his personal ornaments and wore an old and ordinary garment instead. The traditional definition of what makes a person better off would seem to have been turned on its head in this case. But the principle actually remains valid, for the person is now receiving psychological (in this case spiritual) benefit of equal or greater value in return. One is therefore quite safe in assuming that each trade *always* makes each party to the trade better off.[22] This is a major assumption, since it underpins all creation of wealth.

What about transactions not deemed to be legal by a society? In my definition of markets, you'll note that I included only the exchange of legally permitted goods and services. What about drug dealers buying and selling drugs? Is that part of the market? After all, a drug dealer and the drug addict both become 'better off' in their own way as a result of the trade. The same applies to prostitution, smuggling, gambling, or trading in beef, alcohol, tobacco, pornography, banned books and so on. These are areas where a government, presumably representing the views of the majority of the people, has declared some of these 'markets' as illegal, or otherwise restricted their operation. Without commenting on my personal view on any of these 'markets',[23] let me state that illegal trades do not constitute a market for the purposes of this book because these are not recognized markets. There is no place for lawlessness in a free society. Even if we disagree with restrictions imposed in a free society, citizens cannot disobey the laws, but must work democratically to modify them.

The most important thing about free markets is that they are entirely compatible with our freedom, since our individual choice is given the greatest possible consideration or regard. Even the richest man can't force me to buy his products or to work in his company unless I choose to. I am king of myself – of my kingdom of one. Each of us participates in markets consciously and as a complete equal of all others in the independence of our decisions. This equality of status which acknowledges people's dignity is a hallmark of markets. Free markets are truly democratic. Ludwig von Mises described market democracy thus:[24]

> Within the market society the working of the price mechanism makes the consumers supreme. They determine through the prices they pay and through the amount of their purchases both the quantity and quality of production. They determine directly the prices of consumers' goods, and thereby indirectly the price of all material factors of production and the wages of all hands employed [...] In that endless rotating mechanism [i.e. a market society] the entrepreneurs and capitalists are the servants of the consumers. The consumers are the masters, to whose whims the entrepreneurs and capitalists must adjust their investments and methods of production. The market chooses the entrepreneurs and the capitalists and removes them as soon as they prove failures. The market is a democracy in which every penny gives a right to vote and where voting is repeated every day.

Now we examine how these democratic markets actually work.

INDIVIDUAL ETHICAL FAILURES IN THE MARKETPLACE

For both parties of a trade to genuinely become better off, they must both conduct the trade in good faith. If one, or both, deceive the other, then that interaction amounts to cheating, or worse, it can't be counted as a trade. The smooth flow of markets thus depends critically on our personal integrity as actors in each transaction. Some people claim that markets are moral since very few people renege on agreements in their interactions with others. That is true, but the problem with this view is that it implicitly assumes that immoral transactions are also part of the market. But immoral transactions are excluded from markets by definition – markets comprise *only* those interactions that are both voluntary and moral. Just like assaults and murder can't form part of social interactions, markets must exclude cheating.

But problems of cheating do arise and we need to discuss them. Problems can arise if there are discrepancies between what was agreed to and what is delivered. In some 'trades' people could get injured or even die. In others, the buyer or seller, or both, pass on costs to those who were not involved in the trade. To solve such problems we must hark to the theory of justice, not to the theory of market failure found in economics.

Free societies require individuals to uphold their accountability voluntarily. If they do not close the *loop of accountability* (see Appendix 1 for a discussion), the state must step in to provide justice. No free citizen is entitled to cheat, hurt, poison, maim or kill others. Such things, as we have seen, are not 'market failures' but *individual* failures of freedom. The government's job in such cases is largely limited to ensuring justice after the event. The failure must be punished, preferably proportionately. Where a strong argument for deterrence exists, punishment could potentially be disproportionate, noting that disproportion is, in principle, unjust.

However, this is not considered to be sufficient by some people. They want the government not only to dispense justice, but to prevent individual failures. A free society does not buy into such arguments. Preventing ethical failures is not the job of the government. Our ethical behaviour is an individual choice that each of us makes each day. The government is neither our master nor our nanny. Therefore a government is not required in a free society to establish an army of inspectors to detect individual failures before these occur. An inspection implicitly assumes that the organization being inspected is potentially riddled with ethical failures which the inspector has come to detect. While this may be true in a few cases, this is not so for the vast majority of businesses. Therefore expeditions by inspectors to fish around for potential ethical failures are unacceptable. Not only do they pre-judge normal law abiding citizens, they impose unnecessary costs both on the businesses inspected and also on tax payers who foot the bill for such fishing expeditions.

In a free society no law-abiding citizen or organization is inspected randomly. The onus is on the state to prove that an individual or business is potentially guilty before taking away even one minute of an individual's life for questioning. We tend sometimes not to consider an inspection as a penalty, but it is one – an imposition on our time and hence on our life. Diminishing our life even by one minute is a penalty which should be imposed only if there are good reasons. Detailed inspections should therefore occur only after preliminary evidence of failure has emerged. The focus of an inspection would then need to be exclusively on finding the evidence relevant to a prosecution. If an inspection doesn't yield a successful prosecution, then the concerned business or citizen must be compensated for his or her time, and the head of the inspecting agency dismissed (or at least asked to apologize and explain). That is the standard of regulatory excellence expected of a free state.

At the same time, as we have noted, the vast majority of transactions are completed honestly and without incident. That is because a trader's (whether buyer's or seller's) reputation is crucial to his business. A trader who wants to succeed has to focus on building his reputation and displaying good character,[25] or else that business will collapse. Indeed, in developed markets like the USA and Australia, reputational effects are so strong that most large trading organizations and franchises routinely take back products they have sold, and fully refund the sale price – no questions asked – for up to a month or more from the date of purchase. This is done even though it may be obvious in some cases that the products being returned were negligently damaged by unethical customers. This good behaviour of businesses, arising largely because of fierce competition for customer loyalty, must surely confirm some of our 'faith' in markets.

But then there are *bona fide* errors that take place; namely, accidents. Such accidents happen to all of us; they are not, strictly speaking, ethical failures and should hopefully not undermine our 'faith' in markets. For example, we sometimes go back from a shopping trip and find a rotten egg among the dozen that we bought. Indian roadside egg-vendors will usually verify the quality of each egg they sell by eyeballing it, i.e. looking through the egg against the flame of a candle to confirm that its yolk has not curdled. If, after that inspection, one egg out of twelve turns out to be bad when we start cooking it, we don't go asking for government intervention, and generally ignore that error unless this sort of thing has been happening too frequently with the same vendor. Indeed, on our next visit to the shop, if we mention this bad egg incident, the vendor will most likely give us an extra egg free of charge, quite readily.

At other times, a seller may inadvertently under-quote and find later that he will make a small loss because certain inputs turn out to be dearer than he had anticipated. The seller will most likely take a small loss in such a case, and move on without expecting us to pay more. In brief, small departures from what was agreed to and what is delivered do not make us lose sleep about capitalism and free markets. Statistically, these two types (honest transactions, and those with minor errors or mistakes) taken together probably comprise 99.9 per cent of our experience (999 out of 1,000 trades).

* * *

Now to the problem found in 1 out of a 1,000 cases of deliberate cheating and serious accidental failures. Primarily, three types of such failures take place:

1. significant variation in promised economic value;
2. unintended but preventable damage to human life and health; and
3. damage to people not involved in the transaction.

For the most part, markets establish preventive solutions to these potential failures of individual accountability on their own. As far as the government is concerned, its best contribution to these problems is to dispense justice quickly and effectively. It may, however, also have a facilitative role in establishing preventive mechanisms in some cases. Let's discuss these three so-called 'market failures' – but in fact ethical failures or accidents – one at a time.

Significant variation in promised economic value

Relatively large departures from what was promised and what is supplied are of concern, whether these are accidental or deliberate.

Freedom means each of us being held to account; no one can make the excuse that there was an error in not supplying what was promised, and get to walk away from a major discrepancy. Such situations can also lead to litigation and conflict and waste a society's time and resources. A free society generally tries to minimize such discrepancies through its voluntary initiatives.

The role of a government in such cases is largely restricted to creating an efficient legal mechanism for compensation. But while some such failures merely need to be compensated such as through liability insurance, others could be deliberate fraud, being ethical failures. Slightly less than one per cent of the human race seems to suffer from significant shortcomings of personal character.[26] Such failures in character spill into the marketplace equally as they infect other interactions of such people, as in a marriage. In other words, these people cheat in markets equally as they cheat in their relationships. These are morally challenged people. They could be sellers, but also buyers who steal from shops. While we tend to focus on ethical failures of sellers, we should not forget that customers, or buyers, are required to be ethical too. Large department stores have to invest heavily in security because, given a chance, about one per cent of the buyers will steal.

Markets work hard to minimize such failures through self-regulation. Following is an illustrative list of actions that markets voluntarily put in place:

- Consumers ask others, or check the internet about what others are saying about a company they are contemplating to deal with.
- Businesses and customers record in great detail the specifications they have agreed to, so there is no confusion about what is being purchased. Similarly, at the time of delivery, all sorts of signatures are usually taken.
- Businesses send out surveys to get customer feedback so that bad practices or bad staff members can be weeded out.
- Businesses formulate voluntary codes of practice and establish standards to be adopted as part of good corporate governance. These include the standards of the International Standards Organisation, a non-governmental organization whose membership includes private companies.[27]
- Businesses develop internal practices to comply with voluntary industry standards. These practices include internal audits and quality audits carried out by external parties.
- Businesses join voluntary accreditation systems. A psychiatrist who plays fast and loose with his vulnerable patients, or a

company that manipulates the true picture of its accounts, can adversely affect the reputation of that entire industry. Therefore psychiatrists form associations which accredit only good psychiatrists. These associations then identify, warn and ostracize unsuitable members.

All this, and much more, happens on its own, without the free society's government getting involved in any way. Where businesses do not voluntarily act to minimize failures of accountability, and frequent instances of deception are found to occur, a government may have to consider a more active, temporary strategy:

- It may be productive use of the taxpayer's money in some cases (very rarely, though!) to pay business associations to develop the capacity to self-regulate and undertake self-monitoring processes. They could also be subsidized initially to educate their members on best-practice.
- It may sometimes be productive use of a government's time to get involved by providing comment on an industry's self-regulatory practices to ensure consistency and alignment with community expectations. The goal in such cases is to maximize the quality of industry self-regulation.
- If an industry is demonstrably incapable of self-regulation despite such support, governments may need to directly regulate and establish 'rules of the game' temporarily; things like mandatory best-practice prudential norms or self-audit standards. A paper trail of compliance with these rules can then unerringly help to identify the specific person or persons within a business who has or have perpetrated a deception. Setting these norms would not necessarily require a government to conduct preventive inspections. For instance, the annual audit of company accounts to an agreed standard by chartered accountants should suffice to identify economic crime.
- Direct preventive government inspections may become necessary in order to enforce regulation where there is a very high likelihood of proven ethical failures. An instance may be the currently unregulated area of political party accounts in India. The political industry in India has failed to self-regulate. So a government could potentially not only impose regulatory requirements on the industry but also establish a limited programme of inspections – with advance notice and focussing on high risk issues. Penalties for default would have to be high as well.

The last two regulatory approaches are getting increasingly heavy-handed and should be scrupulously avoided until absolutely necessary. As far as action after the incident is concerned, where the matter is significant, consumers can be asked to appeal to the business first, and if that doesn't work, apply to the government to remedy the situation. The justice system then needs to kick in immediately and deliver effective punishment and compensation.

On the other hand, where the compensation will be less than the cost of obtaining justice, consumers can be encouraged to accept the loss and move on, noting that this does not preclude seeking justice where a person feels strongly about it. This situation can be remedied also by lowering the cost of providing justice. In both such cases, consumers can also dent the reputation of the business by denying future custom to the business and by telling others about the incident. Publishing the bad-incident story on the internet or writing letters to editors is also a good idea. This can make such accidental or ethical failures really costly for the business, and act as deterrence.

Unintended but preventable damage to human life and health

A second type of major failure in individual accountability takes place when a trader (buyer or seller) compromises the life or safety of another party through actions that are preventable with due diligence, caution and knowledge. Life is the ultimate yardstick of value – the most important thing of all. If someone has the knowledge or access to such knowledge on how to prevent a potential physical injury or death either in the workplace or during a trade, but does not diligently act to prevent such injury or death, then this category of harm is best treated as criminal negligence.

The wages that the owner of a coal mine pays to miners are for the services they render by digging up coal; the wages are not payment for the miners' lives. If the owner has access to knowledge that can potentially prevent a coal miner's death but either does not seek that knowledge or, having sought and obtained it, does not apply it adequately, thus accidentally killing the miner, then we must conclude that there has been an abuse of the employer's freedom of action to engage the services of the miner. Accountability will then fall squarely on the owner of the mine, and require severe punishment. While there may have been no intention to kill, no one is free to be negligent when human lives are at stake.

While workplace safety or consumer safety can be enhanced through self-regulation, the fact that lives are potentially at risk calls for a higher focus on prevention. As the purpose of our having a government is to preserve our lives (preserving our freedom is only a consequential or derivative purpose), the government can place reasonable restrictions on our actions to prevent us from negligently injuring or killing others.

Examples of good self-regulation do exist in this area. For instance, large food companies generally maintain very high internal standards for food handling and storage. Given that I keep getting hit by diarrhoea germs even at relatively expensive restaurants in India, I prefer to stick to the much cheaper but hygienic McDonald's or Nirula's restaurants. Another example would be the International Safety Management Code developed by the International Maritime Organization (IMO). While its content is periodically vetted by member governments of the IMO, and to that extent it is not exactly self-regulation, the implementation of the Code is largely left to the industry.

Preventive intervention by government on health and safety matters can focus on two main areas:

- **Disclosure**: Failure of disclosure of harm is a major ethical failure. Where businesses fail to voluntarily disclose the details of harmful effects of their products, it may become necessary to mandate such disclosure. This is particularly important as such information is generally not in the public domain. The onus must be on businesses to disclose harmful effects as soon as they discover them, with heavy penalties if it is found later that the businesses deliberately hid such information. Cigarette companies knew for long that cigarette smoking is related to significantly increased risks of lung cancer but did not disclose this information, killing millions of people in the meanwhile. It bears repetition of the fact that freedom is not license to kill.
- **Mandatory duty of care**: Employers must do their very best to prevent the accidental injury and death of their employees. Doing so cannot be optional. The government of a free society can therefore set performance standards, mandatory prudential rules[28] as well as audit standards that will unerringly point to culpable negligence if and when it occurs. Such an imposition on our freedoms is acceptable particularly if it is tailored appropriately to the level of risk and achieves the safety outcomes efficiently. In other words, regulations relating to traffic safety,[29] public health and occupational health and safety, that *seemingly* restrict our freedom, are the standards we agree upon as a free

society to protect our lives and, thus, our freedoms. These standards ensure that not only is accountability clearly specified, but accountability can easily be traced to the responsible person where failures occur. These regulations must, of course, be supported by a very effective criminal and civil justice system.

Damage to people not involved in a transaction

A third type of failure in accountability occurs when either the buyer or the seller or both – either through collusion, ignorance or negligence – pass on significant costs to others not involved in the transaction. This is the well known case of *externalities* (correctly, *negative* externalities) which has become increasingly more important with mounting evidence of the adverse impacts of mankind's actions on the environment. The seller or consumer need not have knowingly harmed others. Even accidental pollution imposes real costs, as the greenhouse gases predominantly emitted by Western societies since the early years of the Industrial Revolution have imposed.

Do these greenhouse gases actually impact global climate? Yes, they do, though perhaps not to the extent suggested by most scientists.[30] The science of global warming has not been perfected yet. The impact of CO_2 being logarithmic, there is likely to be a narrower upper bound, of around 2 degrees, on increase in global temperature irrespective of CO_2 emissions, even as polar areas heat considerably more. Many species of life living in icy cold conditions will be adversely impacted. People who live there will also be adversely affected along with those living in low lying areas.

Since freedom is not a license to harm others, such damage *must* be compensated. Unfortunately, the problem of justice becomes complex in this case. The party, or parties, who engage in such harmful transactions often do not voluntarily disclose their polluting activities to others since both parties may have colluded to pass on costs to others. The affected parties may, of course, complain, but if the people affected are poor, as is often the case, their voice may not be heard. In some cases entire societies pass on costs to future generations knowing that these parties can't complain at all, not yet being born! Each of these kinds of externalities is an injustice. A free society does not tolerate attempts to pass on costs to others.

The problem is that we are all guilty, to a lesser or to a greater extent, of such violations of justice. Our collective neglect of the environment has now created a situation where many animal and plant forms are seriously threatened, apart from the damage caused to millions of other human beings. As an example, each time we buy products made from a tree that has not been fully replaced, we pass on at least the following (small) costs to others:

- the cost of increased flooding and damage to topsoil is passed on to those who live downstream of the forest from which the tree was culled;
- reduced opportunity to make a living by those who make a living off the by-products of trees, such as *tendu* leaves used to make *bidi*s (that *bidis* are themselves a cause of an externality is a separate matter);
- slightly less oxygen to breathe for all citizens of the world; and
- slightly higher temperature and excessive climatic variation consequent to the reduced absorption of carbon dioxide – faced by all citizens of the world.

In addition, there is a loss to the food chain in the wild, as well as loss of habitat provided by that tree to birds, bees and other animal and plant life. While I leave out the interests of plants and animals in the discussions here, these should not be ignored in a free society since our lives are intricately bound by the continuing success of all other species of life.

We note in this example that most affected parties are not likely to complain. More problematically, it is not practical for a government to identify the individuals who perpetrated this negative externality. It may, in any event, not be sensible to punish someone who may have purchased, say, only a few reams of paper in a year.

We note that the mere existence of such difficulties does not automatically create a role for the government. When the affected parties are mutually identifiable, externalities can be often resolved by the affected parties negotiating with each other. This suggestion was first made in 1960 by Ronald Coase in his *The Problem of Social Cost.*[31] For a wide range of negative externalities, however, the government is best placed to ensure accountability and provide justice. It can do so in the following manner:

- *First, obtain compensation for the damage caused.*
  Where possible, a government can tax the parties that are likely to cause the damage and apply the tax towards compensating

those affected. This method of securing justice is known as a Pigovian tax, named after the economist Arthur Pigou (1877–1959) who first discussed externalities. In the example cited above, a tax can be levied on each product made from trees that have not been fully replaced. The total tax should (proportionately) add up to the amount that the government would pay to those affected to clean up for the damage from flooding and to replenish oxygen in the atmosphere through subsidizing new tree plantations. We note that each tax has its own cost of administration and enforcement, so there has to be a judgement made about which product is taxed and which is not.

In the *Online Notes*,[32] I have argued against the concept of excise duty or other product-based taxation in favour of taxation of incomes and wealth. However, where negative externalities have been identified in relation to a product, Pigovian taxes on products ensure that the buyer and seller will, together pay the true cost of the product. These taxes are best seen as a part of the *system of justice,* not part of revenue generation for public goods.

- *Second, where it is not possible to identify the parties that caused the damage, or to levy a Pigovian tax, or if the damage done exceeds the net value of the original transaction, then it could become necessary for the government to prohibit such transactions altogether.*
  An example of this sort would be the prohibition on smoking in bars. In such cases, the small damage potentially caused to bar workers by second-hand smoke from individual customers adds up cumulatively to precipitate lung cancer among some workers. Because particular individuals cannot *specifically* be held liable for such cancer, therefore there is a sound case to prohibit smoking altogether in bars.

- *Third, there is the much more difficult case where damage is caused to a person or persons by people living across an international border.*
  Countries which were the first to make technological advances in the use of coal and oil products are 'guilty' of having (unwittingly) caused the emissions of large amounts of greenhouse gases. It is true that they are similarly 'guilty' of making the technological advances that have saved the lives of hundreds of millions of children across the world and helped to extend human longevity. The difference between these two, however, is that the West has

been paid through the market for its scientific advances; and those transactions are therefore 'complete'. In the case of externalities, though, the external costs imposed by the West have not been absorbed by the West. While we are not in a position to pursue an individual's family for justice on behalf of a guilty dead person, nations, which are living associations of people, do not 'die' in that sense unless they are completely restructured. Therefore countries that have polluted the globe in the past are accountable for their actions and must step forward to compensate the rest of the world for this negative externality. This is particularly important given that the effect of increased CO_2 emissions is logarithmic, meaning that most of the damage is caused by the early emitters.

The problem is that there are no cross-border governments. Social contracts do not run across nations. Consequently, neither compensation nor a reduction in the current level of emissions can be enforced. Compensation in such cases depends critically on good faith. But when large groups of people such as nations compete with each other, they sometimes lose sight of their own larger self interest. Various models have been proposed, such as the global trading of carbon emissions within agreed caps, but each solution works only to the extent that most (if not all) countries participate in these programmes.

My view on this type of externality is that advanced Western countries must abide by the principles of justice and freedom they themselves espouse, and show good faith in compensating the rest of the world before asking others to join them in a global emissions trading order. That will bring about the desired good faith response from countries like China and India. Absence of compensation is likely to make this a tit-for-tat race to the bottom and will expose the weak underbelly of the concept of nation states.

Where would such compensatory funds come from, for money surely doesn't grow on trees? The answer is fortunately very simple: from funds currently deployed as foreign aid. There is simply no basis for Western countries to continue with their extremely misguided concept of foreign aid[33] (see Box 1). Funds deployed in foreign aid should be almost completely stopped and diverted into greenhouse gas emission compensation.

Box 1: Compensation, *not* foreign aid

If they really want to, poor countries can easily transform themselves into wealthy countries in less than one generation by applying basic principles of freedom outlined in this book. That these countries consciously violate common sense and choose poverty and corruption instead is entirely their own problem. Their children will be really sick; their people will multiply like rabbits; and most of them will be hungry. But if these people refuse to take the right medicine from the Adam Smith Pharmacy and go to the village quack instead (Karl Marx and Co.), why should we care about them?

The other, more practical problem is that foreign aid which is allegedly intended to alleviate poverty invariably makes poverty *worse.*[34] Throwing money into socialist dens of corruption only increases the power of corrupt leadership and bureaucracy which sucks the blood of the poor while hypnotizing them with slogans of socialism. What happens is that foreign aid is fungible. While some foreign aid is used for food, most of the money these countries would have spent on food on their own is then diverted to buying guns. If battling poverty really matters to rich countries, they should throw open their markets fully instead of hiding behind trade barriers and subsides for their farmers.[35] They should also vigorously promote the message of classical liberalism.

After doing that, the foreign 'aid' that is currently being thrown into the black holes of corruption and encouraging the purchase of more arms should be redirected to compensate selected developing countries for greenhouse gas emissions. Only those countries which have stable rule of law and which permit the direct funnelling of this money into private businesses, that grow new forests, should be subsidized. Providing this money to governments in any form or manner will exacerbate all kinds of problems, exactly as foreign aid does. A market mechanism with international standards of quality control will need to be devised to allow this money to be directly paid to private tree-growing businesses. Western governments could then buy an appropriate number of carbon sequestration certificates from this market.

It is worthwhile to remind oneself again that negative externalities are *ethical failures*, not 'market failures'. We therefore need to build systems and mechanisms to ensure that everyone is held to account. Freedom is intimately related to good governance; without it no country can hope to be free. A brief word on regulating the regulators. There is compelling evidence – including from the experience of India's history over the past six decades – that regulatory bodies created by governments to protect us often end up protecting entrenched business and political interests instead, being 'captured' by them. In India, policy was often designed, if not tailored, to meet the anticompetitive needs of specific businesses which had bribed these regulatory bodies. The scarcity of goods and services that India faced during the peak years of socialism stemmed from the government's preventing competition through its licensing and quota schemes. The poorly paid and ill-trained inspectorate in India is also often bought out by businesses, nullifying the purpose of their existence. Such regulatory bodies merely increase the cost of goods and services apart from squandering taxes without providing a commensurate benefit of risk reduction or product disclosure.[36] The free society therefore has learnt to keep its regulators in check. It does so by asking for greater disclosure of outcome indicators from regulators, scrutiny by Parliament and seeking contestability of policy advice. The regulator is not to be the provider of policy advice to government, merely a stakeholder. At the most basic level, though, good governance cannot be provided without good political representatives, which, unfortunately, we don't have in India. Ensuring good governance is a major task cut out for us. I discuss some ways to meet this challenge in chapters 4 to 6.

WRONG REASONS TO REGULATE MARKETS

We can define markets that are minimally regulated in the manner discussed above, as 'free markets'. This is what was meant by the qualifier 'almost free' used in relation to markets in the beginning of this section. In other words, governments provide post-incident justice and minimize individual ethical failures through regulation. In addition, there is a role for the government to specify the locations where markets can be established; this would be related to the zoning of towns and cities. This entire package creates highly disciplined free markets and generates the maximum possible wealth in a society. Regulating beyond the 'free-market level' of regulation has a great downside. It can only lower a country's wealth potential without providing any additional benefit to the people.

In particular, there is no justification for intervening in markets on two commonly cited grounds: promoting perfect competition and promoting equality. Unfortunately, these reasons are cited even by most relatively free Western societies, and this approach holds them back from their maximum potential.

THE TRUTH ABOUT MONOPOLIES

I have discussed at length various concerns about monopolies and cartels in the *Online Notes.*[37] The summary of that discussion is that monopolies are almost always created by governments which shelter certain businesses and prevent others from entering the market. Monopolies and cartels cannot sustain themselves without government support. In independent India we have seen many monopolies in the public sector. The quota system created private sector monopolies as well by protecting some of them from competition. Indian socialist governments also blocked competition on the basis of infant industries needing shelter, or the market being 'too small', or the investor not belonging to our country.[38] Further, as a rule, business lobbies oppose competition. It is far cheaper for relatively inefficient businesses to persuade the government through a threat of some sort (such as loss of jobs) to regulate it in a boutique manner that shields it from competition. Similarly, it is lucrative for politicians in league with businesses to set up huge bureaucracies to protect *their* (the politicians and bureaucrats) own empires. Letting citizens harvest the rewards of freedom is opposed by many powerful forces in society. In brief, free markets automatically destroy all monopolies and cartels; we therefore don't need to worry about such things. But we need to be very worried about collusion between business and government.

Leaving aside the red herring of monopoly, there are numerous other actions of business that should draw our attention. Most India businesses are mindless worshippers of Mammon; bribing politicians and bureaucrats, and not paying their taxes, comes naturally to them. Very few of them are value-driven. They are the typical 'capitalists' whom Nehru disliked, but from whom he did not hesitate to take money for his political party. In general, Indian businesses have preferred to support corrupt socialist parties and bribe their way to success, rather than allow markets to judge who is better. They have never supported advocates of freedom; at least so far, for they fear that freedom brings along with it justice, which they dislike. And yet in the pursuit of freedom one must advocate even their freedom to produce whatever they like and to set the prices they wish to – so long as they do not practice deception and or injure people.

In order to strike the right balance between freedom of businesses and freedom of their workers and consumers, the government should severely and efficiently penalize businesses for all violations of justice. Tax evasion and corruption by businesses must be stopped. Business owners who injure their workers must be put behind bars. When justice is prevalent in India, the ethical businesses of India will find it easier to succeed, and a virtuous cycle will be generated.

In summary, a free society needs competition, not 'perfect competition'. India's challenge is to get its government to focus on delivering justice more broadly than looking at alleged monopolies, and to get out of all needless regulation. Many absurd regulations created by previous socialist governments are being dismantled now, but the battle has barely been joined.

THE PROBLEM WITH EQUALITY

Everyone knows that 2 = 2; a trivial equality. Its use in driving our life's goals is very limited in consequence, for it is merely a *tautology* – a statement which uses words to pointlessly say the same thing. What does it matter if two equals two? What can we derive from it?

Similarly, economic equality among people is neither here nor there; a trivial curiosity. Attaching an 'equal to' sign between our incomes (or wealth) does not add any significance to our lives; it doesn't say whether we are free, whether we are experiencing a high quality of life, whether our children are likely to succeed. If two people achieve equal income through the free markets it is of no import; it is a mere statistical coincidence.

The key question that we need to ask is: did these two people get to function in a free society with equality of opportunity? If they were provided with an equal opportunity then their equal outcome is unexceptionable; albeit coincidental. The more common and expected outcome of a free market, though, is a vast increase in individual wealth accompanied by significant inequality among individuals, noting that this inequality does not remain static. Unlike in a feudal society, the level of economic inequality as well as the persons who are wealthy or poor changes dramatically with time in a free society. The children of workers can become far richer than the children of people who are rich today, depending on how diligently they apply themselves.

The key driver of a free society is justice. Our economic worth is a function of justice, not some tautological concept like equality. While our lives have infinite intrinsic worth and we are all equal in the eyes of law, our economic worth must be determined in the market by the balance between the demand and supply for the services we provide. We may find ourselves 'valued' by the market on the basis of our beautiful voice that people like to hear, our philosophy that people enjoy reading about, or because of a drug we invented to save people's lives. In each case, the fair and just price for our service is what is negotiated and agreed to in a free market.

Where wealth of any sort is acquired by trading our services in the marketplace in this manner, where all trades make the parties to the trade better off, there all outcomes of these trades are just, and therefore morally superior, irrespective of the society's Gini coefficients and Lorenz curves.[39] Equality is not an issue that is considered even in the passing in a free society; justice drives all understandings. Indeed, honestly acquired wealth is virtuous wealth; it must be applauded through a standing ovation. Each great singer, each great philosopher, each great inventor, and each business leader becomes rich by his or her own effort; each of them is worthy of that wealth. Who cares whether that creates inequality in society? Why should the inequality created by Lata Mangeshkar's voice bother anyone?

And yet equality is relevant in a free society, at the commencement of the 'race'. Everyone must be given a similar opportunity to run, to sing, to invent, or to play. But at the end of the race, only the *best* athlete, singer, inventor, or tennis player must win. The effort put in by an individual and his contribution being perceived as valuable by others tells us about the justness and morality of the acquisition of wealth. That is very important. For instance, wealth acquired through corruption is not just, and is therefore immoral. John Ruskin[40] said that 'the beneficialness of the inequality depends, first, on the methods by which it was accomplished; and, secondly, on the purposes to which it is applied'. On Ruskin's second point, we note two things:

- We note that the very process of generation of inequality through ethical trades is beneficial. We, the consumers, benefit through the products made by hard working innovative people. Most of us will find purposeful employment through jobs that such people create.
- Second, if left to their own devices, many wealthy people promote the arts and sciences as well as other forms of philanthropy. They don't have to do so, though, since they have contributed enough if their wealth was acquired through ethical trades.

Inequality is not the same as poverty. Extreme poverty diminishes our capacity to act freely and reduces equality of opportunity. A free society needs to take strong action against poverty. On the other hand, even the most extreme inequality does not in any way diminish anyone's freedom if all people are well above the poverty line. In the USA or Australia, which are relatively freer than India, some people are extremely rich, but most are at least well-to-do.

Therefore India must banish poverty if it wishes to be free. Reducing inequality on the other hand, is neither here nor there; it is but idle talk for a few jealous people who are afraid to put in the hard work needed to succeed. Indeed, each of us must aspire to be dramatically unequal to others; to be rich, to be happy, to be great! A free society doesn't countenance these utterly feeble ambitions of equality. It teaches its children to be great, to be better than others in every way; not to seek trivial equality with others. And the way a free society encourages infinite ambition in the minds of its children is by way of its government completely getting out of the way!

Indeed, equality should be banished from our list of priorities because it is extremely dangerous. Equality is not an innocuous concept – something to be had if we can: 'And oh, yes, by the way, can I get a glass of equality with two spoons of sugar?' Equality invariably takes us on the path to perdition. It is a poison that allures us with a strangely beautiful fragrance; but a society that drinks of it will be racked by endless pain; its members will lose their intellectual prowess and die an early death. Its people will multiply like flies; its rulers will be cruel and rapacious. Anyone who is sane and healthy flees a society where equality has poisoned the minds of its leaders.

The reason equality is dangerous is because the only mechanism available to us to create genuine equality is to redistribute wealth, not to create it. That can only be done by plundering those who are richer than us. But to steal and plunder is violation of the fundamental principles of freedom; it is an attack on our life itself. It is a crime no matter whether it is committed by an ordinary robber or an elected prime minister.

And therefore economic equality is associated only with those political ideologies which oppose freedom and which disrespect life; ideologies that do not hesitate to violently coerce others to cough up their property. The main such ideology, of socialism, aims to abolish property rights and vest all property in the state. But there is only one way to abolish property: through the use of force. Hence, socialists do not hesitate to decapitate the rich or otherwise threaten them with state-controlled violence to grab their property.

Indeed, property is anathema to socialists because of its dangerous disease of equality. If they could, they wouldn't allow anyone to even own a pen, for even a pen or paint-brush can spew unbelievable wealth. Socialists probably hate J K Rowling with all their heart for creating Harry Potter, and Pablo Picasso for making his paintings. And they almost certainly hate Lata Mangeshkar with all their might; if they could, they would rip out her vocal chords to stop her from getting rich. The great problem from the socialists' perspective is that no matter how hard they divest us of property and force us to become equal, then put us together inside a box, lock the box and throw away the key, inequality always springs out like Houdini – strong and triumphant.

Their problem is that the aspiration to be unequal to others, to be richer than others, to be faster and healthier than others, is *unique* to the human species, and cannot be abolished. Each of us spends a lifetime yearning for greater wealth, wanting to be at least equal if not better off than our neighbours. We seek the best jobs; we want to look smart and dress up in flashy clothes; we want to drive around in a fancy Porsche. Just look at the craze for lotteries – the millions of people who plunk their hard earned money into the dream of inequality; the dream of becoming richer than others. Even those who seek God, seek to be selected by God ahead of others; they want to achieve nirvana before countless other lesser qualified souls. Inequality is our deepest ambition; no amount of socialism will rid us of it. Only some silly politicians seem to want such equality, but even they actually yearn to be our rulers and to be remembered by others. Stalin and Mao were not interested in equality of fame – they ruthlessly destroyed their competitors in order to remain the rulers, and as to wealth, their wealth was unlimited. Even Nehru's family wealth is not equal to others; its scale is unknown, but it is nowhere near the per capita income of an Indian. Socialist ministers grab money with both hands and build untold wealth their family has ever seen before.

Since inequality is like a starfish whose arms grow back no matter how many times they are cut off, a socialist society has no choice but to continuously plunder. The socialist society must also tell people what to produce. Picasso must be licensed to produce any painting at all; and then he is to be given a quota on how many paintings to produce. Having done that, the socialist society then has to take away his paintings so that he cannot become rich.

The socialist society has an impossible task laid out for it. Starting with an abundant faith in the idea of equality, it degenerates rapidly; its leaders fight among themselves and often kill each other; its people finally rebel against the decadence and corruption they see around themselves, as they did in the erstwhile USSR, and they will do in India upon reading this book (!). In fact this book itself is a rebellion against the much milder, but equally problematic Nehruvian socialism. Socialism comes to grief in the end for what we really crave for is freedom; not equality.

We could, under a distasteful counterfactual scenario, be persuaded to tolerate the ideology of equality could it be demonstrated to unequivocally increase our wealth to an astounding level – well beyond what free-market capitalism routinely generates. But socialism fails bitterly on this front, too. Human beings are not robots. We work hard to generate wealth only if we are free to think, free to produce what we wish to produce, and free to keep the rewards of our efforts. Creativity and innovation decline precipitously under socialism; socialism impoverishes entire societies and makes it hard for them to recoup their energies for decades. India's example is in front of us, but there are many worse examples. When the Soviet Union tried to collectivize its agriculture in order to make each farmer 'equal', it quickly came on to its knees. The entire Soviet Union could not produce enough to feed itself. Tens of thousands perished of starvation. Its mighty armed force and secret service (KGB) were able to compel its scientists, under close observation, to produce, or rather, to steal the design of weapons and spacecraft, but until its end the socialist USSR could not produce enough bread for its people.

Taken to the extreme, as with the (erstwhile) Soviet Union, Maoist China, or Naxalites, socialism physically assaults and kills people. Millions of people have been murdered by Marx's equality-driven ideology over the twentieth century. If we add to this the far more numerous indirect killings – namely deaths through hunger and preventable disease arising from socialist mismanagement in countries like India – then the number of people killed in the cause of equality runs into the hundreds of millions; possibly a couple of billions. Equality is not a hot cup of coffee that we may order if available. It is deadly poison. Once this disease of equality infects somebody's mind, the consequences for that society can become extremely bad. People infected by equality are infinitely more dangerous than those who go berserk and shoot people at random. Equality is as bad as religious fundamentalism in its disastrous consequences for society.

Socialist countries are also some of the most unequal, the difference being that their inequality is derived from corruption and the misuse of power, and is therefore immoral inequality. Corrupt politicians in India have misused socialist controls to acquire untold wealth and create great immoral inequality in India. Our socialist ministers never hesitate to loot even those public funds intended to assist the poor. I talk about this from personal experience, including one involving a Chief Minister.

Plunder need not be pursued through physical coercion alone. It can be more sophisticated, such as under the guise of 'welfare' socialism. One of the most apt descriptions of socialism comes from Frédéric Bastiat (1801–50) who fought Karl Marx's ideas tooth and nail even in Marx's time. Unfortunately Bastiat died very young. Had he lived longer the world might have been saved from the killing fields of socialism. Bastiat noted in 1850 that:

> [L]egal plunder can be committed in an infinite number of ways. Thus we have an infinite number of plans for organizing it: tariffs, protection, benefits, subsidies, encouragements, progressive taxation,[41] public schools, guaranteed jobs, guaranteed profits, minimum wages, a right to relief, a right to the tools of labour, free credit, and so on, and so on. All these plans as a whole – with their common aim of legal plunder – constitute socialism.[42]

The message for us is simple – be *extremely* wary of anyone who preaches equality. You never know when this person is going to shut your mouth, steal your wealth and property, and kill you and your children. There are some Indians who 'accept' equality as a good thing *if it happens* by itself. Such people are merely misguided for statistical equality is meaningless and can never be 'good' in isolation of the reality of that society. But if someone genuinely believes in equality, then run for your life as fast as you can! Freedom is as basic to us as life itself. Equality is simply nowhere in that league. It is a curiosity for economists who idle their time making Lorenz doodles. To consider even *slightly* diminishing our freedom in order to promote equality is like throwing away a priceless pearl necklace and picking up a slithering, poisonous snake to hang around our neck, instead; a snake that will bite us while we are sound asleep.

And yet, socialism will *always* remain tantalizingly hypnotic to people who have not understood the magic of free markets and equality of opportunity. By painting a rosy but false picture of the world, socialism ensnares children every day and continues to have a vast following among those children who never grew up. The arguments of capitalism require enormous critical thinking since the invisible hand is *actually* invisible! Not being a socialist is hard work for our brains. I will try to make the invisible hand a bit more visible in this book so that more of us can see through the great pitfalls of socialism.

But one need not be ashamed of having been a supporter of equality sometime in our life. The disease of equality strikes almost everyone once, like chickenpox. I too caught this disease momentarily during one of my early years in university. Who isn't fascinated by an ideal world where all of us are somehow blissfully equally competent and equally resourced? Some residual virus of this disease remained in my head until as recently as 1995 when, during my mid-career PhD studies, I expressed concern about economic inequality among nations in one of my term papers. What I should been have concerned about, instead, was about the *self-inflicted poverty* of nations like India which *insist* on being poor despite the prescriptions for wealth being available off the shelf.

There is a strong leftist bent in most academic discourse which arises largely from desktop academics who never grew up; never got rid of their chickenpox. They have a dreamy-eyed view of politicians, bureaucrats, armed forces and the police. These academics project their own virtuous feelings about other human beings on government functionaries; and in doing so they make a fatal blunder. The good thing about Nehruvian socialism is that being a less extreme form of socialism than Russian communism, it has probably *inoculated* us. Once India fully recovers from its socialist fever and its head clears up, it should remain free of equality and socialism forever, unlike Russia which may yet revert to communism once again.

The thing we really want, when we talk of equality, is the eradication of poverty. That also remains a matter closest to my heart; and it is to a discussion of removal of poverty that I will now turn to. Just a brief comment first – poverty *cannot* be eliminated unless we foster conditions which *create great wealth and great inequality.* We need sufficient numbers of *extremely* rich people whom we can tap into, both as taxpayers and high calibre experts, to help us banish poverty.

* * *

Summarizing the discussion of this section so far, the two reasons often used by governments to intervene in markets, namely the quest for perfect competition and equality, are very bad reasons. Criminals and fools flourish under the guise of these two excuses.

ERADICATING POVERTY

Eradicating poverty is a matter of fundamental importance. We cannot be truly free without equality of opportunity; and we cannot have equal opportunity without a minimum standard of living for all citizens including a high-school education of decent quality for all our children.

But why does freedom get compromised when equality of opportunity is compromised? It depends on the basic requirement for the exercise of our freedoms. The assumption behind freedom is that we are fully functional humans. We must be alive, and indeed, fully alive, which means that we should be able to think for ourselves. Animals are not capable of exercising free choice which requires careful thought and deliberation. They are not in a position to consider alternatives rationally, and systematically plan for their future. We can do so, of course, but only when our bodies and minds are fully functional, i.e. when we are at least reasonably healthy and possess a reasonable amount of knowledge of the world around us. Only then can we make informed choices in genuine freedom. In our poverty stricken, uneducated, tribal state, we are unlikely to be able to think critically and thus to be truly free.

I am not suggesting a very high hurdle here. While illiteracy prevents people from the careful consideration of alternatives, it does not diminish their mortal capacity or imply they don't have at least some basic knowledge of the world around them. I am therefore not implying that illiterate adults should not be able to vote or to pursue their business interests; or that they are not accountable for their actions. Illiteracy and malnutrition, no matter how problematic, are not in the same league as mental incapacity or disability which can actually limit our liability – in law.

But I suppose we can see now why poverty reduces our ability to be free. Poverty significantly diminishes the basis of our humanity. When an illiterate poor mother does not administer oral rehydration therapy to her dysentery-stricken child because of her ignorance of its benefits, and the child then dies, we must wonder to what extent the mother was free. She does get to face the consequences of her 'free' choice, but surely her's was a choice made in deep ignorance. With informed choice, the outcomes both for the mother and child would have been infinitely better. Being poor also makes a person vulnerable to exploitation and discrimination. In brief, poverty poses a serious hazard to freedom. A free society must create a platform where everyone can make informed choices and be genuinely free.

While Nehruvian policies are the primary cause of continuing poverty in India, some poverty will remain even upon changing from Nehruvian socialism to comprehensive capitalism. Some people will remain who are not in the physical or mental position to compete in the marketplace and support themselves and their children. And so, if such people, having done their best (i.e. they have not been sitting around doing nothing), fail to achieve a level of income agreed to by a society as the minimum standard for ensuring equality of opportunity, then other, more capable people, should step in to support these unfortunate fellow citizens to the point when they are empowered to stand on their own feet and resume normal activity in the marketplace. That minimal level of support will ensure that they can survive in frugal dignity and that their children can get the opportunity to grow into healthy and well-educated adults, ambitious to take their place at the head of the table of the wealthiest people in society.

Elimination of poverty will need deploying taxes appropriately. Will that not amount to redistribution? Not quite. Richer people are in a position to contribute disproportionately more than those on more modest levels of income, taking into account the marginal utility of money. Hence a free society legitimately resorts to progressive taxation as a general principle. Second, some of the taxes raised can be used as social insurance premium to provide coverage to members of the society against critical adverse events that are largely uninsurable in the marketplace. These events can be things like natural calamities or large-scale terrorist attacks; and poverty. It is in the nature of free societies that as a result of competitive efforts in the marketplace, some middle-class and even rich families will regress into grim poverty even while those who were poor earlier begin to flourish and become rich. While well-off families are expected to insure themselves against poverty, once a family does become poor, it will tend to lose the capacity to further insure itself, particularly its children. A small portion of the taxes paid by everybody is therefore best visualized as insurance premium to cover such contingencies; this premium can be applied to ensure equality of opportunity for poor families.

The free society needs to eradicate poverty while ensuring that people do not become dependent on state support. Free societies don't spoon-feed – they respect their citizens too much to do that. Charity is demeaning. A free society has honourable citizens, not beggars, nor parasites. It is a principle of good faith that people must work and achieve their best outcomes first. Everyone is responsible to work as hard and effectively as they possibly can before their insurance claim for poverty can be considered. No one is free to be deliberately poor in a free society.

The formula for ensuring equality of opportunity in a society is therefore:

- Expect everyone in the society to produce the greatest possible wealth they can through free markets.
- Transfer a sum directly to those who failed to rise above the poverty line despite their best efforts, through an objective and non-discretionary process that will bring their incomes above the poverty line.

We note that the direct transfer of funds to the poor has to be linked to a requirement that the concerned person has worked to the best of his capacity. The second thing we note is that in the two-stage process outlined above, the consideration of equity, or more correctly of equality of opportunity, comes into the society's overall decision-making only once. This consideration occurs at that point of a free market outcome when we have sufficient information to allow us to keep the poor above the poverty line.

Why must the payment be made directly? Because indirect alternatives involve endless fine-tuning of a host of mutually incompatible 'welfare' policies, subsidies and the like. These indirect schemes not only do not reach the intended persons but are wasteful and always interfere with free markets, leading to completely unintended outcomes. Tragically, indirect schemes are a fertile area for every policymaker's imagination; such fertile imaginations have led to a quagmire of complex and inefficient regulations, programmes and subsidies in the name of the poor.[43] These policies include the public distribution system, an alarming range of poverty alleviation programmes, subsidies of all sorts, forcing private builders to set aside houses 'for the poor', preventing rents from rising, preventing parts of industry from using power looms and so on; there are thousands of such policies in India. Such policies, which incur mammoth administrative costs and involve high levels of corruption, have depleted India's capacity to provide equal opportunity to those who really need it. Bureaucrats and politicians steal crores of rupees from such programmes, in league with corrupt businesses.

A philosophical problem with these policies is the paternalism involved. The intended recipients do not get to choose how they will spend the money they are forced to receive as a loan or a subsidy (i.e. if they are lucky enough to actually get the intended benefit). This force compromises their freedom to choose what is in their best interest. If we really want to assist the poor, we must treat them as our equals and trust in their judgement except when there are individual indications to the contrary. It is wrong to second-guess our fellow citizens merely because they happen to be poor today.

In Box 2, I have outlined a method of direct poverty elimination for India. This method, which is fully compatible with our freedoms and does not interfere with the free market, will lead not only to the complete elimination of poverty but also to the shutting down of thousands of expensive programmes currently undertaken in the name of the poor.

Box 2: Eliminating poverty in India: a direct method

Poverty in India can be eradicated in the following seven steps:

1. Identify the people who may need such assistance during a given year, in advance of the actual requirement, i.e. based on estimate income.
2. Find out how much is likely to be needed to meet the gap between their expected income and the societally agreed poverty line (this gap is generally small, for even the poor earn at least above starvation in most cases).
3. Tax the rest of the community in a way that will meet this gap. In the early stages of capitalism, this money can be borrowed against future government revenues.
4. Transfer the precise amount identified in step 2 directly to those identified in step 1 in an automated, fortnightly manner into their bank account. As such a transfer can potentially create adverse work incentives, the poverty level must be kept low; just sufficient to provide extremely frugal dignity, no more.
5. At the end of the year, use the income tax return of each person to automatically adjust what was paid out; obtaining a refund of overpayments made, if any, or slightly reducing future payments.
6. Stop all corruption-ridden subsidies and poverty alleviation programmes, and remove all 'equity'-based policies.
7. Audit the people receiving the antipoverty moneys to ensure they have been participating in the market to the best of their ability and not simply sitting idle.

This is not an impractical suggestion even though it sounds like one. Given India's huge population, the most obvious 'flaw' in this approach appears to lie in steps 1 and 2. However, I am confident that there are several effective ways to use modern technology to implement this proposal. Programmes very similar to this are already running in the USA (e.g. earned income tax credit) and in Australia (e.g. family benefits and related assistance).

It is quite possible to determine the village level household income for each household in India with a fair degree of accuracy. As an illustration, during 1986–8 I organized intensive household income and asset surveys of all registered voters at the village level in selected villages of Dhubri district in Assam and created perhaps the first[44] such computerized database in India. After that survey, the data were sorted automatically in the computer using pre-set criteria, and the sorted data was verified in a village meeting by at least two independent functionaries. This verified income data then generated the final list of the poorest of the poor in that village. This kind of survey was feasible even then. By using far better technology and analysis, it should be quite feasible to identify each of the poor individually and to clearly estimate the distance of their income from the poverty line within a narrow range of accuracy.[45] In fact, in 2000, I outlined a detailed implementation plan[46] for this proposal, calling it the negative income tax method (NIT for short), after Milton Friedman's terminology.

My preliminary calculations, based on data I collected from the Finance Ministry and other official sources, showed me that if the money India squanders annually in the name of the poor is directly spent on funding the poor in the outline given above, we can abolish poverty virtually overnight. I have no doubt that if this plan is refined and tested properly, it will lead to a working solution for the complete elimination of poverty from India and help us to get rid of thousands of utterly useless programmes that currently turn our taxes into rubbish.

THE MECHANICS OF THE MARKET

We now come to the 'formula' for wealth creation that Adam Smith discovered in 1776. Two key features of this formula are the division of labour and the freely adjusting price system. Adam Smith noted that there is considerable division of labour in wealthy societies. People specialize; tasks are broken into many smaller processes. Smith observed that merely ten people, each working on a small part of the process, can together produce thousands of pins in a day compared with barely one pin a day they could have produced otherwise, each attempting to produce the entire pin. In Smith's own words:

> Each person, therefore, making a tenth part of forty-eight thousand pins, might be considered as making four thousand eight hundred pins in a day. But if they had all wrought separately and independently, and without any of them having been educated to this peculiar business, they certainly could not each of them have made twenty, perhaps not one pin in a day.[47]

The division of labour is an outcome of the incentives generated in free markets. It is a response to the profit and price signals in markets, signals that motivate people to continuously improve productivity. By each of us working in our self interest, each desiring to maximize our own profit, we are motivated to make better products, to sell cheaper, to produce more; and thus to produce wealth.

Adam Smith's main discovery was of the 'Invisible Hand' of the price system which brings about the natural coordination of all such wealth-producing activities. A fully functional and freely adjusting price system is the single most important mechanism of a free society. It is crucially important that we 'see' it's functioning as clearly as we see physical things like chairs or tables. This price system allows billions of people to co-ordinate their activities in an almost mystical symphony of all prices and preferences at each point in time across the entire world. I'll outline the price system in some detail below, but in addition to this, I will also discuss related market processes later in this section. But now to the most magical thing in the world next to life itself – the price system.

THE PRICE SYSTEM

The price system is the counterpart of our body's autonomic nervous system or the instinctive brain. This system instantaneously regulates millions of transactions in the world every second. There is no conscious effort needed to ensure its success. This fabulous price system is not the product of human design, but a 'natural' feature of the human world, something like language which is a universal feature of all societies. Indeed, Friedrich Hayek observed in his paper of 1945 on

'The Use of Knowledge in Society'[48] that if the price system 'were the result of deliberate human design, [...] this mechanism would have been acclaimed as one of the greatest triumphs of the human mind'.

Indeed, this paper by Hayek provides us with perhaps the finest description of the price system provided by anyone so far. Hayek showed in his paper how the price system captures information not only of our personal preferences, our relative valuations and our knowledge of local conditions and special circumstances, but also how it then transmits the relevant part of this information to everyone else in the world who needs to know through a sequence of negotiations and trades. He then showed how the changes to the information which is relevant to us flow back rapidly in the form of the prices we pay locally.

The system succeeds in this enormously complex task by offering the right 'inducements which will make the individuals do the desirable things without anyone having to tell them what to do' (Hayek). Because of the exceptional power it commands over people, governments seek to influence our behaviour through this system, either intuitively or from cussedness. They lower prices through subsidies, increase them through taxes, or at times even fix prices directly.

As the Invisible Hand is perhaps not as visible as we would like it to be yet, let's hear the arguments from Hayek himself:

- [T]he economic problem of society is mainly one of rapid adaptation to changes in the particular circumstances of time and place.
- In a system where the knowledge of the relevant facts is dispersed among many people, prices can act to coordinate the separate actions of different people.
- Through it not only a division of labour but also a coordinated utilization of the resources based on an equally divided knowledge has become possible.
- Prices act as 'a kind of machinery for registering change, or a system of telecommunications which enables individual producers to watch merely the movement of a few pointers, as an engineer might watch the hands of a few dials [...] [in this way] a solution is produced by the interactions of people each of whom possesses only partial knowledge'.

It is crucially important that every Indian citizen is able to visualize the Invisible Hand clearly in his or her mind's eye. So let's put on our hats. Off we go to Africa!

* * *

Hello! We are now standing on the outskirts of Yelwa in Nigeria.

Let's assume that China has suddenly increased its demand for steel as the production of its new car – the pilot of which was a closely guarded secret – starts to ramp up. As this sudden increase in demand for steel was not anticipated by the market, prices of steel jump up in response.

Now let's meet Moremi. She is a poor housewife living on the outskirts of Yelwa, blissfully ignorant of this trivia about new Chinese cars. All she knows is that suddenly her careful plans have gone awry. Moremi had been mulling over the past month about upgrading from her terracotta cooking pot to a metal one for which she had been saving some money. But she now finds that the price of the steel pot she had wanted has suddenly increased.

What has happened, of course, is that the relevant information on the new Chinese car has been passed on to Moremi by the market. The Nigerian manufacturer of steel cooking pots has had to pay more for steel inputs. The local grocery shop, experiencing the higher wholesale price set by the manufacturer, has had to pass on this increased cost to consumers. In this manner, the production of new cars in China has changed things in Yelwa – Moremi is forced to rethink her choices. Steel is now deployed towards its most profitable and hence most productive use, diverting it from the production of household pots and pans. Given the higher price of steel pots, she can now either sacrifice other domestic needs and buy the high-priced steel pot or she can choose a cheaper aluminium pot instead, and keep the change. Moremi considers all options and opts for the aluminium pot.

So, is that a bad thing to have happened? Yes, our sympathies are with Moremi for not having achieved her most preferred outcome. But we also notice that everything that has happened has been *just.* Free peoples have made their individual decisions based on relevant information, with each of them working in his or her self interest. No one has cheated any other person. Also, everyone has become better off through these trades. For instance, by buying the aluminium pot Moremi has become a little bit better off than before; she is now more productive in her domestic work. The local grocery shopkeeper is a little better off than before, having marked the aluminium pot up to the price that is sufficient to allow his business to survive in the competitive retail market. We note that the free market doesn't guarantee we will get what we want. It does ensure, though, that everyone involved will become at least a little better off each time they decide to trade.

More importantly, a number of things happen after Moremi buys her aluminium pot. Her choice is quickly communicated to all relevant producers in all parts of the world; people who have never heard nor will hear of Moremi. No emails or letters are sent by anyone; instead, with all other 'Moremis' (namely, buyers placed in a similar position to Moremi) of the world substituting towards aluminium pots, the demand for aluminium pots now begins to rise. This raises the price of aluminium metal by a wee bit. That increase in price then sends a signal to aluminium suppliers in distant Australia to increase their production of aluminium to take advantage of this higher price. More people are hired in Australia and start digging up more bauxite. In this way the entire world shifts, ever so slightly, in an invisible but exquisitely coordinated manner, to a substitute metal – aluminium.

In this magical way, thousands if not millions of people worldwide act in ways they would not have, had China not decided to produce more cars. Most importantly, these direct effects also have second order effects down the line. Since Moremi had some spare change left over after buying the aluminium pot, she takes her family out to the movies. That shifts the demand for movies and more movies are made the following year, in response; and so on. Thus, the entire world is integrated and coordinated by prices – each decision affecting every other decision. And thus, in choosing whether to eat cereal or fruit for breakfast, or in deciding upon the amount of milk or sugar we put into our tea, each of us impacts the demand for, and supply of, all products in the world.

It is this dissemination of relevant information from hundreds of lands and thousands of people back to everybody's doorstep in every corner of the world at an amazing speed that Hayek was writing about. Only a free market can accomplish these amazing feats through the price system. Nothing else has the ability to always produce the locally optimal outcome for all parties involved in a trade, down to the level of crushed-ice candy sold to a child by a bicycle-riding vendor in a hot and dusty village in Bihar – a village that can only be reached after travelling through miles of narrow, bumpy roads.

In this manner the prices of all things in the world and all quantities of products and services produced in the world are in tenuous balance or equilibrium. Even the slightest change is communicated to everybody else but only to the extent that these other individuals need to know. This balance is called the (competitive) general equilibrium of all world markets operating simultaneously and optimally at each instant. This general equilibrium represents the ultimate outcome of the

Invisible Hand, which has thus coordinated, unerringly, the optimal production and consumption decisions throughout the world by ensuring that everyone's preferences and budget constraints are instantaneously in equilibrium, with prices communicating the relative values of things. Technically we say that at such a point the marginal rates of substitution[49] for each of the *n* products in the world are equalized for each of the *n* individuals on this planet.

Indeed, if a supremely intelligent and knowledgeable 'social planner' could replicate the entire series of incidents and information leading to a particular set of purchases, then people would end up buying exactly those goods they have been actually purchased. That is the only just outcome. That there is no possibility of such a social planner existing should of course be obvious by now. No one can or should attempt to replace the Invisible Hand.

RISKS OF INTERFERING WITH THE PRICE SYSTEM

As massive flows of price-related information rush across the globe instantaneously without any coordinating individual, no government can imitate the phenomenal agility and justice of markets. Alternatives to free-market capitalism that try to interfere with prices, or otherwise try to apply brakes on the market, lead to completely unintended consequences, and that society then goes down the slippery slope to self-destruction. Governments simply cannot improve upon, in any way, the natural agility and merit-based reward processes of free markets.

Sadly, governments are often arrogant, believing they know better for us than we do for ourselves. Many immature Third World governments find it extremely hard not to interfere with the price system. (Even the 'mature' First World can't stop giving subsidies to its farmers as in the case of USA and Europe, thus making these unfortunate farmers globally uncompetitive). Interference with prices has great pitfalls. The basic problem with such interference is that normal incentives are distorted and people stop doing their very best, leading to sub-optimal outcomes for everyone.

To examine what can happen if we interfere with the price system, let us stay with Moremi. In a twist to the original story, let's assume that Nigeria is now a socialist country, its government being driven by the objective of equality. Out of the sheer concern they feel for Moremi's 'plight' in not having been able to purchase the steel pot, the socialist leadership of Nigeria decides to influence the price system in order – in the words of Minister Sodeinde – 'to set things right'. Following is a description of what the Nigerian Government did and what happened then:

- **Price fixing:** The first thing the government did was to fix a maximum retail price for steel pots, at a price equal to what was prevailing for these pots prior to the rise in world steel prices. But the Nigerian Government clearly could not control global steel prices, and so the prices for steel inputs used by the Nigerian pot manufacturer did not budge by one kobo (100 kobo=31 Indian paise). The wholesalers wouldn't pay the producer one more kobo either since the maximum retail price had been fixed by the government and retailers wouldn't buy from wholesalers at a higher price than before. Each pot produced thus led to a loss for the producer who had no choice but to tell the government he was going to shut down, throwing 100 workers out of work.
- **Direct government subsidy:** Realizing that this would lead to a major political problem, the Nigerian Government quickly changed this policy. The government promised to lower excise duties for all users of steel. The pot manufacturer resumed making pots. But the government's revenues fell. As a result, a long anticipated bridge over a stream in Yelwa had to be scrapped. There was no money left for it. That then led to significant public protests on the streets.
- **Forced private subsidy:** Reeling from these street demonstrations, the Nigerian Government restored the excise duty. In its place, it made a law by which the only electric company of Nigeria, which had not yet been nationalized, was required to subsidize electricity supply to all Nigerian industry. In order to meet the very significant increase in costs arising from this compulsory subsidy for industry, the electricity company then had no choice but to raise electricity prices for consumers. That was disastrous, for it led to a massive nation-wide protest!

And of course, while implementing these policy changes the government had to hire tens of new bureaucrats to write hundreds of pages of new regulations. That not only wasted tax-payers' money but also squandered the productive time of businesses that now had to read those hundreds of new pages of regulation and were burdened with additional record keeping requirements. (Such are only a few of the socialist nightmares we have gone through in India!)

This whole fiasco turned out to be a very expensive lesson in elementary economics for Nigeria (read: India, of course), leading to the lesson that there is no free lunch. Somebody has to pay for the 'benevolence' of governments, which means robbing Peter to pay Paul. Robbing people distorts the incentives in a society and people do not take optimal decisions. It is better not to rob people. Even a toddler can see that. And yet it is a mystery why most grown-ups can't understand that.

Fortunately for the Nigerian people, its government quickly realized that interfering with the price system was becoming counterproductive. It then switched completely to capitalism. The happy ending to our trip to Africa is that Nigeria is now the world's purest capitalist society, and the world's richest. Moremi now lives in a large beautiful house with four bedrooms and a lovely garden. She has three computers and two cars. There are long queues in the West of highly skilled professionals desperately wanting to migrate to Nigeria.

So what did the Government of Nigeria do to ensure that poor Moremi became a wealthy citizen? We'll, it did (almost) nothing! Its new and highly successful policy was called *laissez faire*, or leaving the people alone. As Moremi was not desperately poor, she did not need direct funding through a negative income tax. She was therefore free to develop on her own. The previous welfare programmes did no good to anyone but merely sapped the self-respect of the poor and encouraged rampant corruption in society. The government scrapped all kinds of social welfare programmes.

Being left alone, Moremi felt motivated to think for her own future. Her self-awareness and capacity grew greatly over the next two years. With thrift and good personal character, Moremi took advantage of the many opportunities thrown up by her newly free society. She attended night classes and obtained a law degree at the age of 42. Then she quickly established herself as the best lawyer in Yelwa. She later joined politics and become the Prime Minister of Nigeria. In her time, Nigeria went to a level of greatness that no socialist leader could possibly have dreamed of. Moremi's government scrapped all regulations that were not fully compatible with freedom. In doing so, Moremi completely liberated the energies of the Nigerian people.

Moremi became the role model for all women all over the world. Moremi finally became the secretary general of the United Nations (UN) and was instrumental in shutting down the scandalous, corruption-ridden welfare programmes of this completely unaccountable, bureaucratic behemoth. Consequently, the UN is no longer in the business of welfare but follows Moremi's strict guidelines. It insists on freedom (capitalism) as the sole principle of governance in poor countries that seek its help. It teaches people how freedom will help their society become wealthy through their own effort. It explains to people why charity is almost invariably the worst form of human abuse.

THE ROLE OF PROFIT

Profit is the direct signal that a society – indeed the world – gives to each of us to provide the particular product or service. The producer who gives us the most value receives our vote in the market each time we buy his product. That producer then becomes profitable, which means he continues to exist, even expand. In this way, only the best providers of goods and services for each rupee spent get to stay. Providers who fail to provide us with value, at least relative to other providers, are politely shown the door. We don't like to kill them for underperformance because we are a civilized society. We simply bankrupt them.

By ensuring that only the best producers survive, everyone benefits. Rewarding only those who give us the greatest value is obviously a very sensible thing to do. In this manner, an entire society becomes smarter, more effective and more productive; and enormously richer. Profit is a critical market signal that must be allowed to flourish by governments which should step aside completely and let businesses become as profitable as they can possibly be; and each person as rich as he can possibly become. That is the sure recipe for the success of a society.

SOME OTHER FEATURES OF A MARKET

There are numerous other features of a market which are of great interest. These include the workings of a flexible labour market; the role of education in a free society; how entrepreneurship works in a free society; and how planning an economy is simply not possible or desirable. Given paucity of space, I have skipped a discussion of these features in this book, but I have provided further discussions in the *Online Notes.*[50]

SUMMARIZING THE FINDINGS SO FAR

Recapitulating, a free society generates wealth by the simple expedient of letting markets function without undue hindrance. It creates institutional frameworks to govern markets with a view primarily to ensure justice. India should seek to build market governance institutions of this nature; these institutions must remain fully accountable to us. However, even Western societies find it hard to manage regulators who often hijack policy and start enforcing things they were not asked to. The government and citizens, together, must strongly curb such tendencies.

Given space constraints I do not discuss how these institutions are to be created, but we can learn much from the experience of the West and from their literature on economic reforms. While endorsing most of the standard literature of economics and economic reforms, I would like to suggest a few words of caution:

- Our future is too important to be left to economists. We must never let economists monopolize the thinking that we need to put in as concerned citizens. The literature of economics should be used to supplement our holistic thinking; not as a primary source of policy ideas.
- Economists are driven primarily by the goal of economic efficiency. They do not base their advice purely on the principles of freedom. They are therefore likely to propose interventions by governments on grounds of market failure, information failure, information asymmetry, 'equity' and so on. We should soundly reject such advice. We need to back off from any intervention by the government unless it is proven without doubt that such intervention will improve our freedoms including our accountability. Let us follow the imperatives of freedom and we won't go wrong.
- Next, we should never use the pretext of 'equity' more than once in society's decision making. If poverty is being addressed by a branch of the government (say, which is implementing the negative income tax), then all other parts of government should provide whatever it is they are required to provide, without reference to equity. Let there not be a thousand policies each trying to remove poverty. That will significantly increase poverty.
- Finally, policy makers are usually very weak in their understanding of good governance and how to implement things. Policy makers, indeed each of us, must therefore learn more about what drives bureaucrats. We must ensure that bureaucrats have the right incentives, and we must tightly control our bureaucrats.

On the whole, it is relatively easy to build free markets. All we need to do is to get out of the way. *Laissez faire*! On the other hand, the next big mechanism of a free society, democratic governance, is very hard to build.

CREATING AND SUSTAINING DEMOCRATIC GOVERNANCE

The second major mechanism of a free society is the process to give voice to each citizen's concerns during national policy development. This is done through the formal institutions of democracy and consultative governance. The key instrument for a citizen to influence such policy is through his or her elected representative, but in a free society there should be many other opportunities to raise concerns. There are many good reasons why we can't get a good democracy easily:

- First, the society faces the same problem that a central planner would face in arriving at optimal decisions for the entire society. Such a decision would be reached when everyone's needs and demands are optimally met, at each instant of time. However, there is simply no counterpart of the price system to effortlessly capture all relevant information on a regular basis; then resolve all competitive tensions (supply and demand) and finally aggregate our collective preferences into one optimal decision for the entire society. The government must therefore make decisions in ignorance of the relevant details.
- Second, there is the great problem of engagement. When we buy or sell in the market, we are fully engaged in the process, and our views are taken into account appropriately in matters relevant to us. But there is no practical method for citizens to engage intensively with a policy making body on matters of interest. A single MP in India can represent around ten lakh voters. We therefore feel helpless about national policy choices even if we have legitimately elected representatives. But how can a representative possibly consult with ten lakh people on every issue? Democracy is very hard.
- Third, there are major problems of accountability in most democracies. Even at the basic level, accountability is very difficult. We can hold a particular business to account simply by walking out of its shop and taking our custom elsewhere. But we get to choose governments only once in five years. We have to live with their choices for this entire duration. How can that help in achieving accountability?

The field of democratic representation and governance of a society is therefore a minefield of arbitrariness. None of its institutions are solidly backed by strong theoretical foundations. Fundamentally, the objective of democratic institutions is to maximize our freedom while minimizing government intervention, maximizing policy stability, minimizing costs, maximizing input from citizens, maximizing responsiveness in defence and security matters, and so on! Democratic institutions are at best *ad hoc* attempts to be reasonably representative and to balance competing objectives and must therefore be continuously reviewed and improved upon. Metaphorically, at one time a Winston Churchill is best suited to deal with a country's problems; at other times a country may need the great Clement Attlee's approach.

Also, almost all concepts found in a democracy, such as simple majority, two-third majority, first-past-the-post, proportional representation, preferential voting, direct representation, indirect representation and so on, are entirely arbitrary. Some of this arbitrariness arises from economizing. Societies build institutions which minimize the costs of electing governments and the subsequent costs of arriving at decisions. If unanimity among all citizens were to be sought in every decision, then no action could ever be taken and the society would come to a grinding halt. Societies also have to consider the need for continuity in government policy. We may be fickle with our favourite film stars, but government policy needs to be far more stable – else it will confuse everyone and prevent citizens from making long-term decisions. Rapid change is best avoided in government-related settings.

Even the most advanced countries continue to wrestle with their democratic processes and no nation has got this element of their society perfectly sorted out. Indeed, there can never be such a thing as perfection in democratic governance; only constant shifts as improvements are attempted. There is constant churn in the institutions of democracy.

There are many other problems with designing democracies as well. Citizens are often easily swayed by tribal interests ('group' interests being tribal). Conflict based on ethnic, racial, linguistic, or religious competitions comes easily to us. This can result, if appropriate checks are not put in place, in people with strong ill-feeling toward certain sections of the population being elected to power. Nazi Germany is not an exception; such failures have been repeated endlessly all over the world, including in India over the past 60 years where many of our representatives have been hate-mongers, not men of peace and wisdom.

As a result, democracies, even in the West, which are not structured very carefully, degenerate surprisingly quickly into mobocracies, or worse. The Germany which Hitler ruled was notionally a democracy, as was Soviet Russia where the Communist Party regularly received 99 per cent of the votes polled. Germany slid down the slope to mobocracy in only five years from 1928. Hitler held only 12 seats in the 1928 Reichstag, which increased to 230 out of 608 in 1932 – still not a majority. After that, political machinations took him to power and then to total dictatorship. A critical design flaw in the German constitution allowed Hitler to become Chancellor after which he never looked back, and the rest is history – a history of the brutal killing of millions of people across the world.

Democracies therefore need to be structured to prevent their being hijacked by mobs. India's democracy clearly shows signs of early onset of mobocracy, with many communal elements elected to high positions in its Central or State Government(s). By communal elements I not only refer to those who preach religious extremism, but also those who divide us by caste, colour, place of residence (such as rural or urban) and tribe. Such people stoke the tribal undercurrents in our nature and ride the turbulent waves so generated to electoral victory. As a result of their 'divide and rule' policies, unchecked by opposition from alert citizens, who seem to have tuned out from politics, India tends to burst into mob frenzy at periodic intervals when tall flames lick the night skies and muffled screams of terror and hatred resound into the desolate distance.[51] The great challenge in India today is to stop further degeneration into a mobocracy.

In the broader sense, though, freedom crucially hinges on the level of vigilance exercised by citizens. Unfortunately, most voters in India are disinterested in politics. While they do vote once in a while, few exercise the vigilance needed by a free society. They are busy with their day-to-day lives and do not have the time to examine the broader public interest or examine the impact of government policies on their freedom. In doing so, they forget that this negligence will cost them dearly. Without resistance from citizens, politicians are able to hijack a society's institutions to serve their personal ends, as has happened in India.

* * *

These, then, are only some of the many difficulties faced in designing good democratic institutions. India's real problem lies with the poor design of most of its governance frameworks. Our democratic model creates strong incentives for corrupt people and ruffians to enter politics and rise to the top. Indeed, I will show in chapter 4 that there is currently no possibility for a totally honest person successfully entering our political system.

This poor design has a lot to do with our leapfrogging many steps of political development. We face the consequence of going straight from primitive monarchies to a Westminster-style democracy without any political philosophers of freedom to tell us why we needed this change. There was no one to tell us that the purpose of these institutions was to get back our freedoms from 'rulers' who had taken these away from us thousands of years ago. No one told us that democratic institutions are not a fashion but have deep significance for the way we think of life and our place in the world. We have therefore failed to internalize the reasons for a democracy. We copied British institutions without knowing why. And so we don't know how to change them to suit our needs. And we don't exercise vigilance. There is very little civil society as well; no opposition to the rampant misuse of political power.

If we learn anything from the experience of history of freedom and representative democracy, it is this that genuine freedom and democracy can only be built upon the time-consuming edifice of debate, reflection and understanding among citizens. 'Instant democracy' – of the sort that we got in 1947, or of the sort that has recently been attempted in Iraq by the USA – is not the way democracies take root. Even if notional democracy has sent down some roots into India's soil, its reason for existing, namely, to help preserve our freedoms, has not been understood, and so we don't have real democracy.

Take the case of religion and politics in India. The links between these two were never broken in our past, nor was the divine right of kings questioned. The fact that our partition took place on religious grounds further emboldened the mix of religion and politics. Gandhi did no one a favour by talking of *Ram Rajya* when he should have been talking of a modern secular society grounded in freedom. In that regard, Nehru at least spoke the right things, though the Hindu laws enacted in his time put his understandings of the role of the state into question. This inflammable mixture of politics and religion now explodes in our face at periodic intervals.

Similarly, inherited roles continue to be accepted readily across the Indian society. These feudal characteristics create significant risks of dynastic rule which nullify the concept of democracy – we see that happening in Indian politics and in the film industry, apart from business. In genuine democracies like the British that fought each step on its long journey to freedom, people have internalized the dictates of freedom. Things like political dynasties and communal rioting are unheard of.

But we have not gone through the basic stages of political development and now are faced with the challenge of reforming our corrupt democracy. Today most Indians are reconciled to political corruption in India in perpetuity. No one thinks or believes that this will change. But that has never been the way of freedom. Free societies don't tolerate the mess of the sort we find ourselves in. The good news is that our problems of corruption and communalism are eminently fixable. We are not the first to have encountered such problems and so we can learn from others' experience. Our having missed a number of steps in democratic evolution need not prove a barrier to success if we dispassionately review our democratic experience, look outside India for good models, and make the necessary changes.

* * *

Before I review Indian democratic institutions in the next three chapters and suggest what we could do to improve things, I would like to briefly touch upon the question of presidential, proportional, or other representation models for India – a question that for some unfathomable reason exercises our minds more than questions of how incentives operate within our existing governance system. We periodically seem to go on a wild-goose chase looking for other models that appear, on the surface, to function better than ours. But the mere *form* of democratic representation, whether Westminster or presidential, whether proportional or first-past-the-post, doesn't really matter in the end, given the complexities and competing objectives that democracies need to serve. While models are important, the quality of governance in a society ultimately depends on the design of the incentives deep inside the entrails of these models.

Two democratic frameworks that look exactly the same on the surface will operate radically differently and lead to opposite outcomes based on the incentives generated by their supporting structures. A comparison of the performance of the Indian system with the Australian proves this point easily. While these two models are quite similar on the surface, the Australian model performs unimaginably better because its incentives and mechanisms are different at the detailed level. Improving the incentives in our current Indian model of democracy will similarly yield dramatic improvements in our outcomes.

For those interested, I have explored the following two key mechanisms of democracy at some length in the *Online Notes*[52]:

- keeping policy making and ideology separate from the social contract; and
- providing the right incentives to elected representatives and holding them accountable.

While I elaborate on these challenges in chapters 3, 4 and 6, we can make a mental note for now that India has done particularly badly in designing its institutions of democracy and governance at the detailed level.

SUMMARIZING CAPITALISM

This is a point that is approximately near the middle of this book. It is a good time to look back at the first two chapters and review some historical facts as well. Do sit with me on this nice rock here and have a coffee while we enjoy the beautiful vista of Free India rising in the near distance.

The main thing we have found so far, much to the surprise of some of us, is that capitalism or the overall mechanism of freedom, which comprises free markets and democracy, is infinitely better than what Karl Marx (1818–83) portrayed in his 1848 *Communist Manifesto.* I would like to digress for a moment here and explore this rather interesting and earth-shaking discovery!

In political philosophy, the age of thirty at which Marx wrote his *Manifesto* is considered very young. Marx was a baby philosopher then; quite immature and unable to plumb the depths of the ambitions for freedom of the human spirit that philosophers who preceded him had first articulated. It can be stated with some confidence that political philosophers should try to gain life experience at that age, not pen inflammatory pieces that overemphasize their ignorance. Unfortunately, through sheer repetition of the wild claims made by Marx in the *Manifesto* it appears that his deadly ideology of communism persuaded many people to stop investigating the truth about capitalism. Given the vigour of the *Manifesto*'s expression, Marxism became the new Gospel for many people, particularly its later *avatars* of Fabian socialism in India. And so Marx's followers diligently killed or made poor millions of people for 150 years while at the same time claiming that capitalism was to blame for these deaths and poverty.

But let us look at Marx's arguments more carefully, though briefly. It may come as a surprise to some of us, but Marx pointed out a number of good things about capitalism in his *Manifesto* even as he painted a gloomy picture of its allegedly insurmountable shortcomings. Marx said that 'capitalists' – a word which to him included industrialists, landlords, shopkeepers and pawnbrokers (but which to me is much narrower, meaning those who understand freedom) – were part of 'the modern bourgeois society that has sprouted from the ruins of feudal society'. Now,. at first blush it would seem that, if nothing else, sprouting from the ruins of feudalism is a step in the right direction. Capitalism was surely on to something! Some other quotations from Marx are noted below, with my comments italicized in brackets:

> 'The bourgeoisie cannot exist without constantly revolutionising the instruments of production' [*technological innovation is good*]. '[It also has] the need of a constantly expanding market for its products' [*this is a competitive and productive endeavour that enhances the wealth of nations*].
>
> 'The bourgeoisie, by the rapid improvement of all instruments of production, by the immensely facilitated means of communication, draws all, even the most barbarian, nations into civilisation' [*that is a great achievement, to be a civilizing force*].
>
> 'The bourgeoisie has [...] created enormous cities, has greatly increased the urban population as compared with the rural, and has thus rescued a considerable part of the population from the idiocy of rural life' [*here's another important feature of capitalism, though this statement needlessly insults people who may choose, upon having considered various options, to live in rural areas*].[53]

In general, we can agree with these parts of Marx's characterization of capitalism. If so, why did Marx go on to oppose capitalism and want to topple it? Well, what seems to have happened is that after noting its many advances, Marx began to doubt – quite wrongly as it turned out – whether a worker in a capitalist society would ever get to acquire ownership over property. He wrote, 'we Communists have been reproached with the desire of abolishing the right of personally acquiring property as the fruit of a man's own labour, which property is alleged to be the groundwork of all personal freedom, activity and independence [...] [h]ard-won, self-acquired, self-earned property! [...] [D]oes wage-labour create any property for the labourer? Not a bit' [*False!! – this being my heated exclamation of protest, obviously*].[54]

Marx actually went wrong by a mile here; off on a complete tangent. He was, for some unknown reason, not aware of the growing evidence of the dramatic improvements in the lot of workers even in incipient capitalist societies. For example, writing about the changes to the conditions of agricultural labourers and factory workers during the early stages of industrialization, the great economic historian, Rondo Cameron,[55] notes, 'That factory workers received higher wages than either agricultural labourers or workers in domestic industry there can be no doubt'. England also experienced a 'rapid rise in population during the early stages of industrialisation'. This indicates that relatively better nutrition and sanitary conditions prevailed in urban areas at that time, particularly better access to health. Public health initiatives were also starting to make a significant dent on infant mortality. For instance, in 1847–8 the British Parliament adopted a sanitary code for all of England and Wales excluding London. A few years later, Louis Pasteur of France proved beyond doubt that germs led to disease. Cameron then notes, 'the general trend of real wages was upward' at that time. These, then, are the high-level facts of the time of Marx which indicate that rapid scientific and economic advances were taking place exactly when young Marx was hastily jumping to wrong conclusions.

But 100 years of experience then available to Marx was perhaps somewhat mixed. Why don't we look at the facts prevailing now and see what happens in capitalist societies? In 1848, the theory of freedom and its practice, namely, of democratic free markets, had barely found a foothold. Today we are able to call upon 250 years of experience. Early trends found in Marx's time have become totally obvious. Today we are able to note unequivocally that the average worker in a capitalist society is much better off than an average worker under any alternative system. There are no two opinions about this fact of life.

In addition, there are great equality incomes at the professional levels. In a modern capitalist society, all occupations pay almost equally well at that level. For example, a good professor and a good plumber earn about the same (both earn above $100,000 in Australia today). That is due to the extremely high productivity of plumbers in these countries who are extensively trained in modern, productive technology. Morarji Desai made his first visit abroad in 1958, to Britain, USA and Canada. He found that capitalist societies were very equitable, more so socially. He remarked to Welles Hangen, an American journalist, after his trip, that 'In your country the manager and the worker sit together without any embarrassment. Many times the worker's clothes are as good as his boss's and the car he drives to work is also as good'.[56] Marx simply did not live long enough to see the long term impacts of capitalism; and like a bad scientist he ignored evidence of the increasing prosperity of workers in capitalist societies in his lifetime.

On the other hand, workers in feudal and socialist society remain pathetically poor, albeit equally. Only the corrupt are rich in such societies. Incomes in capitalist societies are highly unequal, but as we have seen, this is *moral* inequality, in that it is based on justice and voluntary, non-coercive trade. Such inequality is superior and even, arguably, desirable. In this manner, the level of overall morality in a society is perhaps the strongest signal of capitalism. (Now that I think of it, I should have put *morality* as a key indicator in Chapter 2; but it is implicit in the discussion on the culture of free societies and in the high levels of corruption found in socialist societies.) The main point is that inequality in capitalist societies doesn't remain fixed over generations as with feudal societies; an unskilled worker's children can easily become entrepreneurs and prosper through diligence. At the same time, it is not uncommon for a wealthy person's children to regress into penury.

We have seen that a capitalist society rewards people objectively through the balance of demand and supply for their contributions through the market. Rewards are not dependent on who one's father was, or on the colour of one's skin. Bill Gates' father could have been a 'lowly' black cleaner, and it would have mattered not one bit to Bill Gates' future. He would have still become the richest man in the world and equally respected. Capitalism is a fair system which gives everybody an equal chance to excel and prosper. Everyone can be rich in a free society. And happy.

Indeed, the classification by Marx of the society into classes such as workers and the bourgeoisie is completely unsustainable today. Capitalism has rich texture; it is not unidimensional like socialism. In a free society a person can become rich and poor in the same lifetime. And today, managers are a kind of worker; and knowledge workers are a kind of manager. There are no distinctions of class possible today.

These, then, are some of the true facts regarding capitalist societies. Unfortunately, based on his serious misinterpretations, or misrepresentations of the truth, Marx asked workers of the world to revolt against capitalism. He did not recommend making improvements to capitalism through peaceful, voluntary negotiations. He wanted capitalism abolished. He rallied workers: 'Workers of the world unite; you have nothing to lose but your chains'. According to him, workers needed to divest capitalists of their wealth (through violence, of course), and take charge of productive resources. Marx did not give directions on how the management of factories would change hands. Would the managers – who are also workers, but skilled workers – have to be demoted, and those without such knowledge and ability promoted to lead factories?

Was merit to be turned on its head? Whether he wanted it this way or not, that is exactly what happened at least under India's socialist regime in our public sector undertakings.

Marx's implicit recommendation was clearly to encourage plunder. Anyone with wealth was now to be game for our envious passions. When discussing this comment about socialist plunder, one of my friends asked me, 'The rich don't plunder?', to which the answer in a free society should be given in the following way: 'First, to be rich is not a crime. Indeed, profit earned through just means based on persuasion and voluntary exchange, where each party to a trade becomes better off, is philosophically *just* and eminently *moral.* It can't be related to plunder in any way. Plunder requires coercion to be employed. Second, a free society does not assassinate the character generally of all rich persons as a group. The issue of plunder has to be tested objectively in each individual case. Plunder is a definite crime in a free society and no one is exempt from punishment on being found guilty of plunder. Our inquiries may find that some of the rich have plundered; but perhaps not all have. We may also find that some of the poor have plundered as well; but that not all have. In brief, *whoever has plundered* must be tried and punished'.

Communists prefer to use force to obtain their objectives. According to that vile communist, Mao Zedong, 'all political power flows out of the barrel of a gun'.[57] Nothing could be more abhorrent and revolting, coming from a political leader. Leaders should speak the language of moderation, peace and freedom; not of violence. Such messages of hate and disrespect of life are in gross opposition to the philosophy of freedom. Freedom demands respect for life and everyone's freedom. Violence is never a part of it. It treats life almost as a sacred thing.

From the time of Marx, capitalism acquired a bad odour about it. In India, Nehru led a crusade against this word. At least two generations of Indians have now been poisoned against capitalism. But we know now, at last, the real truth that capitalism is an ethical, just and equitable system built on the foundation of freedom and equality of opportunity.

* * *

Having said that, we note that wherever there is smoke, there is bound to be some fire. It is possible that Marx did not see things as clearly as we see them today because, during his time, the characteristics of morality and justice we talk of today were at times not self-evident. Arrogance, racism and imperialism were often on display. So what was going on in the political environment in Marx's time? Despite workers' wages growing at a significantly faster clip than they had ever grown in the past, the early to mid-1800s, which Marx saw while growing up, were exploitative of workers by our standards today. Well-entrenched vestiges of British feudalism continued to have significant impacts on the culture of those times. The following points elucidate this:

- *Though the ideas of freedom had started to take root, these had not percolated into day-to-day governance.* Many battles for freedom were being waged across the world around that time. There was the American Declaration of Independence of 1776; people like Edmund Burke (1729–97) spoke about freedom and free trade in the British Parliament; the mechanisms of capitalism and free trade had been articulated by Adam Smith in 1776. Freedom had begun its hesitant march, but not yet found root.

- *It takes many generations for complex ideas such as the ideas of freedom to be internalized.* The ideas of freedom had not been internalized even by the propounders of freedom. Even Thomas Jefferson (1743–1826) held slaves and did not act on his own beliefs (he had made a passionate assault on slavery in his draft of the Declaration of Independence, an assault which was ripped out by others).

- *While freedom depends on high quality democracy, the British Parliament had barely started standing on its own feet by 1848.* It was so badly unrepresentative at that time that thousands of Irish had to die of starvation in the mid-1800s before the mercantilist British Government, controlled by landowning parliamentarians who benefited from high prices of wheat, permitted imports of wheat and potatoes from Europe. The voice of the 'common' people was definitely not being heard in 1848 in the British Parliament.

- *The newly rich business leaders of England of that period knew nothing about freedom.* Marx was wrong to assume that every so-called 'capitalist' would be a spokesperson for liberalism. Many systems of accountability had not yet been developed in capitalist societies. Its governance structures were very weak.

- *Some developments were taking place to advance accountability even as Marx penned his poisonous Manifesto.* Since workers had limited political and economic freedoms at that stage, it was left to trade unionists and thinkers like Robert Owen (1771–1858) and Thomas Hodgskin (1787–1869) to raise and address the many practical problems thrown up by incipient capitalism which had not yet internalized the meaning of freedom.

At a stage like that it was critical for thinkers like Marx to advance the cause of freedom. A vigorous defence of freedom was needed, not a misguided attack on the hard fought work of a few philosophers. It was also too early in capitalism's long journey to make firm judgements about its future. But Marx had made up his mind when he was young that he wanted nothing to do with freedom. He wanted equality, and wanted it now! Rather unfortunately for the hundreds of millions of people whom his ideas maimed or killed, Marx chose to throw out the baby (freedom) with the bath water of feudalism. If, instead of arriving at his hasty conclusion that capitalism needed to be overthrown, Marx had helped to improve the mechanisms of capitalism and accountability, including things like collective bargaining, or had helped to bring about improved governance of markets, he would have been acknowledged in a positive light today. Freedom is very hard to obtain even under ordinary circumstances. To have a confused person block out freedom through his fascination for objectives which oppose freedom can create a great setback.

But capitalism kept improving despite Marx. As a consequence of people like J S Mill – his writings speaking independently and boldly for freedom, unrelated to Marx's misguided attacks – a range of measures to improve the level of freedom in England began to be implemented by the British Parliament. It was as a result of various parliamentary battles in England and elsewhere that the conditions of workers in the capitalist world are now better than ever before. Apart from the abolition of slavery (which had already taken place in the early part of the nineteenth century in the UK but which took place much later in the USA) and the extension of suffrage to working men sometime later, the voice of women began to be heard in the early part of the twentieth century in England.

Entrenched vested interests that had long resisted accountability in feudal times continued to resist democracy and equality of status for as long as they could. Finally, businesses were brought under the umbrella of freedom (accountability) through the Factories Act. The modern system of industrial relations also came into being, a system that is still evolving. These are a few of the many things that helped to minimize the exploitation of workers by the so-called 'capitalists'. Today, the safety of workers is much better looked after in capitalist Australia, for example, than in socialist India or China. Workers in capitalist societies are generally rich and healthy, and their children can become a Bill Gates if they have the calibre to become one. None of these great improvements had anything to do with Marx.

Fortunately for mankind, Marx's followers, including the communists and socialists of the world, could not kill off everyone on this planet during their long massacres. The human race has survived the ravages of Marx. The truth always triumphs in the end, and today capitalism shines again in most parts of the world, brighter than ever before, acknowledged as the political and economic system of freedom; the beacon of hope for the great future that lies ahead for mankind and this planet. Capitalism has emerged smelling of roses after a struggle lasting 150 years. It will take many more generations to iron out all the shortcomings in the practice of capitalism, but at least 'Baby Freedom' has been retrieved from the bin Marx threw it into, and is now growing up sturdily.

* * *

It is very important to highlight that India is by no means a capitalist country today, despite economic liberalization. Capitalism is not merely the economic system of freedom. It refers to the entire system of freedom which includes institutions of good democracy. Capitalism is wedded to democracy. Freedom to speak and be heard (democracy) and freedom to act (justice, markets) are really one and the same thing. Capitalism also means preserving our physical and natural environment. Our planet sustains all known life; without its good health we cannot hope to live.

To be a capitalist is not to be an industrialist or a moneyed person. As a geologist is to geology, or an economist is to economics, a capitalist is to capitalism – the practice of freedom. While some of us may not be willing to 'rehabilitate' capitalism on this grand scale, we must remember that we are talking about a theory of freedom with credentials grounded in some of the greatest achievements of mankind; all of them achieved without recourse to violence. Science, innovation, peace – all these are the branches of capitalism. I suggest, therefore, that we discard all socialist beliefs and accept freedom and equality of opportunity as our core beliefs. Having done that, let us ask our socialist leaders and politicians when they have last thought about our freedoms?

It is time for us to move in detail into the Indian landscape. We need to explore where India lies today in relation to freedom and consider how we can lead it to freedom. The remaining four chapters of this book are devoted to the examination of India's governance and finding ways to improve it. In Chapter 4 I ask why we are unable to attract people who understand freedom into our political process. In Chapter 5 I ask why people found in our governance system (the bureaucracy, politicians) are so ineffective and corrupt. We will begin this exploration of India by examining the strengths and weaknesses of the most significant Indian document – its Constitution.

Chapter 3

Problems with our Constitution

> I shall strive for a constitution which will release India from all thralldom and patronage and give her, if need be, the right to sin.
>
> Gandhi[1]

Even if it is not specifically called a social contract, a democratic nation's constitution comes closest to representing the mutual agreement of all its citizens to the establishment of the nation. The primary purpose of a constitutional social contract is to establish a system of self-governance by which citizens are able to preserve their life and freedom. Where the constitution has been signed by the representatives of the people, as with India, this agreement is implicit; where the citizens have endorsed it through a referendum, as in Australia, this agreement is explicit. Where a dictator or king has promulgated an alleged constitution, for instance the 'constitution' which was created by Saddam Hussain, we cannot recognize it as a social contract for it is not a mutual agreement of citizens whether implicit or explicit.

India decided to move away from its monarchical roots after the British left in 1947 and chose to become a modern republic. Our first social contract, i.e. our first Constitution, has served us reasonably well by providing us with an agreed set of rules, similar in many ways to the rules the British governed India with. It has given continuity to our governance and acted as the glue to keep the country together. Further, its ability to respond to evolving social pressures, without letting go of the core principles of parliamentary democracy, a federal structure, the rule of law and judicial review, has enabled India to move in fitful starts from a feudal society to a relatively modern one. Our Constitution was very welcome and it has done us far more good than harm, particularly given the low starting point of freedoms in India.

But few of us know much about our Constitution. It is an abstruse and distant document not easily understood nor of much interest to most of us. It is too long, being the longest in the world; too detailed;

too pompous; too legalistic. But most importantly, it doesn't talk in a simple language of meaningful things that we can relate to. We search hard to find a coherent story. 'What is this Constitution all about?', we wonder, as we turn its hundreds of pages.

It doesn't quite belong to us in the sense that the crisp and short American Constitution belongs to the Americans. American children study the highlights of their Constitution as early as in the fifth standard in school, particularly its references to freedom. Australians also own their Constitution, primarily because it was adopted after a referendum. But we did not have a referendum either, it being perhaps impractical to hold one in 1949. Our 299 representatives who constituted our Constituent Assembly agreed to it on 26 January 1949 and it was given effect on 26 January 1950. And of course, we are not modern enough to have a system by which each generation can review and re-adopt the Constitution. As a result, except for a few Supreme Court lawyers, very few Indians are interested in it, which is regrettable since there is really no document more important in India than this.

On evaluating its merits, I find our Constitution to be a mediocre product. Yes, there are surely a few good parts – among them the original fundamental rights which were based on the classical liberal philosophy of freedom. Unfortunately, some of these are no longer available, having been repealed or amended significantly. The Constitution has some parts which could do with significant simplification. Finally, it has some extremely poor parts which had no business to be included in the Constitution in the first place.

Consider the original Preamble for a moment (the one that didn't have socialism ensconced in its midst). While it did mention liberty and equality of opportunity, it clearly wasn't focused exclusively on these two principles. It wandered off into strange rhetoric about things called 'fraternity' and 'equality of status'. The former makes no sense whatsoever, or is at best subsumed under liberty. Whether we fraternize with each other is a personal choice; a Constitution can't force us to do that. The latter, equality of status, is a trivial corollary of liberty and equality of opportunity. Equality of status implies equal treatment under the law. No one can be free without each citizen being treated as an equal in law. So we should have stuck *only* to two things – freedom and equality of opportunity, noting that equality of opportunity is a derivative of freedom. In reality we needed only one thing – protection of our life and freedoms.

Most unfortunately, though, the Preamble distorts liberty itself by talking of a completely indefensible and vacuous thing called 'social' and 'economic' justice. But social justice is a totally meaningless term (even assuming that economic justice merely represents justice in commercial undertakings). Justice is always individual, not collective or social. 'Social justice' is not based on consistent logic. Indeed, this phrase has a deeply socialist origin, and has laid the seeds of terrible corruption and continued poverty in India. Most bad policies in India have been justified by the pursuit of social justice, even as we did practically nothing to ensure equality of opportunity. Equality of opportunity requires the eradication of poverty and educating of all our children. None of that happened because people got distracted by the whimsical 'social justice'.

The further problem with the rhetoric found in the Preamble is that its good parts such as liberty and equality of status are violated at numerous places in the Constitution itself. There is only partial equality of status in law in India. People are differently treated in the Constitution based on tribal and caste distinctions. And the restrictions on freedom imposed in the Constitution make a farce of the word 'liberty'.

Only a year after the Constitution had been given effect, Nehru decided he needed to significantly reduce the freedom of businesses to operate in India.[2] It was fortuitous for him but unfortunate for the nation that Sardar Patel – who had a stronger grasp of the purpose of independence than Nehru did, and who would have probably opposed Nehru's socialist approach to the economy had he lived longer – passed away in December 1950. In the meanwhile, Gandhi, the other opponent of Nehruvian socialism, had been assassinated. That left Nehru with untrammelled power to open the floodgates of his cherished experiments of socialism. The Indian Constitution has now been amended 94 times. Unfortunately, these amendments did nothing to remove any of its glaring defects. Instead, many of them added new defects. Luckily, despite this intensive mauling, the Constitution still resembles its original form and structure and retains some of its liberal founding principles.[3]

While this document has served us reasonably well by increasing the awareness of democratic principles in India, it is now well past its 'use-by' date. The time has come to completely review and remake our social contract. Some could argue that since the Constitution is not fully broken yet, we shouldn't fix it. But that is exactly when you fix and renew a thing – before it has completely broken down. Also, a document as important as this needs to represent current expectations and focus explicitly on the fundamentals of liberty. It needs to be completely freshened up, not patched up. In this chapter, I will make a few suggestions which could inform such a total overhaul. I also propose a practical way forward to get a social contract relevant to our times. But let us begin with a review of its key problems.

INADEQUATE FOCUS ON ITS PRIMARY PURPOSE – FREEDOM

As already indicated, our Constitution doesn't have a uniting theme, a theme to focus each of its words towards the advancement of our freedoms. The ideas of freedom of expression, property rights and habeas corpus haplessly mingle with ideas that oppose freedom. It dabbles with a number of second order, even tertiary and mutually incompatible, ideas – things like social justice, socialism, casteism, tribalism, policy whims and directives, etc. All kinds of strange animals find a place in our Constitution. It is a veritable *khichri* with small irritating pebbles that crack our teeth as we start 'eating' it. Some of these pebbles, like socialism or social justice, are poisonous and have actually caused us endless grief. We need to spit them out. It is definitely not a simple and therefore well-made *khichri*, flavoured only with the deeply satisfying aroma of pure freedom, like pure ghee melting all over it.

The debates[4] of the Constituent Assembly indicate that the forces of freedom were very weak when this document was drafted between 9 December 1946 and 26 January 1949. There were too many muddled up aspirations in the minds of our representatives. The Constitution we got was a hotchpotch compromise between the whims of the 299 people on our Constituent Assembly; not the resonantly clear voice of freedom. Our Constitution is ungainly. If it were a building, it would look like an incoherent mix of radically opposed architectural styles juxtaposed into a precariously balanced structure, straining to avoid an impending collapse.

Nowhere to be found in our Constitution is the piercing depth of understanding of freedom and simplicity of expression that Alexander Hamilton and James Madison brought to the American Constitution in 1787. 'We the People of the United States, in Order to form a more perfect Union, establish Justice, insure domestic Tranquility, provide for the common defence, promote the general Welfare, and secure the Blessings of Liberty to ourselves and our Posterity, do ordain and establish this Constitution for the United States of America.'[5] No confusion between freedom and justice – two sides of the same coin. No intrusions by social justice and fraternity; no need to mention equality of status. Such clarity permeates the entire American

Constitution. In consequence, the American Government has restricted its focus to defence and freedom over and above a bit of social welfare (equality of opportunity, primarily). That is it. That is all that is needed to achieve greatness.

I also don't understand why we replaced the word 'freedom' with jargon like 'fundamental rights'. While the contents of our fundamental rights are important, none are fundamental. None can be deduced in isolation of freedom. But freedom does not give us any rights at all. When we advocate freedom, all we say is that everyone has the 'right' to be free – the pure act of being free. Its limits do not depend on 'rights', but on accountabilities. It does not generate 'fundamental' rights. Everything listed under 'fundamental' rights is at best a derivative implication, a mere tangential illustration of the concept of freedom.

In fact, the language of 'rights', even the glorified term 'human rights', misleads us badly and takes us down a blind alley. The word 'rights' is dangerous because it conjures up a free lunch; as if we have something given to us for free on our being born. It is easy to extrapolate this language to the 'right' to work and things like that, making a mockery of the fundamental principles of freedom. But all we ask is to be free to choose and to act. We are free to breathe so long as we let others breathe; free to speak so long as we let others speak; free to earn our livelihood so long as we provide a service that is actually sought from us. We have no rights to work. We don't even have fundamental rights. All we have is the 'right' to be held to account for our freedoms of action.

What our Constitution should therefore have clearly demanded and boldly stuck with as its key principle are freedom and – its obverse – justice. From this single concept, clearly explained, any ordinary human being should have been able to derive implications of the sort which we so laboriously and mystically seek to embellish as 'fundamental rights'. The concept of 'property rights' is, for instance, nothing but the attribution of the outcome of our actions. Freedom makes its own accountability and lives as one – like Yin with Yang (see Appendix 1). These two, together, are complete and whole, one with each other. That is the only logical foundation of a society where people do not go about taking undue advantage of each other. Once we have stated this principle of freedom and accountability, we would not need 'fundamental rights'. We could have created a few 'illustrative examples of the freedoms and accountabilities of Indian citizens'.

Despite the language of rights being misleading or pompous, I continue to use 'rights' in some of its more traditional senses in this book, such as when referring to property rights. However, I steer well clear of terms such as human rights, where dangerous animals like 'social justice' or the 'right to work' often lurk just below the surface.

INFLEXIBILITY

Ideally, the social contract of a free society should allow each generation the freedom to think for itself and create institutions of governance relevant to its needs. But our Constituent Assembly did not quite believe we could be trusted to make our own detailed laws. And so it paternalistically told us everything about how we should govern ourselves, including how we should run our public services. Our Constitution is extremely prescriptive; not focused on outcomes. Given that it is a Constitution and not an ordinary law, it becomes very hard to change its prescriptions. The jungle of detail found in our Constitution has made it very hard to modernize our governance. As a result, our governance structures have remained practically frozen as they were designed in 1950 (noting that many of these structures had roots in British India's laws and institutions, going back into the 1850s. We are effectively forced to do today what the British had done 150 years ago!).

Countries with short and flexible constitutions have breezed through many experiments in governance and radically improved their governance. But in our case, our 299 'wise' people of 1949 still dictate to us how we shall do things for the next million years. 'Thou shalt use a bullock cart even if thou art in a position to use jet engines or time machines', they seem to be saying to us.

CITIZENS NOT PERMITTED TO ENGAGE IN A BUSINESS OF THEIR CHOICE

On 10 May 1951, Nehru brought to our provisional Parliament[6] the first Constitutional Amendment Bill to amend Article 19 of our Constitution. His aim was to limit our freedom to trade with each other. This amendment not only empowered the government to enter into any business it wished, but enabled it to prevent citizens from undertaking such a business. There may be a justification to exercise oversight over specific businesses, e.g. when citizens set up their nuclear plants and arms factories,[7] but this amendment was not introduced for such oversight. It was intended to push aside citizens to allow the government to operate ordinary businesses such as making bread, or running bus services.[8]

It appears that catching thieves and ensuring the rule of law was not challenging enough for Nehru's government – maybe it was too hard and not exciting enough. Socialist governments always fail on fundamentals such as law and order, anyway; they prefer to drive around in buses, picking up people from bus stops, tootling away at their horn. And so Nehru told the Parliament:

> The citizen's right to practise any profession or to carry on any occupation, trade or business conferred [...] is subject to reasonable restrictions. *While the words [...] are comprehensive enough to cover any scheme of nationalisation* which the State may undertake, it is desirable to place the matter beyond doubt by a clarificatory addition to article 19(6)[9] (italics mine).

The amended Article 19(6) now reads as follows:

> [...] nothing [...] shall affect the operation of any existing law in so far as it relates to, or prevent the State from making any law relating to [...] (ii) the carrying on by the State, or by a corporation owned or controlled by the State, of any trade, business, industry or service, **whether to the exclusion, complete or partial, of citizens** or otherwise (emphasis mine).

That the freedom of citizens to set up a business and engage in a legal trade, and thus earn their livelihood, is a basic freedom that a government must always defend, was lost on Nehru. He was engrossed in taking us to his Heaven of Equality, a strange Heaven in which government officials would drive buses and bake bread instead of providing us with security. And with this amendment, our legal freedom to engage in a legal trade, business, industry or service of our choice came to an end. Not only would the state henceforth produce shirts and bread, instead of producing justice and security, it would also regularly oust us from such businesses. It was through such frontal assaults on the relatively liberal 1950 Constitution that Nehru and his successors laid the foundations of misgoverned India.

We also observe with a sense of astonishment how state-created monopolies were deemed not to deprive us of freedom, but at the same time a great deal of fuss was made about some smallish businesses that India had managed to grow indigenously in its private sector during British rule, such as the Tatas and Birlas. These were extremely small in comparison with American and European companies, but were labelled as monopolies under the MRTP Act of 1969. The government then sat, open-handed (as opposed to even-handed), soliciting bribes in return for sheltering such companies from competition through the license *raj*, accentuating whatever little monopolistic powers these companies may have had.

FUNDAMENTAL RIGHT TO PROPERTY ABOLISHED

To Nehru, socialism was to be brought about by 'the ending of private property, except in a restricted sense'.[10] The interpretation of this 'restricted sense' was left to his personal whims, making it difficult to pin down what he had in mind. Property rights are purely freedom-based; this is a capitalist concept. From John Kenneth Galbraith we know that Nehru's views on property reflected the opinions of Harold Laski, a professor of political science at the London School of Economics. 'The centre of Nehru's thinking', said Galbraith, 'was Laski', and 'India the country most influenced by Laski's ideas'.[11] Maybe if we read Laski carefully we will understand what Nehru really meant by 'restricted sense'. Laski said:

> [...] the existing rights of property represent, after all, but a moment in historic time. They are not today what they were yesterday and tomorrow they will again be different. It cannot be affirmed that, whatever the changes in social institutions, the rights of property are to remain permanently inviolate. Property is a social fact, like any other, and it is the character of social facts to alter.[12]

Thus, Laski clearly did not recognize freedom as the supreme good. Hobbesian in approach, to him the state was supreme, with our role being to serve it and to be regulated by it. According to Laski, 'The state [...] is the crowning-point of the modern social edifice, and it is in its supremacy over all other forms of social groupings that its special nature is to be found'.[13] But in the dictionary of freedom, the state is nowhere in that league. It is a creature of our convenience operated by governments paid to do our bidding. The state exists merely for our convenience; for the specific purpose of protecting our freedoms and enforcing the accountability that accompanies freedom. If the state does not guarantee our freedoms and property rights, we have no allegiance to that state – we will make another one, or leave.

In that sense, John F Kennedy was wrong when he said, 'ask not what your country can do for you – ask what you can do for your country'.[14] In a free society, obligations lie with both parties. The state or country, represented by its government, must behave responsibly and defend our freedoms diligently in order to retain our allegiance and participation in dangerous enterprises like the defence of the land. A state loses legitimacy if it destroys the freedoms for which it was created. Laski's arrogant state that believes it doesn't have to protect our property rights and freedoms is destined to be a failed state. It will not only be defenceless against external aggression as its best people abandon that state, but even those that remain will rebel and destroy its foundations through corruption and anarchy.

Laski turned the primacy of freedom on its head, claiming that property was a mere cultural artefact. That is absurd, but such were the Muses of Nehru and the Indian socialists. Nehru's younger fellow party-man, Siddhartha Shankar Ray (SSR), similarly argued that while life and liberty are innate natural rights, ownership of property is not. He said that since the right to property and freedom to contract did not pre-exist the Constitution these should be deemed to be of lesser import, presumably to be cast out from our Constitution with the flick of a socialist finger.[15] Many of our judges also did not distinguish themselves as protectors of our freedom in those primitive times. Justice Hidayatullah of the Supreme Court lowered the stature of his office when he said that 'it was a mistake' to have property as a Fundamental Right.[16] But this fact, that other political leaders in India also shared Laski's views, does not diminish Nehru's primary role in promoting these ideas in India.

Let us, even for the sake of argument, momentarily agree with SSR's view that 'modern' freedoms and property rights did not pre-exist our Constitution. Was it then not obligatory on the leaders of independent India to ensure that these 'new' freedoms were introduced and 'passed on' to us? If some freedoms did not exist in a feudal, imperial India, how could that justify our not having them in independent India? Was the purpose of our struggle for independence merely to continue with the limited set of freedoms that the British had allowed us to enjoy? Was our independence merely an occasion to substitute arrogant and brown sarpanchs in place of imperial, white rulers? I must admit that at times I am unable to distinguish clearly between Nehru and his godchildren on the one hand, and the British rulers of India on the other. It is difficult at times to conclude who was worse for India in the end – having to work with totally corrupt Indian ministers as one's bosses at work, or having honest but arrogant imperial British rulers in their place.

Implementing his whimsical arguments about property rights, Nehru launched his assault by enacting land ceiling acts, called, euphemistically and misleadingly, 'land reforms'. After Nehru's passing away, Congress leaders strengthened this attack. The argument they made to support their attack was that 'rights' of the society were more important than our freedoms. Mohan Kumaramanglam said, 'The clear object of this amendment [25th] is to *subordinate the rights of individuals* to the urgent needs of society' (italics mine). This was in relation to the 25th amendment of the Constitution in 1971, which removed the concept of compensation upon acquisition of people's lands,[17] yet another destruction of property rights. But except in situations of war when the overall need of the society arguably predominates that of an individual, the freedom of individuals cannot be subordinated in a free country. This was not a war-related withdrawal of freedoms.

The socialist flood was now nearing its fullest season. All stops had been pulled out. There was the monopoly of loss making public sector businesses, there was the nationalization of privately operated businesses, there was land acquisition without market compensation and there were land ceiling laws. 'In the months after the [25th] amendment [...] coal, coking coal, and copper mines were nationalised, along with steel plants, textile mills, and shipping lines – totalling hundreds of nationalisations'.[18]

This plunderous socialist rampage was fully supported by all political parties in India except the Swatantra. After Swatantra shut down in 1974, these principles continue to be supported today by all major parties in India; none of them has suggested returning our freedoms to us. The biggest blow to property rights was therefore not administered by Nehru or by his Congress party, but by a rag-tag bunch of socialist factions calling themselves the Janata Party, in 1978 (this included Bharatiya Jana Sangh, the predecessor of the current socialist group called Bharatiya Janata Party, or BJP). While we remain indebted to this motley bunch for reversing some of the more blatant impositions against freedom by Indira Gandhi's Emergency, they simply added one more nail to the coffin of freedom in India. By the time the Janata Party formed the government, only a sliver of property rights was still left in India.

Land reform legislation had already not only been enacted but had been placed under the Ninth Schedule of the Constitution, sheltering it from judicial review. However, the risk, no matter how remote, of a constitutional challenge to these laws prompted the Janata Party to abolish the right to property through the 44th Amendment of 1978. In particular, Article 19(1)(f), that had till then, even through Nehru's time, guaranteed to the Indian citizens a right to acquire, hold and dispose of property, was repealed.

No sensible reason was offered. To assuage people's fear, it was announced that property, 'while ceasing to be a fundamental right, would, however, be given express recognition as a legal right, provision being made that no person shall be deprived of his property save in accordance with law'.[19] This is an extraordinarily weak protection. The law is a malleable thing in comparison to the Constitution. Citizens of a free country should not have to depend on the whim of their ruling governments for the defence of their freedoms, and thus of their property. Socialists have never understood why they can't do such things when they still stick with the word 'liberty' in our Preamble.

FORCING THE POLICY CHOICES OF THE PAST ON US

A Constitution is not a forum for social or economic policy discussion. Policy lists are relevant to someone's personal writings, such as in books like this, but they are completely unacceptable in a social contract. A multitude of whims of a few people of the past find mention as the Directive Principles of State Policy. Some of these are extremely ill-thought-out and have added fuel to the fire of existing divisions in the Indian society. The Uniform Civil Code (UCC) comes to mind as one such gratuitous policy.

The basic question that arises is why we care at all about what the members of our Constituent Assembly thought about policy? In what way is our generation less capable of deciding its policies for itself? As a matter of fact, these 299 people knew much less, on average, than what we know today, in the same way that our generation knows much less than the following generations. These folk were asked to draft our Constitution, not to create policy advice. They should have stuck to their task and done it well.

Most amazingly, in 1955, Nehru added to the confusion by advancing the bizarre claim that the Directive Principles can have a higher status than fundamental rights. He declared, 'It is up to Parliament to [...] make the Fundamental Rights subserve the Directive Principles of State Policy'.[20] I suspect our leaders would have removed all protections of our freedoms had they been able to get their way. Mercifully, a few upright High Court and Supreme Court judges opposed this madness, and the 'basic structure' of our

Constitution has survived the ravages of socialism. We still retain a whiff of freedom, though one can't say that with a straight face to someone who has been detained illegally for months, then tortured and beaten, and finally killed by our own police forces in a fake encounter. I wish I had the space to narrate instances of governmental brutality that I know of from my own experiences in government.

Let's now look at a couple of the policy dabblings in the Constitution:

THE UNIFORM CIVIL CODE

Article 44 of the Constitution states, 'The State shall endeavour to secure for the citizens a uniform civil code throughout the territory of India'.

One may well ask, 'What is wrong with this innocuous statement?' To keep the record straight, we first note that the subject under discussion is not about civil law. We already have a consistent framework for such matters. It is about a civil code. But what exactly is a civil code? It turns out that it is all about personal law. Civil code is 'code' for 'matrimonial matters, guardianship, adoption, succession, and religious institutions'.[21] Even before we think further about it, this must raise a red flag. Personal law is surely a dangerous thing to demand uniformity about in a free society.

An individual's choice of a religion, if any, and actions taken by that individual to manage the journeys of his or her soul as part of the requirements of that religion, is surely a purely personal matter. Among related matters, marriage as a religious sacrament is clearly a human relationship in which, unless a very good case can be made for it, the state has absolutely no business to intervene. The government's role of providing justice relates largely to damages we cause by commercial improprieties and criminal actions. We do not want a government peeking inside our family unit without either a commercial impropriety being involved or a criminal action. In any event, we don't need a government to tell us how to marry for the institution of marriage predates modern government by fifty thousand years or more. On the other hand, I agree with the Supreme Court which said on 14 February 2006 that registration of marriages must be made compulsory. Registration of a marriage would be a public record of the facts, including which type of marriage was performed. Registration does not lead to uniformity.

All societies have developed their norms of marriage, including relevant principles of accountability. These principles of accountability are often designed to balance the economic liabilities of the two families or communities that come together through the marriage. There is no uniquely 'correct' way to bring these liabilities together; plenty of flexibility and scope for negotiation exists. These accountabilities are largely a creature of convenience and consensus within the boundaries of particular religions or social structures. It cannot be up to a government to decide which mode of consensus is appropriate for an entire segment of society. In general, therefore, I should be in a position as a free citizen to negotiate suitable agreements in a marriage which would then bind, explicitly or implicitly, all parties in the relationship. As long as a group of free people 'self-regulate' in this manner, and accept a particular norm for balancing their liabilities, no outsider, including the government, can have cause to get involved.

Many social norms relate to matters on which for a government to legislate will make it look silly. For instance, we cannot legislate the level of affection that must exist between husbands and wives, equally as we cannot legislate that a father must invariably provide for an equal bequest to all his children, irrespective of the care and effort that the children took of their parents when they were alive, or irrespective of the obligations enjoined in the parent's religion. These are matters of personal judgement and belief. The state cannot have a role in these matters.

Indeed, if I am not free to choose my religion, my culture and my own way of life, I would question the point of my existence itself. We must be free to live, and to be what we want to be, not what the state coerces us into becoming. A free citizen must be free to choose from among an array of competing suppliers of marriage laws, religions and cultures; just as the citizen is free to choose between different brands of shampoo. A state can legislate minimum standards for shampoos to prevent people from putting in poisonous ingredients, but it cannot tell us which shampoo to buy or how to shampoo our hair. And we must also remain free to use our home-made shampoo as well.

This freedom implies that those who are not satisfied with the traditional norms of existing social groups must always be free to explore and adopt, or to create alternative norms. As a feeble example, I should be able to choose to marry under the Special Marriage Act (which is what I chose for my marriage) if I do not subscribe to any religious practice (which I don't). But more generally, I should be free to create my own rules of accountability for marriage. A marriage contract that meets socially acceptable minimum standards should be equally binding as any religious or other form or marriage.

We must be very sceptical of attempts to impose a mythical 'best' way on us to marry or to pass on our inheritance. The free society's government does not standardize things merely because it can do so. Uniformity among personal laws is not a virtue but an unwarranted imposition, just as demanding uniformity among various brands of shampoo is not a virtue. This 'hands-off' approach may appear to allow for continuation of problematic things like dowry, but that is not how it will play out. Madhu Kishwar has demonstrated that dowry is often used as a way to prevent the equitable transfer of inheritance to daughters. Therefore a system without dowry but with equitable inheritance, which takes into account the extra costs incurred by sons (or daughters) in looking after the elderly parents, is a much fairer system. However, rather than having a government prescribe such a thing, I suggest that left to itself Hinduism will move on its own to a system without dowry but equitable inheritance, particularly as children get more educated. The point therefore is that people must be free to choose any appropriate norm they please on personal matters. We can't have a government telling us what to do. On the other hand, if I were to harass someone for dowry, or cause a dowry death, then that would be a criminal matter to be dealt with under the usual criminal law. Either way, the message for the government is – stay away from uniformity or prescriptions in these matters, and let societies evolve their own understandings.

I have a feeling (I may be wrong) that Article 44 was introduced at the behest of some Hindus – not all of them – to compel conformity by Muslims to their evolving views on monogamy and succession. If that hunch is true, then it was an insidious imposition of majority rule; an example of mobocracy. Originally, some of the religious leaders, whose views BJP presumably now represents, opposed both the Hindu laws as well as the UCC. The Rashtriya Swayamsevak Sangh (RSS) position is outlined by K R Malkani in his 1982 book, *The RSS Story*:

> Shri Guruji [Golwalkar] went so far as to say that Muslim Law could continue separately, without being replaced by a Uniform Civil Law, as laid down in the Directive Principles of State Policy. When subsequently asked whether uniformity of law would not promote national integration, he said, 'Not necessarily'.[22]

The BJP should move away from a blind faith in uniformity and for the sake of uniformity think of the underlying issues. Article 44, being incompatible with freedom and democracy, must be scrapped.

* * *

There is a potentially legitimate concern underpinning this Directive Principle. It is possible that things like bigamy and practices in Islam that (apparently) do not take appropriate care of divorced women drove the inclusion of this Directive Principle. The way for a government to deal with such evolving social expectations is to shift the agreed minimum standards of individual accountability. An umbrella of minimum standards of civilization can be established, not complying with which can be deemed to be criminal. Creating a minimum standard is not the same thing as having a UCC. It creates uniformity in outcomes and not in processes; and it is not a code, but a prohibition. This would be a mechanism fully compatible with freedom and flexibility of social evolution.

Left to themselves, societies and religions will constantly evolve. Ethical standards will also evolve. For instance, slavery is no longer acceptable whereas it was a part of most societies in the world till about 150 years ago. It was abolished only in the mid to late 1800s. As a society evolves, it re-defines the boundaries of individual accountability. Each society can therefore abolish, over time, 'primitive' social norms not compatible with civilization, including things like bonded labour, *sati* and child marriage. These prohibitions limit our choice but only in the interest of accountability and of equality of opportunity, and thus foster our freedoms; particularly the freedoms of children and women.

We know that polygamy (marrying more than one women) was equally practised among all communities in India till the 1950s. The abolition of bigamy in Islam is one of the demands of the votaries of the UCC. Bigamy is now a potential candidate for such prohibition. However, there is a need for discussions and negotiations first. I have discussed the issues that potentially arise in this regard in Appendix 3 in the *Online Notes.*[23]

In a similar fashion, not as a set of prohibitions, but as a set of minimum acceptable accountability standards, a society can legitimately establish a requirement that women shall be looked after well after divorce, or such things. Citizens can always choose to deliver to themselves standards that exceed these minimum standards. I believe that these two methods, combined, will address all the underlying 'needs' of the votaries of the UCC. It is important to note that such generic methods to resolve underlying social concerns are topics for potential policy debate, which need to be discussed by each generation's parliament. These are not matters for inclusion in a country's Constitution. That can only be disastrous.

I would therefore urge the RSS and BJP to work with others to agree on these two sets of minimum standards for India. In closing this discussion, I have provided my suggestions for a personal law framework that will be compatible with freedom in the *Online Notes.* This manner of generic treatment of outcomes, not of processes, will also help to repeal the Hindu and Muslim laws enacted by the Parliament – something which it should never have done in the first place, for such matters are none of its business.[24]

GOVERNMENT EMPOWERED TO MEDDLE IN RELIGIOUS MATTERS

In numerous places our Constitution recognizes a range of religious 'minorities', specific castes and 'backward' groups, as well as specific religions such as the Hindu, Sikh, Jain and Buddhist religions. It also discusses religious matters such as prohibition of cow slaughter and opening up Hindu religious institutions. In this manner, the Constitution implicitly enables governments to enact a range of religious laws; that is presumably why Hindu laws[25] are not unconstitutional. Our government is also empowered to operate religious institutions. A government officer manages the Tirupati temple as its executive officer.[26] The government also organizes and pays subsidies to Indian Muslims for their *Haj* pilgrimage. Rampant dabbling by Indian governments in religious matters has made a complete mockery of India's claim of being a secular nation, or a free nation. There are many other problems with such Constitutional arrangements:

- This has created a great deal of confusion in the society about the proper role of the state. The state and religion are totally different spheres of our life. The state has a geographical boundary; religion is infinite, beyond all boundaries. These are two radically different jurisdictions. A government must therefore be religion-blind (as in colour-blind) if it wishes to perform its role of justice without blemish. The rule that suits a free society best is, 'Render unto Caesar the things which are Caesar's, and unto God the things that are God's'. In other words, a government cannot even recognize a religion, leave alone helping people specifically on the basis of their religion. It is the job of religious believers to support their own religious practices like the *Haj* or manage the Tirupati temple; the government can never have anything to do with these matters. Politicians can, of course, individually be as religious as they wish to be. But their role in government is exclusively to govern and provide justice.

- The current practice forces citizens like me who do not have any religious beliefs to subsidize those who are religious. This is truly bad policy, sufficient to make people like me want to rebel and stop paying taxes to the government. I am happy to pay to raise the poor above poverty; but not one paisa for anyone's religious practices.
- The religious pronouncements of the government, which thinks as a committee and knows very little of anything, are full of inaccuracies. For instance, the Hindu laws combine independent world-views like Buddhism, Sikhism and Jainism together under one religion, Hinduism. To mix these distinct offshoots of Hinduism with the main religion is the height of absurdity.
- Government religious laws lead to false implications in some places. For instance, according to explanation (a) under s.2(a) of the Hindu Succession Act, 1956, I am deemed to be Hindu since both my parents are Hindu. 'The following persons are Hindus […] by religion: any child legitimate or illegitimate, both of whose parents are Hindus.' But I am neither a Hindu nor a member of any other religion. My being deemed by a Parliamentary law to be a Hindu is amusing, *if not disturbing.* At the least it amounts to interference by the state in my private affairs. The government should stay completely clear of all religions matters if it doesn't want to give offence to all and sundry.
- Such laws are anticompetitive and block competition among various religions and branches of religions. As usual, all long-term monopolies are always created by governments. Nehru, who avoided religion and definitely disliked its excesses, seems to have helped a particular brand of Hinduism to get a legal foothold in India. I just can't figure out what he was thinking at that time!
- Freezing religions practices such as Hindu caste practices in the schedules of the Constitution has simply blocked all

> possible reform of Hinduism. No one wants to get rid of the caste system any longer; for how else will some people get the 'benefit' of being a 'scheduled' caste? Didn't it strike the Constituent Assembly that dong so would simply pour cement on the caste system?

Constitutional and Parliamentary interference in religions in India has dramatically aggravated the religious divides of this country which would have eased off had they not been given such elevated status in the law and focus had been entirely given to the primary business of promoting freedom. As a result, the so-called religious 'card' is now played feverishly during elections by many irresponsible politicians wanting a quick route to power by rousing our tribal emotions. The BJP's repeated demand for a UCC[27] and its infamous 'rathyatras', which are the lowest form of mixing of religion with politics, are cases in point.

The solution to this chaos is simple – the Indian Government should never talk or write about religion or discuss this issue in any of its laws, statistical publications including its census or other reports and documents. Religion is a purely personal matter for each of us; it is none of the business of the government.

INJUSTICE OF THE 'JUSTICE OF YESTERDAY' AND SOCIAL JUSTICE

To rationalize his ideology of socialism, Nehru used other related arguments as well. He called for 'not just the justice of today, but the justice of yesterday'.[28] Of course, he wasn't the only one to make such an argument, for this argument echoes throughout the Constitution. But in claiming that accountability transmits over generations, Nehru, a barrister, made a most fundamental error of all; for people who have nothing to do with an alleged injustice are never accountable for that injustice.

The idea of 'justice of yesterday' can lead to extremely convoluted consequences. Just because someone couldn't catch a guilty person and punish him or her in the past (quite possibly because the law under which that person is being deemed guilty today, did not exist then!), therefore our government must apparently punish the innocent progeny of that guilty person now. It seems that alleged criminals' children and great-grand children who were not even born when the alleged crime was committed, must now be punished without trial by taking away their lands and properties and denying them an equal status under today's laws. The Preamble's assurance of equal status is made completely hollow if such a logic is adopted.

According to such a theory, had Nehru investigated his family history, he might have found that, possibly 50 generations ago, one of his ancestors had treated a low caste person criminally but was not caught out and tried by the law of that time (there most likely having been no such law at that time). Applying Nehru's own principle to himself, Nehru would have had to give himself up to the nearest police station and sought to be jailed for life on behalf of his allegedly criminal relative who died 50 generations before he was born. Even a two-year old can tell us that such justice is absurd!

Freedom hinges on the very simple concept of individual justice – a justice that belongs to our lifetime, not a 'justice of yesterday' wagging its long tail for a thousand generations. Unfortunately, many people in India continue to behave as if common sense is not necessary. There is nothing to distinguish rabid socialists from rabid religious fundamentalists on this form of justice. BJP and Vishva Hindu Parishad used exactly such reasoning[29] to provoke and at least indirectly encourage their followers to tear down the Babri Masjid.[30] Apparently, some primitive barbarian (doesn't matter who – for that person is surely long dead!) demolished a temple that presumably existed at that site and built a Babri Masjid instead, hundreds of years ago. Hence the Masjid had to be destroyed in 1992 by barbarians who, without reference to any legal process, took the primitive concept of the 'justice of yesterday' into their own hands. Should this continue unchecked, we would have a situation of continuous retaliation forever; until possibly everyone is dead! 'Justice of yesterday' stands for revenge, a revenge to be extracted from babies not yet born. Nehru should not have aligned with such barbarism.

While it is unfortunate that a temple was destroyed a few hundred years ago by a primitive barbarian, it is criminal to break down a Masjid by force today. Law and order in a free society cannot function if the concept of 'justice of yesterday' is allowed even the slightest foothold. To the extent that Nehru used this argument, we must hold him responsible for promoting barbarism in India. Nehru only had to open his eyes to find that this primitive concept was no longer being applied anywhere else in the modern world. With Hitler's death, the book of his wrongs was closed and consigned to the archives. Whatever 'extra' punishment Hitler subsequently received in hell, if such a place exists, was a matter between Hitler and God, not a matter for man to consider.

RELATED CONCEPTS: SOCIAL FREEDOM AND SOCIAL JUSTICE

Related very closely to this barbaric concept are the concepts of social freedom and social justice. These are one and the same thing, noting that freedom and justice are always two sides of the same coin. Within the Indian system of governance, both these concepts are totally flawed and based on the barbaric concept of the 'justice of yesterday'. Carrying on his crusade to confound the concept of justice, Nehru said that the 'concept of individual freedom has to be balanced with social freedom [...] and the relations of the individual with the social group'.[31]

But what can this mysterious concept of social freedom possibly mean? It sounds very much like a collectivized version of freedom. If so, just as individual freedom has its matching individual accountability, social freedom must have its matching social accountability. The nearest thing to social accountability, however, seems to be the concept of 'collective punishment' – a very deeply troubling concept. I recall it being mentioned during my training as a civil servant in 1982–4 that collective punishment was practised by some officers in British India. Under this model of 'justice', all men in a village were punished for the crime committed by one of them. But if we did not consider such practices to be just under British India, how could our Prime Minister in independent India possibly advocate this?

In 1982, someone tried to assassinate Saddam Hussein as his convoy entered a village 60 km north of Baghdad. In response, Saddam got 148 innocent people from that village executed. That is collective punishment – social accountability, a dastardly and cowardly attack on the very fundamental concept of justice. Fortunately, we don't condone collective punishment, even if our leaders do not understand what justice means.

In sum, social freedom, social justice and the 'justice of yesterday' are not only concepts without logical content, but are extremely dangerous ideas; we must reject them all and throw them into the ocean. If anyone uses these arguments, we should challenge that person to logically derive any sensible and consistent implication of these concepts.

* * *

I suspect that what Nehru really had in his mind while advocating social justice and social freedom was his concern about two things. He wanted an end to feudalism and an end to inequality of status, particularly caste inequality. But there are eminently sensible ways to solve these problems without confounding the concept of justice.

Feudalism is in violent opposition to freedom and rejects equality of opportunity. It is therefore completely incompatible with a free society. Some would argue that feudal or monarchical societies may need some 'rough handling' of the sort that was applied to Charles I in 1649 (he was decapitated). Freedom has not always taken a linear path, and those who gain from an unearned status quo rarely return their powers without a fight. King Jigme Singye Wangchuck of Bhutan is a rare exception, having voluntarily transferred a few of his powers to the people through a democratic government.

But using physical force is totally inappropriate. Punishment without a specific trial is inappropriate; it merely ends up damaging the cause of freedom. Taking recourse to injustice is wrong. Two wrongs do not make a right. Therefore, Nehruvian socialist methods which include land reforms (land ceiling) and caste or tribe based reservations with the aim of getting rid of feudalism and caste discrimination were wrong. As seekers of freedom and justice, we must ensure that not even one innocent person is ever harmed.

I will now explore both the land ceiling and reservation policies given that both these injustices find shelter in our Constitution (in the Ninth Schedule and Part XVI, respectively), and demonstrate how much better methods to get rid of the underlying problems could have been devised.

Example 1: State sanctioned theft

Gandhi said all when he made it clear that socialism should not achieve its ends by impure means. 'Impure means will result in an impure end. Hence the prince and the peasant will not be equalled by cutting off the prince's head nor can the process of cutting off equalise the employer and the employed. One cannot reach truth by untruthfulness […] Harbour impurity of mind or body and you have untruth or violence in you.'[32] But such niceties were completely lost on Nehru. His First Five Year Plan articulated his socialist arguments to justify plundering those who held land bigger than a specified size, with the so-called 'excess' land being redistributed to the poor. This plan was implemented quickly, and by 1960 most states had introduced ceilings on land.

Despite its reformist title, land 'reform' legislation was anything but a reform. It was a completely regressive step. It created massive injustice in a so-called free society. Land reform was all about reparations for what the ancestors of our current zamindars had allegedly done. Land was therefore 'legally' taken away from people without recourse to a trial; from people who had not themselves committed any crime. This 'reform' was robbery on a grand scale. The state became the Big Thief. If the state legislates a theft it does not make it any less blameworthy. Plunder and crime are not valid merely because these are legislated by a mob of gangsters sitting in the parliament. That is exactly what mobocracies are all about – elected mobs. In a free society, on the other hand, majorities never misuse their parliamentary power to violate individual freedom.

But let us ask ourselves a question – what had India not achieved through its independence movement that it needed to attack innocent members of its society and divest them of their property without trial? Had we not already divested the princes of their monarchical powers and constructed a republic out of a primitive society? Had we not declared adult franchise and empowered the entire Indian community? Could we not have, through equal opportunity and the rule of law, made zamindars completely irrelevant?

In the extremely favourable environment for the advancement of freedom that existed just after independence under the tutelage of people like Gandhi, Sardar Patel and Rajaji, India had a golden opportunity to aspire for the world's highest standards of governance. We had the opportunity to build a new culture of freedom and justice. That would have led us without fail to Nehru's promised tryst with destiny; indeed, it would have led us to a tryst with greatness. But Nehru allowed the baser elements found in our country, those who belligerently bellow for plunder out of the sheer jealousy they experience upon seeing anyone with some wealth, to override the basic reason for our independence, namely, to achieve freedom and give us justice.

But a leader's job is not to follow the mobs. His job is to lead. Nehru let us down very badly by attracting all kinds of thugs into politics. And the less said about his successors the better. Nehru was the best leader we have had in independent India's government. It has been an even more downhill journey ever since.

So you ask what Nehru should have done, instead. He should have ensured that the yardstick of accountability was applied equally to each citizen, irrespective of the citizen's social, cultural or economic background. By equally enforcing the rule of law, the evil of feudalism would have been wiped out in a decade without impinging on anyone's freedom. The following are a couple of measures that could have been taken:

- A strong police and judicial system would have ensured that if a zamindar had personally stolen someone's lands, he would have been punished and the stolen lands returned. If some zamindar committed a murder or rape, that zamindar would have been immediately tried and given capital punishment – or at least jailed for life.[33] Unfortunately, Nehru's shoddy system of law and order allowed brutal bully of zamindars and anyone else with money to run amuck as never before.
- Public finance is hard work, and setting up an effective and honest machinery to collect taxes from all people of a country is very challenging. But socialists have not bothered to build such a machinery that can reliably obtain an income tax return from all citizens of India. A strong land records system coupled with progressive taxes and a wealth tax could have transparently deployed the wealth in India to the public causes to strengthen infrastructure and provide equality of opportunity. But instead of taxing them, zamindars were rewarded by Nehruvian socialist governments with complete tax-exemption; and land revenue was discarded as a source of revenue. Today most people therefore evade taxes and make merry while the government spends time driving our buses and airplanes.

The greatest problem with Nehru's approaches is that they fostered a great muddle in the minds of ordinary people about what is right and what is wrong. On the one hand, Nehru encouraged his ministers and bureaucrats to seize people's so-called 'excess' lands. On the other, he wanted corruption to stop. But if you confuse everyone about what is right and what is wrong, then why will corruption stop? And so ministers and bureaucrats extorted money out of traders and manufacturers on the plea that they were taking away 'excess' money from these 'capitalists'. When ethics are negated even in one case by our leaders, there is no stopping the decay of morals in a society. Corruption received a significant boost in Nehru's time and has never looked back since.

In brief, Nehru's times – which continue till today – are best compared with those of France after its revolution of 1789. Frenzied mobs controlled the government in France after that violent revolution. Today, India is a mobocracy where the entire Parliament is united against freedom. India's policy has been made for 60 years by socialist mobs driven by revenge, not by lovers of freedom and honesty.

In the midst of this wild loot and frenzy, every rich person, every trader, every money lender and every zamindar has been condemned sight unseen as an evil 'capitalist'. But each individual must always be seen as the unique locus of individual responsibility. We may be rich or poor, often both in the same lifetime, but we must be individually accountable. Justice consciously denied by the state to even one of its citizens diminishes all of us. That, unfortunately, has happened for so long now, and in so many ways, that most of us have lost our sense of justice and ability to distinguish right from wrong. We condone corruption as a practical requirement of life; we vote for corrupt leaders; we give bribes; we take bribes. We have completely lost our way. India has lost its moral moorings. By breaking free of Nehru's amoral regime, and by removing the immoral haze that blocks the sun from reaching India's soul, we will once again be able to set our gaze on the lodestar of freedom. That star will then return us to our lost ethics and, more importantly, will return each of us to ourselves. We will find our lost self-respect once again, allowing us to completely renew our life; to be re-born as a different and better people.

As would be expected, under such moral anarchy, India's land reform experience went to seed. Except for a few places like Kerala, where these reforms 'worked' (actually led to enormous fragmentation of land and loss of agricultural productivity), for the most part the so-called land 'reform' legislation could not be enforced. Not having strengthened the government's machinery to enforce the rule of law, this socialist task of stealing land, too, failed, as any other task taken up by India's governments. Since Nehru's socialist functionaries[34] were paid very poorly,[35] given that there wasn't much money left to pay them after 'feeding' loss-making public sector undertakings, they became easy prey to the manipulations, in self-defence, of the same feudal lords whose lands they were supposed to forcibly acquire. Landlords transferred their lands in the names of their dogs and cats with the connivance of local land revenue officials and police. To unearth the truth behind these '*benaami*' deals would have required a machinery with honesty of purpose which the thoroughly corrupt socialist government could never possibly muster. Hence, virtually no land finally got 'stolen' by the 'Impotent Big Thief'.

Indeed, as a result of Nehru's wasteful efforts, the feudal system remains as strong as ever before. Someone has rightly said that India is now a mix of 'hypercapitalism' and feudalism, with neither of these two being founded on any semblance of ethics. We won't find it easy to build a free society in India today; for that would need a foundation of ethics which will now need many years to rebuild. Corruption has increased to such levels today that freedom will have to fight to get a foothold. The wrong ends (nationalized theft) and the wrong means (shoddy governance) have led to very wrong results. Just as integrity and morality are the hallmark of a society founded on freedom, so also subterfuge, hypocrisy, corruption and deceit are the hallmark of a collectivist socialist society founded on revenge.

Indira Gandhi, who had none of Nehru's intellectual prowess, continued his mindless 'justice of yesterday' tirade. In 1971, during the process of brushing aside compensation for acquired land, she asked, 'Compensation for what? Compensation for land [...] for a palace or big house? [...] what about compensation for injustice?'[36] The deadly seed of revenge that Nehru and various other Indian leaders have sown in India has by now morphed into our DNA. Incessant arguments on new ways to redistribute poverty, on how to drag back the wealthy and extract their wealth, swirl around in our disease-stricken heads. We are unable to think clearly any longer of the simple and morally clean arguments of freedom; of ethical ways of generating wealth for ourselves and for our society.

Example 2: Reservations

In its Part XVI, our Constitution has institutionalized social inequality and inequality of opportunity, despite the claims in the Preamble to the contrary. Article 15 (1) states quite clearly, 'The State shall not discriminate against any citizen on grounds only of religion, race, caste, sex, place of birth or any of them'. And yet, the Constitution goes off to do precisely that! On the ground presumably of social justice and of the 'justice of yesterday', Part XVI recognizes multiple classes of citizens, namely, the scheduled castes and tribes and the rest of us – each being treated quite differently from the other through affirmative action such as by Article 335 which enables the 'relaxation in qualifying marks in any examination or lowering the standards of evaluation' for such classes of citizens.

The argument underlying affirmative action is the following – that non-scheduled members of the present generation should legally relinquish their equality of opportunity in order to compensate the scheduled groups for the harm allegedly caused by the forefathers of the non-scheduled groups. This is an untenable argument. The present generation both of the scheduled and non-scheduled groups was not even born when the alleged harm took place. If the current generation of non-scheduled people have harmed 'lower' castes or tribes in any way, they must be punished, but *individually*, not collectively. This is a matter of justice, not a matter of the 'justice of yesterday'.

Ours appears to be a contract between two types of slaves. As Gandhi said, 'A slave is a slave because he consents to slavery'.[37] One claims to have been discriminated against and hence wants compensation from people who had nothing to do with it. The other group offers to be punished for the alleged discrimination that someone else practised in the past! No one can remain free in a society where both parties violate the basic principles of accountability. This masochistic self-flagellation on the one hand, and the opportunistic beggary on the other, diminishes everyone.

On a personal level, I would hate to be a member of a 'lower caste' or 'tribe' who takes advantage of a more meritorious person. It would lower me, demean me; it would reduce my sense of self-worth. Charity is anathema to able-bodied free peoples, an insult greater than no other. I would be unable to get out of a sense of deep anguish at being an able-bodied person given other's charity. Therefore I would say to such foolish 'higher' caste people, 'Stop this! Stop perpetrating this mayhem of charity towards me, you slaves of injustice! Let me find my own way and own level in life through my own effort. Let me be a *man.* Do not treat me as a cripple'. I admire Ambedkar precisely for getting out of the stigma imposed on him by Hindus who called him a lower caste person. He joined Buddhism. Mass-scale exodus of this sort is perhaps one of the most effective ways to fix Hinduism's flawed caste system that deeply insults virtually half its members. I would suggest an exodus to reason as an even better option.

Let India become a place of respect-worthy people and not a land of cowards, each coward begging for a little 'extra marks' from others. If you were to call me backward I would be extremely angry. And yet today, entire groups of people seek to be labelled as backward! This is a clear sign of a great people who have lost their way. Let all men and women of India forget their social and economic past, and stand up as *Indians* – no less, no more. Let each person meet the great challenge of making the greatest possible contribution to society by dint of his or her determination, hard work and merit. Let the best man or woman win in every field of life in India.

I love the story about a young couple, Craig and Helen Elliott, who started with virtually nothing in their pockets in 1995 and have built their own farm in New Zealand which now generates 26,000 litres of milk per day. Between the two of them they milk 900 cows a day; only two of them work on the farm! And they have done this without any government assistance as well.[38] That is the minimum standard of sheer determination that each of us must show. No more of this shameful desperation to be labelled as 'backward'! Let us cast out all charity into the ocean! And throw the person who gives us charity far into the ocean as well. That is the only way we will grow up into humans worthy of living in a free country.

Many things are deeply wrong with Part XVI of the Constitution:

- Sociologists and anthropologists can use terms like tribes and castes, but not a government. A government only recognizes citizens. Period.
- As already indicated, Part XVI perpetrates grave injustice by punishing people who have not, as individuals, participated in any crime.
- By recognizing these castes and tribes in our Constitution, we have effectively frozen them forever. Our culture and society should remain free to evolve and change in any way that its people individually choose to, so long as they remain accountable for their actions. In any event, the time has come for people to move from tribal modes to a modern, individualist mode sooner rather than later.
- Affirmative action increases caste-based inequality. If the caste system would have disappeared on its own in, say, a hundred years in capitalist India, the socialist intervention of reservations will now sustain it for ever. Thus, our Constitution has made it very hard even for the best social reformers of Hinduism to do anything about the caste system now. There has never been greater awareness of one's own caste than in today's India. We don't know our politicians by their views any longer, but by their caste. Perhaps even primary school children think about their caste now.

These things should be completely out of the reach of a government. A government should entirely focus on the economy, on the education of our children, on teaching them the wonders of science. The way to break the back of the invasive and insulting caste system is the following:

- abolish reservations;
- remove all references to any religion, tribe or caste in the Constitution;
- review, and where possible repeal, any law in India with the

words Hindu, Muslim, Christian, Jain or Sikh included in it; and

- ban the census of India from asking us silly questions about our religion or caste. Let us only be Indians. Period. That should do.

* * *

I am not denying the deplorable practice of caste discrimination. I strongly oppose it, it being one of my reasons for choosing not to be a Hindu (I have, in addition, many other reasons for opting out of the business of religion altogether). Nevertheless, eliminating the caste system is not a matter for a government to get involved in – it is a matter purely for social and religious reformers.

Similar discrimination or stereotyping has occurred in the past in every part of the world. Ending these things needs a different approach. Even as George Washington was taking on the role of American presidency after the 1776 Declaration of Independence, he owned hundreds of slaves. Thomas Jefferson, the man to whom we owe the sentiments of the Declaration, also owned over 180 slaves; even as late as in 1824. Similarly, providing equality and adult franchise to women took a very long time coming in the USA. In other words, there has been massive discrimination in the past even in today's relatively free societies.

The lesson here is that while a government can set minimum standards and punish people if they violate these standards, the task of preparing a society to accept these standards requires social reformers to spend decades, if not generations, in preaching the message of reform. Yes, governments can set in place non-discretionary outcome standards, and they should. In the case of caste discrimination, the government can do the following two things:

- Ensure that poverty is eliminated and all children receive education of decent quality up to their twelfth year. This will involve a total revamp of the school education system, as outlined in chapter 6.
- Enact an Equal Opportunity Act in order 'to enforce everyone's right to equality of opportunity; to eliminate, as far as possible, discrimination against people by prohibiting discrimination on the basis of various attributes'.[39] A government can definitely control people's behaviour, even if can't change people's feeling. Such a law will clarify, extend and enforce Articles 15 and 16 of our Constitution. The government would then need to build a very strong capacity to enforce this law.

But to ask a government to do anything beyond these two is not realistic or reasonable. If a government attempts social reform, it faces the following problems:

- Governments are not credible. Their sincerity is questionable. Members of a government are not qualified to touch our hearts and to make us change. People know that politicians are on the lookout for votes.
- The opinions of the political class or the bureaucracy merely reflect existing social opinion. They can't become reformers, anyway.
- Bureaucracies established to 'reform' the society have no interest in eliminating the social problem, for if that problem goes away then they will lose their jobs!

The diagram below tries to distinguish the role of government from that of social reformers.

Our improper feelings

Role of social reformers
to change our feelings that do not regard others equally

Our improper acts

Role of government
to change our actions that are not compatible with freedom

It is therefore up to social reformers to initiate community-based action to educate and change people's minds and hearts. When we feel really bad about the terrible things that continue to happen in Indian society, we can try to do the following few things:

- We can begin by setting aside, in differently coloured piggy banks – labelled separately as 'Ending the Caste System', etc. – all the money that we would have been otherwise willing to let the government take away from us in taxes for the purpose of social reform (say one per cent of our income?). Presently, this money would go towards establishing mammoth ineffective bureaucracies which are focused entirely on increasing the problem.
- Instead of then funding the government through this one per cent increase in our taxes, we can get together with others who believe in similar causes and form associations to promote our chosen causes. There may already be many such associations in existence that need volunteers like us. Let us network with other

like-minded people and expand India's social capital. Let us build civil society.

- Once we are satisfied about the quality of work of these associations, let us then break open our piggy banks and fund these associations.

We will be pleasantly surprised by participating in such associations that social causes are impacted quickly, economically and very effectively. In addition, those of us who belong to a so-called 'high caste' should not forget to clarify to our children that we will be equally happy if they marry a person from a social category considered by unenlightened Indians to be 'lower' than ours – as long as the person they choose is of good character. We can also use non-caste titles in our names. Finally, we can place the entire offending religion on notice and publicly declare that we will abandon it if it refuses to reform.

There is another problem brewing on the horizon. In addition to caste-based affirmative action, gender-based affirmative action is gathering momentum, namely, reservation of seats for women in elected bodies. This, once again, is primarily a matter for social reformers to deal with. There can never be any justification for a government to legislate quotas for women. Reservations for women (or any other group) in Parliament or any other elected body goes against equality of opportunity. Sweden doesn't have any reservation of seats for women, but its political parties have a voluntary norm under which 50 per cent of their candidates are women. As a result, women constitute 45 per cent of Swedish parliamentarians. The way out for India would similarly be for political parties to take the lead and not to have the government do things which are none of its business.

THE FAST TRACK TO AN EXCELLENT SOCIAL CONTRACT

Given some of its shortcomings we have explored, and numerous others that I have not touched upon to conserve space, the Indian Constitution should now be completely remade. Its language and style should be made extremely simple, with its length drastically reduced to a maximum of ten pages. It should focus on the basic principles of freedom and create institutional flexibility and agility to enable each generation to arrive at, and implement, its own policy choices.

How are we to transition[40] to a new Constitution? The steps below can help us get there:

1. First, a new representative Constituent Assembly, comprising 20 persons – say, proportionally from the main five parties from the current Parliament – should brainstorm and arrive at a draft constitution of ten pages. This Assembly should be supported, purely for the purposes of drafting, by ten outstanding experts in politics, law and economics, selected on the basis of their international renown, along with one of our Booker or Nobel prize winners in literature who will do the final writing. It is crucial that these ten pages talk only of fundamental things, which can be explained even to an illiterate person in about an hour. These ten pages should then be put to a vote in the full Parliament, upon receiving the endorsement of which, a referendum should be held across India. Once passed by the majority of Indians, it should be declared to be *The Social Contract and Constitution of India.*
2. Simultaneously, the Parliament should translate, i.e. transcribe without making any substantive changes, the institutional framework currently prescribed by the Constitution into various Acts of Parliament, such as the President of India Act, Legislative Bodies Act, Courts Act, Election Commission Act, Civil Services Act, Reservations Act, Directive Principles Act (yes, even these last two!), Responsibilities of State and Central Governments Act, and so on. The commencement of these Acts should be linked to the date when the new Constitution takes effect. With these two steps, India will have its new Constitution as well as a set of flexible laws that will potentially defend our freedom. However, nothing would have changed on the ground – yet!
3. Change would come as follows:
   a) The Reservations Act and the Directive Principles Act would be repealed by the Parliament, also given that they will become unconstitutional under the new Constitution. Alternatively, any citizen would be able to launch a petition with the Supreme Court to get these two Acts declared null and void.
   b) The other translated Acts should then be reviewed by Parliament in a prioritized manner. Each review can take up to two years including extensive India-wide consultation. At least half the review work can happen prior to the new Constitution taking effect since everyone would know what will be contained in the translated Acts. These translated Acts could then be re-enacted, amended or repealed, as

appropriate. Acts that would likely be modified include the Civil Services Act, Comptroller and Auditor-General Act, and Election Commission Act. Acts that are likely to remain entirely unchanged would include the President of India Act, Legislative Bodies Act, and the Courts Act.

What will this new Constitution look like? I've provided my thoughts on its shape and form in the *Online Notes*.[41] Of course, this is not a matter for me but for the elected bodies. Anyway, a bare-bones Constitution of this type will ensure that it does not need to be amended for its entire life of 30 years. It will also allow our institutions to be continuously improved upon through ordinary legislation. The other advantage of having such a clear and simple Constitution will be that all Indians will understand it fully and genuinely 'own' it, both through the referendum and by signing it before being licensed to vote. The process of renewing our social contract every 30 years will make explicit our trust in the adults of future generations to make their own laws.

* * *

I admit that this approach, being extremely flexible, will potentially create a situation where legislation inimical to freedom can be enacted by a Parliament through simple majority. The big barrier to bad legislation will be the extremely powerful role of the Supreme Court in the new Constitution which could *suo moto* nullify laws that violate our freedom. That should protect us for the most part. In the end, though, freedom can never be protected by a contract, no matter how long or short. Even our 'cast iron' and ridiculously long Constitution was found wanting when the crunch came; it was unable to withstand Indira Gandhi's assault on freedom through the 1975 Emergency. We will therefore need the following two strategies to protect our freedom, apart from the very strong Supreme Court:

- First, we will need to elect representatives who are passionate about our freedom.
- Second, we will need to be extremely vigilant as citizens. Freedom can be protected in the end only by each of us being vigilant and participating actively in the political process.

That none of us aspires for, or wants our children to aspire for, being a representative of the people is a matter of great concern. The next chapter explores why ethical and competent citizens who believe passionately in freedom are unwilling to participate in elections, and why only unsavoury characters step forward to represent us. Clean, policy-based politics determined to protect our freedoms is the lifeblood of a free society. If that lifeblood is contaminated, a society cannot ever be free. Today, India's politics is not just contaminated, it is dirtier than the dirtiest *nullah* or sewer that flows in the most polluted parts of our cities. Even the smell of politics is so revolting that people stay away from it. That has to be changed.

Short note to fellow traveller: We will enter a very dirty sewer in the next chapter. I recommend putting your remaining sandwiches in an airtight container at this stage.

Chapter 4

Causes of Political Corruption in India

No government is better than the men who compose it.
John F Kennedy[1]

Let us move from a general discussion of the extent of freedom in India to an analysis of the governance structures designed by Nehruvian socialists. This chapter primarily addresses the leadership gap in India that was alluded to at the end of the previous chapter. Today we are unable to find good candidates who can become high quality MLAs and MPs for India. This has happened because our socialist electoral laws and systems have made politics a very corrupt profession. Honest and competent people are very reluctant to join hands with such a sullied group of people. After we identify the causes of this leadership gap, we will be able to suggest necessary steps to make politics in India attractive to high quality leaders.

We must begin by asking what a good political representative should look like. The following attributes perhaps reflect a minimum expectation:

- **Intellectual superiority:** As John Stuart Mill wrote in his essay on *Representative Government* (1861), we expect our representatives to be 'in any intellectual respect superior to average'.
- **Prudence and good moral character:** We expect our MLAs and MPs to at least possess a moderate level of prudence and a good moral character.
- **Awareness of their role in relation to our freedom:** Their being aware of the requirements of freedom and of the role of a government in protecting our freedoms is yet another minimum expectation.
- **Awareness of and dedication to good public policy:** We expect from them at least some knowledge of the world's best policy making, as well as dedication to creating outstanding public policy for India.

- **Responsiveness:** Finally, we expect them to be easily approachable and responsive.

This is not an ambitious list. We should easily be able to find thousands of such good people in India at any given moment. But clearly something is wrong, for our democracy doesn't throw up even such moderately good leaders.

Some of the recent literature on leadership has veered around to a view that there are five levels of leadership (see Jim Collins[2]). If we extrapolate this to the political sphere, the lowest level of leader (the Level 1 leader) will be found to have a big ego and moderate ethical standards, while the highest (the Level 5 leader) will have a modest ego and very high ethical standards. The Level 5 leader will be found to be determined to achieve great results for his or her country. Gandhi or Abraham Lincoln come to mind as examples of Level 5 leaders. Given that Level 5 leaders are extremely scarce, we should be content to find Level 4 leaders for ourselves, as our representatives. Of course, leadership is not as rigid or inflexible as these 'levels' may seem to indicate. People can move between these levels based on different situations, as well. In the end, it is quite likely that given human imperfections, no single leader will be a Level 5 leader in all situations. And so, these 'levels' are best visualized as reflecting tendencies rather than absolutes.

But no matter, our average 'leader' today is way down the leadership scale. India is perhaps only able to attract Level 1 leaders or lower, down to Level *minus* 3![3], as its representatives. The N N Vohra Committee Report[4] on the nexus between politicians, bureaucrats and criminals is as explicit an acknowledgement of our shameful reality as anyone can get from within the secretive and circumspect Indian bureaucracy. It states that, 'In certain states [...] these gangs enjoy the patronage of local level politicians cutting across party lines, and the protection of government functionaries'. Our 'leaders' are mostly power- and money-hungry desperados who are not reflective on their use of power, are completely unaware or disinterested in learning about the concept and requirements of freedom and are unwilling to listen to expert policy advice or world-class innovation that may be required to create a free and great India.

We therefore experience a depressingly corrupt and incompetent democracy, where the main qualification for being given a 'ticket' to contest elections by a major party is a modest intellect coupled with serious moral shortcomings. Moral shortcomings in greatest demand are: (a) the ability to play fast and loose with public funds, (b) a close association with the mafia and criminals, and (c) an ability to threaten honest candidates to scare them into withdrawing from elections. In addition, being the son or daughter of an existing political personality is desirable – provided, of course, that the mandatory criteria from (a) to (c) are first met. Since such 'leaders' lack any sense of shame, calling them corrupt does not jar their nerves or make them lose sleep. They probably fall down from their chairs as they rollick across the floor on their back with rumbustious laughter, big belly jiggling, upon hearing that some people in India still consider corruption to be a shameful matter. Having vigorously jiggled their fatty tissues in this manner for a while, they perhaps fall asleep more soundly than ever before.

And yet, we must remain ever grateful that such leaders very kindly allow us to experience a notional sense of democracy and a fleeting semblance of the rule of law. We are in the seventh heaven each time we see these people actually handing over power after losing elections. Even these not-so-good representatives have actually allowed us to become a modestly free society, and enabled a wide range of aspirations to engage with our democratic frameworks. This has meant that India has managed its internal conflicts relatively well. But every democracy manages such diversity of political opinion. Isn't that what a democracy is all about, namely, a method to represent different interests? Even on this matter, we should have been able to manage our internal conflicts much better than we have.

No other well-established democracy generates super-corrupt, even criminal political leaders like ours does. While leaders in democratic free countries command respect, and sometimes even inspire the world, our political leaders inspire utter contempt. Prior to the inception of Transparency International (TI) in 1993, it was widely acknowledged that India was an extremely corrupt country, but there were few systematic comparisons. Since then, using international benchmarking, TI has consistently found India among the most corrupt countries in the world. Between 2001 and 2007 we occupied somewhere between the seventieth and ninetieth position in the world in TI rankings. Even communist China, drug-infested Columbia and genocide-ridden Rwanda have at times been ranked less corrupt than us. Therefore, whatever else we may be today, we are definitely not the world's role model on ethical behaviour.

On hearing this our politicians smirk, and following the footsteps of the World's Great Defender of Corruption, Indira Gandhi, tell us that corruption is a worldwide phenomenon. As if that, even if it were true, absolves them of their key responsibility to identify its causes and to get rid of it. But corruption is definitely not a global phenomenon. I experience a radically different culture in Australia.

There is no tolerance of corruption in Australia. It is recognized for what it is – a deadly poison, a frightening evil, a disease worse than the Ebola virus; and combated ferociously wherever it seeks to grow. Corruption in the police in the state of Victoria in Australia has been reported in the media from time to time but I would agree with the former head of the Special Operations Group in Victoria, Inspector John Noonan, who was quoted in *The Age* on 31 July 2006 as saying, 'There is no grey area. If you take two bob [i.e. indulge in minor corruption], then you are a criminal – you have crossed to the other side. If you make that decision, you are one of them, not one of us'. And, 'The truth is that 99 per cent of police are totally against corruption, and if they see it will do something about it'. But even if Australia were to become totally corrupt, that couldn't justify India following in its footsteps. If we do not want to be the world's cleanest country, then there is a real problem with us.

Having smelt the faint whiff of democracy that we get from our current crop of leaders, we wait for the time when we will actually become a genuine democracy. We wait for great leaders to arise and lead us. In this land which once produced Buddha, Vivekananda, Tagore and Gandhi; in this land to which at least some people in the world look up even now in their search for truth and freedom, our politicians specialize in the *total destruction of truth.* The followers of Gandhi's ethics or resplendent sources of wisdom and values are not our leaders today, by any stretch of the imagination. Since they do resemble humans in shape, as opposed to monsters with fangs and claws, and because they have been actually elected by us, we have learnt to tolerate them as part of our scenery. But we single them out for our children as examples of what *never* to become. And we continue to wait, with ever increasing impatience, for great leaders to finally emerge. A billion people and no great leader. Something is seriously wrong.

THE ICEBERG OF INDIAN CORRUPTION

The following diagram depicts the iceberg of Indian corruption. The diagram shows that a small portion of India's corruption is 'visible' to us, the vast bulk being hidden from view; 'below water'.

The diagram shows that corruption is of three types:

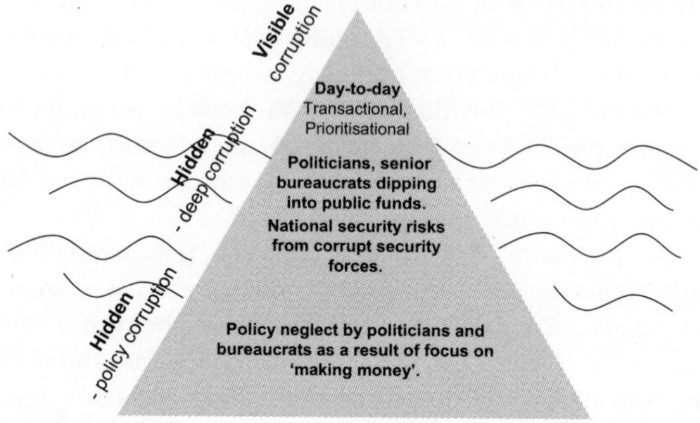

1) Visible corruption

The visible tip of the iceberg is corruption experienced by 'common' people. It comprises many types such as transactional, prioritizational and avoidance.

- *Transactional corruption* is where the people have to pay a bribe over and above the government-established charge to get a service which they were entitled to get without the bribe. This form of corruption is relatively easy to fix, being driven by defects in the design of governance systems, defects which leave open areas of information asymmetry and discretion, which can then be arbitraged by government functionaries through non-transparent and unaccountable decisions. Where information technology has been cleverly used, such forms of corruption have reduced; for example, when the Indian Railways computerized its ticketing system the previously rampant corruption in ticketing dropped precipitously.
- *Prioritizational corruption* is where people get 'out-of-turn' favours through 'speed money'. Such corruption was more relevant in the past where government interventions had resulted in shortages of telephone connections, cars and so on. This kind of corruption has significantly reduced after liberalization. Obtaining gas cylinders now doesn't require bribing a host of people any longer.
- *Avoidance corruption* is where people pay a bribe to avoid a fine or wastage of time. This is still quite prevalent when people

bribe a police constable to avoid a speeding ticket, a tax avoider pays a bribe to an income tax officer, or the truck driver avoids a detailed inspection from the police by handing over Rs 100 at each check post in India.

As a result of some improvements in governance coupled with liberalization, most of us do not face visible corruption to the extent we used to. In any event, the bribe of a few rupees taken by a lowly government functionary – no matter how deplorable – is the least of our problems in India.

2) Hidden deep corruption

Below the visible corruption is an absolutely mammoth amount of possibly increasing, hidden corruption. This is where the bulk of the 'money' is made by politicians, in amounts that run into thousands of crores of rupees each year. The malaise of hidden corruption goes very deep into the vitals of India and provides evidence of its existence from time to time in frightening ways, as it festers for a long time and then erupts. We can't easily 'see' it. But we know it exists when trains smash into each other, roads fall apart, millions of illegal migrants from Bangladesh swamp the country, police perpetrate major crimes and operate as organized criminals at night, and soldiers and farmers commit suicide. Corruption by ministers of police and defence has driven a deep knife into the heart of our security forces. Our border protection and possibly general security are in shambles. It is possible that India's security could collapse one fine day like a termite-riddled house that has been chewed up, if deep corruption is not checked. We see this termite-like, hidden infestation at work in all government institutions such as public works departments, rural development programmes, public distribution system, education and health services. No major file, no appointment, no contract moves without such deep, fully institutionalized corruption.

3) Hidden policy corruption

But there is an even worse, more insidious and dangerous form of corruption not even thought about by most people. Policy corruption, or policy neglect on account of our political leaders devoting their entire waking energy to making money, saps the foundations of our country. Ministers of education spend most of their time in transfers and appointments of school teachers, for a fee. Other ministers consort with tenderers who bid for government contracts with a view to finding out who will pay them the most *dakshina*. That is the 'regular' deep corruption stuff. What happens with all this is that they are able to spend less than 20 per cent of their time on policy making and are forced to delegate policy and strategy to career bureaucrats. Not only are our bureaucrats blissfully ignorant of the world's best practice in policy, their interests are often at cross-purposes with the interests of India. Many of them are focused primarily on wangling a stint in international organizations through their political contacts, when not making money on the side – which is the primary occupation of a large number of them now. Delegating policy to bureaucrats, namely our IAS officers, is a recipe for total disaster for India on a scale unimaginable by those who haven't worked for decades within the government and don't know all about what really happens! I have never seen more shoddy policy analysis than analysis which emerges from Indian government departments.

Ministers display a singular lack of excitement at the great opportunity they have to make a difference to the country. Our representatives simply do not care to question why things are not working and don't care for finding out effective solutions. Policy-making is not why they joined politics in the first place; they joined politics only to make money. No minister I worked with ever asked any intelligent question on the strategic direction of his portfolio, or guided me on overall policy direction. I was on my own. And if, as a diligent officer, I did bring up such policy matters, there was bemusement when I explained various options through professional analysis. The damage done to India by chronic policy neglect by both ministers and bureaucrats, neglect which I call *policy corruption*, is far more devastating in impact than 'regular' corruption. This corruption leads to colossal damage – there are major policy errors such as investing our money in the wrong things, undertaking the wrong activities, not establishing systems to plan cities and infrastructure, non-functioning services and justice, non-existent schools, non-functioning law and order. No society can prosper, even if it has free markets, if its leaders are dishonest to the core and completely disinterested in good policy.

We therefore need to review our democratic system's incentives to find out what it will take to attract some of our best people to politics. If we are to be only led by our most mediocre and corrupt people, then we had better get reconciled to perpetual mediocrity. The greatest barrier to entering politics is at the first gate itself – our electoral system. Tall barriers meet honest candidates who want to represent us, barriers deliberately designed to block out all good and competent people. The good news first – it is possible to remove these barriers, since they are all man-made. The bad news is that existing politicians will never remove these barriers, for that would mean the end to their opportunity to make quick money!

NOT ONE REASON TO BE HONEST

Good governance, like most good things in life, does not come for free, or even cheaply. That is perhaps the central message of this book with regard to the mechanisms of freedom. What we buy from our elected representatives is a process to preserve our freedom. And of all the things we can possibly buy – and freedom can't be bought in that sense, only allowed to blossom – freedom has never, ever come cheap. Throughout history, preserving freedom has demanded the greatest cost from citizens, including, at times, the price of one's life when opposing tyranny.

Freedom is the single most precious, and therefore most expensive, 'product' in the world. Ask any refugee from anarchic Afghanistan, Iraq, Rwanda, Somalia, or Ethiopia who is forced to flee from angry flames of civil war in the absence of security and freedom. Our lives, and the lives of our children, depend critically, in a manner that we rarely visualize, on good systems of governance. To 'buy' freedom – which means buying the rule of law, defence and justice – we must get used to the idea of paying quite steeply. Freedom must precede everything else. It comes well before roads, infrastructure and even education. Leaders who understand freedom and are doggedly determined to defend our freedom are priceless. Once we have freedom, wealth will always arise spontaneously. A good prime minister and his or her Cabinet can generate gains for India of over 1 trillion US dollars or 45 lakh crore rupees per decade; indeed, even in each year, once momentum builds up. India can easily become a $150 trillion economy in 2100 in today's values if it chooses to become the world's front leader in freedom.

What we need to get there is to allocate just one rupee out of every hundred rupees that we earn as a nation, or one per cent of our country's GDP, towards the 'purchase' of the services of high-quality political representatives who will fiercely and single-mindedly defend our freedoms. That would cost, say, Rs 41,000 crore in today's estimated value (as at 2008).[5] This seemingly high amount is a very small price to pay for the enormous benefits we will get from good representatives. At the minimum we can expect a return in excess of 100 per cent per year on this investment. On the other hand, bad governance can sink us into oblivion and cost us trillions of dollars in present and future lost opportunities. Good representation is one thing we'd be foolhardy to save money on.

Apart from paying for and thus making it possible for our best people to lead us, we must also allocate our time to the protection of freedom. Freedom has never befriended those who don't care passionately for it. Only those who are assertively vigilant and aware of the great details of how their society and government function can hope to attract the angels of freedom to their side. Acquiring knowledge of public policy and being vigilant is therefore a citizen's duty. It is of concern that we don't value democracy and political representation sufficiently today, or appreciate the barriers our own laws place on potential good representatives. The findings of this chapter should be a first step in our search to find out more about the processes of good governance.

GOOD CANDIDATES PREVENTED FROM CONTESTING

Conducting a general election costs the Election Commission hundreds of crores of rupees. We are quite happy to support such expenditure. But we quickly baulk at the likelihood that candidates, too, need to spend similar, if not greater amounts of money, collectively, to take their message to us. India is a mega-democracy; each of our electoral constituencies covers an enormous area and population. The population of some of our constituencies equals the population of countries like Bhutan, Kuwait, or Macedonia, comprising about 20 lakh people each. To reach out and persuade each voter is therefore a very expensive task. Costs mount rapidly, and include:

- Organizing and paying for public meetings for the hundreds of workers involved, including paying for their transportation and food, as well as for posters and pamphlets.
- Once candidates are elected, money is needed to look after persons from their large, primarily illiterate, constituency who land up at their doorsteps each night for succour (an Indian MP's official house in Delhi often looks like a railway waiting room with people sprawled about).
- Continuing costs of retaining key campaigners for the next election; MPs and MLAs often distribute significant amounts of personal money to various organizations in their constituencies, such as youth clubs in remote villages, to ensure support for their future campaigns.

Indian politics is therefore very daunting, not only being sweaty, grimy and fraught with risks to life, but also very expensive. The questions that arise are:

- Who ultimately pays for these expenditures?
- Are there limits on such expenditures? If so, why and how are these monitored? What is the penalty for breaking expenditure limits or for not accurately reporting on the funds raised and spent for a political purpose?
- What is the 'take-home' salary of a political representative upon being elected? Is this occupation financially rewarding?

The answer to the first question above is very simple. Indian voters do not have a tradition of joining political parties or of funding them. Therefore, almost the entire money used in elections is purely black money, i.e. unaccounted money; undeclared wealth.

With regard to the second question, legal limits exist on what amounts can be spent in an election campaign. Under Rule 90 of Conduct of Elections Rules, 1961, made in pursuance of s.77 of the Representation of the People Act, 1951, the limit of expenses which can be authorized by a candidate in a parliamentary constituency election is Rs 25 lakhs. Note that this expenditure has to be authorized by the candidate; after that it doesn't matter who spends it. For instance, a candidate's political party can spend the entire amount if so authorized by the candidate. Excluding the travel expenses of leaders of political parties, and expenses made on behalf of a candidate but not authorized by him, all other expenses must be declared. There is a microscopic penalty if someone spends for a candidate without authorization. According to s.171 H, anyone who incurs or authorizes expenses on account of the holding of any public meeting, or upon any advertisement, circular or publication, or in any other way whatsoever for the purpose of promoting or procuring the election of a candidate 'without the general or special authority in writing of a candidate' commits a crime punishable by a magnificent Rs 500! Therefore, on pain of this measly penalty, no one supposedly spends any money on behalf of candidates! Of course that's not true! Indeed, unauthorized spending is the single largest loophole in the electoral expenditure accounting system.

But pausing for a moment, let us explore how well or otherwise the very idea of limits sits in relation to our freedoms. Is this limit of Rs 25 lakhs, or any limit at all, compatible with freedom? And the answer is to be a resounding 'No', for the following reasons:

- As a general rule, a citizen in a free country can spend any money he wants to, on any legal activity. There are no limits on how many shirts a person can buy, or how many advertisements he can take to sell his product. Contesting elections is a legal activity, indeed a basic obligation of citizens. Therefore, limiting expenditure on elections is wrong on first principles. Freedom of expression and belief also calls for scrapping election expense limits.

- There is nothing stopping us from supporting a religion of our choice. Similarly, free peoples are entitled to support political parties with unlimited funds if these parties represent their views. If a party becomes 'rich' through this process, and is able to spend more at the time of elections, that is unexceptionable, since it represents a genuine support base. We are talking of a democratic 'market' for policy here. I should be free to support liberal political parties should I find any!
- Those who seek to limit expenditures possibly do not trust in their own judgement as voters. For trying to block expenditures would imply that Indian voters are influenced purely by the number of advertisements put out by a candidate. This view completely denies that policies matter. And yet we know that the Indian voter is clever enough to take unsolicited 'bribes' from all rich candidates but vote only for the one he or she believes in. The critical thing is to ensure complete secrecy of the ballot. Expenditure on campaigns is never a real issue. And so long as substance and policies also play a role in the minds of voters, we have nothing to fear.
- We must either have a free democracy or have none at all. All this intellectual posturing and putting arbitrary limits smacks of statism and the dictatorship of the elites. Let's get out of this paternalistic frame of mind and start respecting people's choices!
- On a practical note, expenditure limits create incentives to lodge fraudulent accounts of electoral expenses, thus destroying the sanctity of the laws of the land. Today, almost all candidates in India, particularly those from the large political parties, exceed the expenditure limits by a vast margin, in the order of ten times or more than the expenditure limit, even as they continue to sign off on false statements of accounts. The question is, are we adult enough to live with reality? Do we want the truth, or do we want to deliberately pull wool over our eyes?
- There is a practical example that can ease some of our artificially inflated worries about expenditure limits. The US

experience clearly shows that money can't buy electoral victory. US presidential campaigns allow unlimited amounts of money to be raised and spent, so long as these amounts are fully declared. Ross Perot spent over $65 million of his own money in 1992 but got absolutely nowhere. This clearly shows us that throwing money at voters is not good strategy, without substance. The Indian voter is not the same as the American voter, but we must not presume that our 'masses' are fools.

In brief, there are very good reasons why expenditure limits for political purposes need to be abolished. And at the same time, our extremely weak mechanisms to account for political expenditures need to be significantly beefed up. Stringent requirements on the verifiable disclosure of expenditures will force political parties and candidates to stop using tons of black money in elections. If clean money is used to promote political ideas or candidates, then we really have nothing to fear. Good ideas need to be sold too. Even the outstanding ideas of freedom that this book is promoting cannot reach everyone in India for free. If a political party wants to preach freedom, it will have to write and print brochures; people will need to be physically met with and spoken to. Even preaching freedom is not free!

* * *

Despite my strenuous objections to electoral expenditure limits, I will now assume for the rest of this chapter that expenditure limits do exist, and will analyse the impacts of our current system on potentially good candidates. I will examine the linkages between expenditure limits, the actual expenditures, the standards of accountability and their enforcement, and the wages of political representatives. The results of this analysis will show us that the interplay of these factors filters out each and every competent and honest person who may have otherwise considered contesting elections in India.

FILTER 1: MONETARY LOSSES KEEP THE PRUDENT OUT

The largest of these three sieves or filters gets rid of 99% of the people of India from the field of potential candidates. People excluded include:

- rich people who are prudent;
- those belonging to the middle classes; and

- the poor people of India.

To see how this filter works, let us consider the case of Mr Aaaj-ka Harishchandra, aged 50, who is a decent person of good character and also happens to be 'in any intellectual respect superior to average'. He is modestly endowed financially, earning Rs 20,000 per month as a junior accountant in a private firm. Mr Harishchandra had acquired some basic knowledge of economics while in school, but has since avidly read the fortnightly Sunday columns of Gurcharan Das, as well as drafts of this book placed in 2007 on the internet. He is now enthused about reforming India by contesting elections and becoming our political representative.

A small hitch has come up, though. While Mr Harishchandra has a house (on mortgage) and is able to financially maintain his small family, he does not have the minimum spare Rs 25 lakhs needed to propagate his message to voters in the Parliamentary constituency he wants to represent. It is theoretically not necessary to spend such a large amount of money if one is a really good candidate, but Mr Harishchandra finds upon talking to a few past contestants that this Rs 25 lakhs is the bare minimum he must spend to have a serious chance of reaching out to his vast electorate of ten lakhs. In reality, Rs 25 lakhs is insufficient, since most serious candidates will spend many multiples of that. But we live within the law of the land in this book, and so we will leave aside that inconvenient truth.

To meet these funds requirements, he works out that he can collect small donations worth a total of Rs 2.5 lakhs from one thousand supporters. Five big donors have also agreed to fund him unconditionally for a total of another Rs 2.5 lakhs. These are unconditional contributions because Mr Harishchandra has made it clear that he needs the freedom to think independently for all citizens of India once he is elected. Also, he has told people that their contributions must be from declared income; he has warned people not to give him black money or he will report them to the income tax authorities. Mr Harishchandra doesn't belong to any major party given that he doesn't agree either with their ethics or with their policies. That means he must raise the remaining Rs 20 lakhs he needs either by withdrawing from advance payments made on his mortgage, or by taking a personal loan. Either way, he will have to repay this money.

When elections are announced, a hopeful Mr Harishchandra, being the prudent accountant he is, whips out a pen and paper and makes a calculation on the back of an envelope of the costs and benefits of contesting the election. He will contest elections only if he has a reasonable chance, if he is elected, of earning an income that will be sufficient for him and his family to maintain an existing middle class lifestyle, after paying off all election expenses.

As it is early days, Mr Harishchandra doesn't know how many candidates will contest. He assumes that '*n*' number of candidates will contest in all, giving him, all other things being equal, a $1/n$ chance of winning the election. If successful, he expects to be able to represent his constituency for five years. He assumes he will not be assassinated during this period and will live on after his term is completed. Being 50 years old, he expects to live another 25 years upon retirement from Parliament. He estimates that he could lose his security deposit of Rs 10,000 if more than five other candidates contest, but that if only up to five others contest, he will scrape through by getting one vote more than others, i.e. just over one-sixth of the votes polled. In his calculation, he therefore ignores the security deposit, which in any case is peanuts compared to the main expenditure.

Being an MP is almost a full-time job if it is to be performed well, including the time spent to read Bills, to meet his constituents and to prepare for Parliamentary sittings. So he expects to give up his current full-time job and will live entirely on his salary as an MP, which is the following:

- a take-home component of Rs 33,000 per month (actual salary only Rs 16,000 plus some extras),[6] i.e. Rs 3.96 lakhs per year; and
- upon retirement, a Parliamentary pension of Rs 8,000 per month, i.e. Rs 0.96 lakhs per year.

He works out the expected present value[7] (PV) of his 'return' from being an MP, which is:

$$PV_{return} = \frac{3.96}{n} + \frac{3.96}{n(1+\theta)} + \cdots + \frac{3.96}{n(1+\theta)^4} + \frac{0.96}{n(1+\theta)^5} + \cdots + \frac{0.96}{n(1+\theta)^{29}}$$

If $n = 2$, i.e. there is only one candidate contesting against him, and $\theta = 0.02$,[8] then the PV_{return} = Rs 18.18 lakhs approximately. The expected net present value of his 'investment' is then equal to $PV_{return} - 20 =$ –Rs 1.82 lakhs, i.e. he will lose nearly two lakh rupees. That means that after repaying his loan of Rs 20 lakhs, he will receive a net of –Rs 1.82 lakhs in his entire remaining life, which means he will starve to death! That is shocking. He then considers the other scenarios. See the table below:

No. of candidates	Expected loss (in Rs lakhs)[9] of Mr Harishchandra by borrowing Rs 20 lakhs
1	–16.35*
2	1.82
3	7.88
4	10.91
5	12.73
6	13.94
7	14.91
8	15.46
9	15.96
10	16.37

*(i.e. he makes a 'profit'; he can live very frugally on this for the rest of his life.)

In all scenarios except when he is the only candidate, he finds he and his family will starve to death, since he has to repay his loan first and only then can he eat. Given that, at times, people contest elections to become MPs merely for one year when casual vacancies arise, or if the Parliament is suddenly dissolved, and given that most candidates will never get elected anyway, it implies that there is virtually no hope for any candidate in India to recover the costs of contesting elections, even if the candidate spends only up to the legal upper limit. This is true unless almost all expenses are borne by a major political party. State funding, conditional upon the number of votes obtained, is another option – one that I recommend – but it is not currently available in India.

A more complete analysis will include other factors as well, such as:

- the opportunity cost of a potentially well-paying career forgone for six years. This includes a year before elections, being the time needed to familiarize voters of the selected constituency with one's policies;
- risks to life such as attacks by political goondas and terrorists who like killing politicians for the publicity that gets them;
- reduced focus on his children's education during these six years; and, last but not the least,
- an increased risk of divorce since the spouse can become very annoyed with the continuous influx of people into the house at odd hours!

Doing calculations such as the ones above, and finding that representing the people of India is a guaranteed recipe for the ruin of his family, Mr Harishchandra cancels his plans to contest elections. Therefore, this filter, which ensures that people who fund elections by themselves will lose significant amounts of money even if they are successful in being elected, eliminates all those who cannot afford to lose such huge amounts of money.

* * *

At this point, you could very well ask me if this is for real! Is it really possible that all our representatives or political parties lose big money by representing us? Well, this calculation, based on information in the public domain, certainly says that is true. If I'm proven wrong, and it is found to be financially viable for people of ordinary financial means, or people who are rich but prudent, to contest elections without joining a corrupt political party and using black money I'll be grateful for that information. I may even be willing to then review my personal plans and return to India earlier than is feasible at present, with a view to contesting elections and representing you.[10]

The main thing, though, is that if this calculation is correct, it shows that we are living in a 'fool's paradise' if we expect any responsible, prudent, person to lose a significant amount of money in order merely to represent us. While a few people may find spiritual bliss in 'serving' us by going bankrupt and starving to death, no sensible person will do so. As a result, we attract primarily two types of people into the electoral fray:

1. *rich and imprudent people* (such as some erstwhile maharajahs and feudal zamindars, or sons of corrupt socialist leaders who have so much black money that they don't know what to do with it); and
2. *completely unethical people*, being those who have never had, nor will never have, the slightest compunction in misusing their elected office to capture rents from the government machinery and business in order to more than adequately recover their black money investments.

The first group of people, namely, those who possess sufficient money that they could lose well over 20 lakh rupees without batting an eyelid, comprise a very small part of India's population. There is no reason to believe that such people are even modestly competent in public policy. In any event, no free country can expect to be successful by putting imprudent people at its helm. Imprudence is a personal trait which can transmit to the way public funds are handled. We'd rather have people lead us who have worked hard for their own money and know the worth of every single rupee. Even more importantly, we want no favours from anyone; we don't need people to lose money to represent us. Free, able-bodied people do not care for anyone's charity. Charity is poison for such able-bodied people. Rich people who contest elections by throwing money at us insult us. We want good governance services and are prepared to pay what it takes to get them. We must insist on paying these representatives sufficiently, if for no other reason but to make it abundantly clear to them that we are their masters and that they act on our behalf, as our agents in Parliament. We do expect them to lead us, but that is why we employ them.

The second group comprises morally challenged people (MCPs), who comprise less than one per cent of the population. There is a very strong overlap between these two groups. In total, a maximum of one per cent of India's population is therefore eligible to contest elections. 99 per cent of us are knocked off from the contest. As far as the second group goes, namely MCPs, the moment they get elected and become ministers, all hell breaks loose! They frantically begin to work not only to recover their election campaign investments, but to make sure that they build enough reserves for future elections some of which they are bound to lose. Public policy is totally secondary to such people. They enter politics solely to make money. To them, government departments are vehicles to be exploited and sucked dry; not an opportunity to provide us with services. Hence the infamous horse-trading that takes place in India after each election for so-called 'lucrative' departments like public works, education and rural development.

But if recovering electoral expenses and building future campaign reserves was the only thing these MCPs wanted to do, there would eventually be an end to their rampage. They would stop once they recover, say, their Rs 25 lakhs (or two crores, or whatever it is they 'invested'), plus a 25 per cent return, multiplied by three! But from my experience, these are fundamentally evil people. Many of them will not rest without building large mansions in all corners of India and the world during the few years they manage to cling to office. Their families and relatives will flourish in hitherto unprecedented ways. Many of them open hidden bank accounts in Switzerland or otherwise palm off their wealth in *benami* deals. It is common for very poor government school teachers from remote villages to become elected as Chief Ministers and suddenly become wealthier than the richest industrialist in India!

To be true to the facts, there is, in addition to these two groups of potential candidates, a miniscule third group comprising ethical but incompetent people who, by virtue of their hard work and continuous presence at the grassroots, manage to get elected from time to time. These candidates largely belong to parties which have an excellent grass-root network such as the CPI(M). Such candidates are committed to a life of personal destitution and penury. But whether these people are competent in any way is seriously questionable. Predominantly communists, their policy credentials are totally dubious. These are ordinary Level 1 leaders whose ideas are entirely wrong and knowledge pathetic. It is simply not good enough for India to depend on this incompetent category of people for the advancement of its interests.

FILTER 2: LOW SALARIES KEEP OUT THE COMPETENT

This filter gets rid of any potentially competent candidate.

Let us now tweak our story's plot a little bit. A week before the Election Commission notifies the elections, our friend Mr Harishchandra's dear old aunt dies leaving him with Rs 20 lakhs with a condition that it must be used by him only to contest elections. As a result, he becomes a part of the group of rich people potentially eligible to contest elections provided they are prepared to write off significant losses. While extremely sorry to hear of his beloved aunt's passing away, Mr Harishchandra is now able to contest the elections, which he promptly does. As good luck would have it, he also gets elected despite competing against hugely corrupt political parties which invested massive amounts of black money and also threatened to maim him permanently.

Upon being elected, as luck would have it, his vote becomes crucial to a group of parties struggling to form a coalition government. The nefarious local goondas with big moustaches and swarthy faces therefore decide to pause for a few days before they break his legs. Emboldened, he joins the coalition and is made a minister.

But while representing India in his first international conference, Mr Harishchandra learns that the world's political arena is studded with amazingly brilliant minds, people with enormous intelligence and knowledge, quick wit and humour, literary feints and flourishes, and exceptional persuasive skills. All across the free world, some of the most exceptional human minds succeed in politics – except, of course, in India. In conversations that Mr Harishchandra has with his First World counterparts, he feels completely out of his depth; outclassed, out of his league, the proverbial fish out of water. He just can't negotiate confidently with brilliant ex-professors like Henry Kissinger whose strategic capacity and knowledge of world affairs is in a dimension infinitely higher than his own. He therefore realizes that the levels of knowledge, skills and competence he possesses simply won't take India to the levels of development and freedom he was aspiring for. The last I heard was his mumblings under his breath during his return flight to India: 'Why is this so? Why do I get to face such brilliant people? Where are India's brilliant people hiding? Why do they not contest elections?'

Well, here's why. Even if the actual costs of contesting elections were managed through state funding of elections, as should be the case, and even if the limits on electoral expenditures were abolished, as they should be, India will still not attract Level 4 and 5 leaders into politics with the measly salaries we pay our MPs and MLAs. Only those who can expect to earn equal to or less than what an MP earns, namely, Rs 33,000 per month, will think of joining politics. That is the standard of prudent logic we should expect from an ordinarily competent person. For someone with a more profitable 'opportunity set', it makes no economic sense to aspire to electoral politics in India. No one of the calibre of Mr Azim Premji (of Wipro), when considering career options at the beginning of his career, would think of running for electoral office in return for this trifling amount. Sure, an average minister does receive a bit more, say Rs 50,000 per month, but even at this level, the vast majority of the truly competent people are filtered out.

By ensuring that salaries of our MPs and ministers are well below what an educated young person even of slightly above average ability can comfortably command in India at the commencement of his or her career, our democratic system can only attract people of very meagre ability. Of course, we can still hope to get some Level 3 leaders like Mr Harishchandra, for whom Rs 33,000 a month is a great deal of money, provided their rich aunts die at the right time. But even if Mr Premji's hypothetical rich aunt had died just at the 'right' time when he was young, he would surely have forfeited his aunt's conditional money and not contested elections. It would have been way better for him to generate wealth in business than attempt the impossible task of reforming policy as the only competent person in a totally corrupt and incompetent system.

At this stage, a reader might well ask why India needs super-competent leaders in politics. Aren't we better off if our best people become doctors, engineers, lawyers and businessmen? While a general response to such a question has been provided earlier, it may be worth considering this issue a little bit further. I should begin by asking you, first: would you consider flying an airline that pays its pilots poorly? No. We value our lives too much to take such a risk. And therefore an average Indian pilot is paid in excess of Rs 20 lakhs per year in recognition of the skill and responsibility needed for that job. Experienced pilots get even more.

However, a pilot is responsible merely for a few hundred lives. On the other hand, a PM is responsible for a billion lives. The risk to our lives from corrupt and incompetent politicians is infinitely more than the risk from flying a plane operated by a poorly paid pilot. Many more people die from socialist corruption and incompetence than from potential plane crashes. In fact, millions of lives are regularly lost in India due to our corrupt and incompetent political leaders – children who die before the age of five from preventable disease; elderly who die from lack of medical treatment; people bombed by terrorists; people whose murderers are never found; people murdered by the police itself; people run over by chaotic traffic; people run over by the convoys of politicians; people electrocuted; people who have died unnecessarily from heat and cold waves; people who die needlessly in earthquakes, noting that virtually nobody dies in Japan even with much worse earthquakes; people who die when buses fall off narrow hill roads; people who die when running trains plunge into rivers or collide; people who die of starvation; people who are burnt, hung and quartered in communal riots; people who sink without trace inside the deep holes found in our city footpaths; and so on. We don't usually attribute these deaths to our leaders, but we should. These deaths are directly caused by failures in governance. This loss of life is entirely preventable if we get good leaders.

With so much at stake, why do we foolishly insist on paying our political representatives – people at the helm or the 'steering wheel' of this mammoth country – extremely meagrely? We insist on hiring the cheapest PM and ministers. I agree with fellow misers that stinginess has its great merits. I am very stingy. I even take my own sandwich to work instead of buying one from the *deli* (noting that home-made sandwiches are also healthier). But we must draw a line somewhere when our lives and the lives of our children are involved.

And strangely, after hiring PMs very cheaply, we don't hesitate to give them thousands of crores of our tax rupees to manage! We elect pure thieves to office and then complain if our infrastructure and justice are in shambles! Amazing country! One of the unintended consequences of our extreme foolishness is that our bureaucrats, who are, on average, much sharper than our political representatives, manipulate political representatives or fool them sufficiently so that nothing ever gets done.

And so we never get Level 4 and Level 5 leaders. I want to remind us that while Level 4 and 5 leaders are humble and very dedicated to the success of India, they are not saints who will work for free. They are honest, competent and care a lot about getting paid the high salary they deserve. There is no silly posturing about Gandhi dhotis and not one iota of sacrifice in them. Humble but proud, they will not slave for us for free. They are determined to make India succeed, but they will never compromise their personal lifestyles in the bargain. We will never find such truly competent people of this sort contesting our elections until we become sensible enough and unclench our tight fists. You get what you pay for. That general rule applies to everything in a free market.

FILTER 3: PERJURY AS A QUALIFICATION

This last filter removes those unable to sign false statements or perjure themselves, merely to represent us.

This filter is the hardest for people to grasp. Most people simply can't see what the point is all about! Why am I so hung up about perjury? So let me tell you yet another story about Mr Harishchandra. Let us first transform him; give him a make-over. Let's assume that instead of getting only Rs 20 lakhs, Mr Harishchandra now faces no financial constraints whatsoever, being left with a bequest of Rs 4 crores. Therefore, spending any amount of money in order to contest elections is no longer an issue for him. He is also a highly improved version now – very well educated, experienced and competent. On top of that, he is dedicated to good policy and is also quite modest, if not humble. He is close to a Level 5 leader in calibre. What more could we want? Very desirable indeed!

But this is what happened to him during the last elections. Being mindful of the law, Mr Harishchandra tried to keep the authorized expenditure for his election to within Rs 25 lakhs. Unfortunately, due to the price of petrol going up on the last day of the election campaign, the cost of filling his petrol tank tipped his total planned expenditure. He now had spent a total of Rs 25,00,001 on the campaign, i.e. one rupee more than the limit. This became a very serious concern for Mr Harishchandra; a dilemma, even a nightmare. Exceeding the election expenditure limits, even if accidentally, was something he could not possibly condone. He was firmly committed to abiding by the law of the land. By breaking them, he would lose the moral right, in his mind, to represent his constituency and country. This is what his weasel accountant told him: 'Destroy the petrol receipt and pretend you did not canvass in the last hour of the last day of the campaign'. But Mr Harishchandra would never sign on any doctored accounts. He would never perjure himself. He promptly fired his accountant for providing such grossly unethical advice. 'What an astonishing accountant!' he thought, 'Destroying the integrity of the entire accounting profession! Is a rupee not a rupee any longer? Can people so easily cheat and tell lies?'

Mr Harishchandra decided immediately that he could not violate the laws of India and be a lawmaker at the same time. There was no scope for any ambiguity on this matter. If a lawmaker breaks laws he can't be a lawmaker. There is no further need to think on this matter. And so Mr Harishchandra did what has hitherto never been done in India. Moments after the close of the election campaign, he sent a message to all his supporters saying that he was withdrawing from the election. Even though his name remained on the ballot paper, he informed the voting public that he no longer saw himself fit to be their representative as he had broken the election laws of the land by one rupee.

This was an unofficial withdrawal, since the date of withdrawal of nominations had long closed. Therefore Mr Harishchandra was still required to produce his electoral accounts. He faithfully did so, noting that he had exceeded the expenditure limit by one rupee. Upon receiving this information, the Election Commission was completely flabbergasted. No candidate in India had ever before officially declared that he had exceeded the expenditure limits. The Commissioners found this to be a great pain in their sore necks. They were at their wits' end and tore out their remaining few hairs in despair. They had never come across a Level 5 leader; now that they found one, it was a traumatic experience for them. They were completely unprepared, having got used to dealing only with super-corrupt ruffians. Despite wanting to praise Mr Harishchandra, they had to commence a major proceeding against him.

The moral of these three stories is that our electoral law meticulously filters out all the truthful, competent and prudent people of India. Our system is therefore a nightmare the likes of which has never been imagined in any other 'democracy'. Through this book I hope to awaken the interest of Indians who have been sleeping while the people they elect build high walls against honest people. If you think these analyses are correct, then there is no escaping the next step – you must come forward and contest elections with a view to changing the system. Once we finish this book, we'll talk more about that step. You'll not be expected to do this alone.

ACCOUNTING OF POLITICAL PARTY FUNDS AND ELECTION EXPENDITURE

One could well ask: how am I so confident about my claim that election expenditure accounts of virtually all the serious candidates are either an incomplete or untrue record of reality? Where is my evidence to show that legal limits are flouted, given that declared accounts don't show that? I agree that I only have circumstantial evidence; but given similar evidence from a number of sources, I suggest that we can reasonably deduce that this claim is true.

Secondary reports from knowledgeable people provide compelling circumstantial evidence. The following are two important secondary sources:

- Mr T N Seshan, the former Chief Election Commissioner, spoke in 1994 of cases where the actual campaign expenses, based on information informally gathered by him, exceeded the official limit by orders of magnitude. 'Seshan revealed that he had been personally told by a woman candidate for the Delhi assembly elections that she had spent Rs 55 lakhs on election expenses even while stating in the mandatory government form that she spent a mere Rs 483. Another candidate for a parliamentary seat had told Seshan that he had spent Rs 50 lakhs and one Telugu candidate reportedly confided to him that he had spent 8.5 crore rupees on his elections' (Mr M V Kamath reporting in *News India Times* on 4 February 1994).
- Arun Kumar's 1999 book, *The Black Economy of India,*[12] provides a detailed analysis of actual electoral costs based on interviews with 14 politicians. Many of these politicians 'commented that their first act after winning elections was to tell a lie'.[13] The average expenditure per constituency came to Rs 1.29 crores, hence exceeding the then prescribed limit of Rs 15 lakhs by over eight times. This expenditure included voluntary contributions and expenses borne by the state and local committees, noting that no unauthorized expenditure is allowed to be made by anyone. If a candidate knew about these expenses, then these should be deemed to be authorized; hence these candidates flouted the law quite badly.

My conclusion is also informed by first hand circumstantial evidence; information I have personally come across between 1983 and 2000 in various roles. My evidence includes the following:

a) As a junior officer (Assistant Commissioner), I observed significant misuse of the government machinery by ruling parties in Haryana and Assam. This misuse included taking thousands of people to political rallies in buses commandeered, and in one case, paid for, by the district administration. This is an illegal subsidy for political purposes.

b) Among my other duties as Sub-Divisional Magistrate (Sadr) of Guwahati, it was my job to supervise the Guwahati Circuit House in 1984–5. In August 1985, Rajiv Gandhi announced the Assam Accord and the subsequent elections in Assam. With the election fever came a huge inflow of money to local units from the Congress (I) 'high command'. A room bearer who serviced the room of a nationally renowned young central minister told me that he had seen a briefcase full of hard cash in the minister's room. As this was a common occurrence for the room bearer, that observation was mentioned merely in passing. I haven't seen the 'smoking gun' myself, but I have no reason to disbelieve the room bearer since I have directly witnessed, elsewhere during the same period, the handing out of Rs 100 notes in a major political leader's office in Assam to villagers who had brought in various petitioners from villages. In 1985, a Rs 100 note was a very big thing. Such liberal use of cash (most likely black money) by very senior politicians indicates that their expenditure statements of elections are likely to be fraudulent. Cash flows like water around big politicians.

c) As a Commissioner in Shillong, during a conversation with one of my more friendly ministers in 2000 on a long trip by road and air from Shillong to Delhi, the minister told me how he had spent well beyond the limit in his election. This person was a fine gentleman. His source of funds seemed to be genuine. I believe he falsified his accounts only because the law forced him to do so. Without such limits, he would have disclosed the full amount.

d) In observing the behaviour of most of the ministers with whom I have worked, I found them ceaselessly engaged in making money through corruption of all sorts. In one case I was summarily dumped from my role as Director of Rural Development in Assam when I did not follow a particular (*very* senior – hint!) minister's directive to award a cement contract to a particular private sector company. I was asked to 'cook up' reasons to reject the lowest bidder and to give the contract to the private company even though its cement would cost more. While this does not tell us about election expenditures, it tells us about the incessant generation of black money by politicians. And where else do they really like using it except in elections?

e) In 2007, a worker of a major political party met me to discuss this book. He agreed with many of the things I have written. He told me in passing about how he had distributed Rs 35 lakhs in cash during a single night among voters in Mumbai a few years ago, along with his fellow party workers. Apparently that was to no avail as his party lost that election. (This point additionally supports the argument that voters are not stupid; they do not vote only on the basis of the money a party throws at them.)

With all this evidence coming from different directions, I am sure you'll agree with my conclusion that electoral expenditure accounts are almost invariably falsified.

* * *

But leaving aside the issue of actual expenses, which I really wouldn't care about if these were not based on black money or corruption, let me talk of the much more important issue of account keeping. Election expense accounts are required to be declared under Section 77 of the Representation of the People Act, 1951. An inspection or a full copy of these accounts costs only one rupee.[14] But since all of us 'know' that electoral accounting laws are violated, not many of us seem to bother to actually get a copy of these accounts.

I spent one rupee on 1 December 1999 to obtain a copy of the election expenditures declared by candidates to the 1999 Shillong Parliamentary Constituency elections. A brief letter to the Returning Officer of Shillong along with a formal receipt for one rupee lodged with the appropriate account in the district Treasury did the job. I received a complete photocopied set of the accounts on 3 December 1999. The data were illuminating, indicative of potentially serious issues both with account keeping and with the overall system of monitoring of accounts. I have summarized these accounts in Appendix 2. As this information is (was) readily available to any member of the public at extremely low cost (well below cost, in fact), I am deeming this information to have been published, and have not hidden the candidates' names from my analysis. I am discussing systematic issues here and so the names are entirely incidental. To be perfectly clear I would like to state that I am not in any way pointing fingers at the named individuals; on the contrary, I applaud them for having the gumption to contest elections despite the barriers imposed by our laws. They deserve to be thanked for keeping our infant democracy alive and ticking.

Anyway, back to the issue of accounts. These accounts actually raise more questions than they answer. My discussions with the then Chief Electoral Officer of Meghalaya and with a Deputy Chief Election Commissioner in Delhi did not answer my questions either. While I note that some improvements have subsequently been made to the system of accountability, most of my initial comments are still valid.

- One of the candidates spent Rs 4.5 lakhs from his or her own personal account, while that candidate's political party reportedly spent nothing. That is not believable. Why would a candidate agree to represent a party that does not offer even the minimal financial support for the campaign?
- There was one candidate whose party spent Rs 6.05 lakhs while the candidate spent nothing on his own. I don't believe this either, as political parties tend to demand at least some co-contribution; there is an element of risk-sharing involved.
- Five of the nine candidates provided incomplete accounts, or accounts that were improperly filed. Three of the nine did not submit accounts at all till the date I received a copy of these accounts – these were definitely delayed beyond the mandatory 30 days.[15]
- The information provided did not permit me to cross-check whether expenses declared to have been incurred by political parties had been recorded in the expenditure statements of those parties. The reason this can't be done is because no political party in India discloses its accounts publicly (Loksatta party has disclosed an outline of its accounts on the internet recently: well done!). Of course, such disclosure is a given in most Western societies. Further, political party income tax returns (which can't be a substitute for such detailed accounts) are deemed confidential in India and therefore even the Election Commission does not have access to them. A promising development has taken recently place in India. According to news reports of 1 May 2008, the Central Information Commission has ruled that one can 'seek information regarding funding of political parties [...] from the Income Tax department using [the] [...] Right to Information'.[16] This development potentially opens the door, even if only

slightly, for the verification of political party expenditures on elections.

- In order to determine whether the payments mentioned had actually been made by cheque or were otherwise traceable one needs a level of detail that is not available. The Election Commission also does not audit these accounts, nor asks them to be audited before submission.
- The Deputy Commissioner of Shillong informed me verbally on 24 April 2000 that no action was contemplated against any of these *prima facie* violations which I had noted and circulated in the form of a discussion paper[17] among all senior officers in the Meghalaya Government including the Chief Secretary and Chief Electoral Officer.

The violations I found were of two types: (a) failure to submit accounts, and (b) improper accounts. That no one audits these accounts at all is another issue.

Failure to submit accounts

If the Election Commission had agreed to launch an inquiry into the cases of candidates who did not lodge accounts, it could have, under section 10A of the Representation of People Act, 1951, disqualified those candidates for a period of three years. As on 1 March 2004, 114 persons were barred across India from contesting Lok Sabha elections, although, in my opinion, many more should have been disqualified if diligent compliance were to occur in India. The problem is that this penalty is too low and therefore meaningless. One can spend crores of rupees, not lodge accounts, and still get to contest in the following elections which usually take place after five years. In my view the failure to submit accounts – and accounts will be needed even when election expenditure limits are scrapped – should be treated as a serious criminal offence leading to imprisonment for at least six months. Our trust should not be trifled with by candidates so lightly.

Improper accounts

On this issue the position is murky. There are penalties including imprisonment of up to three months for some types of electoral offences, but it is not clear upon a casual perusal of the law whether improper accounts will attract a penalty. Under the current law it would appear that if, after due processing, accounts are found not to have been kept, the Election Commission could prosecute the errant candidate under s.171 I of the Indian Penal Code. A successful prosecution would then lead to a fine of *at most* Rs 500! Expenditure limits: Rs 25 lakhs. Penalty for failure to keep accounts: Rs 500! (The law says: 'Failure to keep election accounts: Whoever being required by any law for the time being in force or any rule having the force of law to keep accounts of expenses incurred at or in connection with an election fails to keep such accounts shall be punished with fine which may extend to five hundred rupees'.)

Note that this law doesn't talk of improper accounts, or of exceeding election limits. I suspect the Commission has probably not tried to prosecute anyone under this section, since it appears to be too hard and not worth the effort. If our honest Mr Harishchandra had been prosecuted for disclosing an expenditure of Rs 25,00,001, the court would probably have dismissed the case since complying with the limit appears to be irrelevant under this particular law. All that is relevant is whether Mr Harishchandra kept accounts; which he did.

For the philosophy of freedom, deeply grounded in the principle of accountability, the current situation involving weak monitoring and toothless enforcement is unacceptable. The current accounting system is a total farce. While I strongly disagree with putting limits on political or election expenditures, we should expect complete disclosure and independent audit of all political receipts and expenditures. Accountability in a free society cannot be made into a plaything; our most basic freedoms are at stake here.

In brief, our rotten system requires candidates to falsely swear allegiance to socialism, to lose money in the process of serving the country, to tell lies in their electoral accounts statements and to compromise their personal integrity in innumerable ways throughout their political career. Each of these is a legal requirement! Why would any good person want to join Indian politics?

REFORMS OF POLITICAL REPRESENTATION

While Equality (socialism) and corruption are lifelong buddies and room-mates, Freedom (capitalism) and corruption are arch enemies. A free India can't condone even the tiniest bit of corruption. We must become the least corrupt country in the world if we want to be called free. The following four actions will help to eliminate political corruption and also dramatically improve India's governance:

- Raise the wages of MPs and MLAs at least by a factor of ten while simultaneously getting rid of all of their 'perks'. Let us pay the Prime Minister of this great nation at least what a middle level business executive of a very large multinational firm gets, say Rs 1 crore per year, and MPs Rs 20–30 lakhs each. As it is unpopular for politicians to raise their own salaries, we can help them by setting up an independent commission that would determine their wages. There is also a tendency among politicians to add to their perks if their wages are kept low by public pressure – this is a significant problem for India. In India some MPs also allegedly sell some of their perks, such as their free air tickets. That is surely criminal. Perks are also expensive to administer. Let us therefore get rid of all perks once salaries are raised, and only reimburse actual expenses incurred on the job, for instance, eligible travel expenses. Let openness and transparency on such basic matters prevail in India; a free society can't expect anything less than that.
- We must fund our elections differently – through state funding. The purpose of the wages of MPs or MLAs is not to cover the expenses incurred during elections, but to pay them competetively for their responsibilities. Even if wages are hiked, we will still need to find a way to make the electoral expenses manageable. We can do so by state funding of elections. A simple and effective method that will pay Rs 25 or thereabouts, at current values, for each valid vote cast in favour of a candidate is outlined in Box 3. A system similar to this operates successfully in Australia, where about $2.10 (about Rs 66) is paid at present by the government for each valid vote polled by a candidate.[18]
- Third, we need to abolish election expense limits while simultaneously building extremely strong audit systems for monitoring the contributions received and expenditures made during elections.
- Finally, a wider set of reforms of the electoral system will be needed, such as making public the property returns of our candidates in the interest of greater transparency. These and other such reforms are touched upon in Chapter 6.

Box 3: State funding of elections

Let us revert to Mr Harishchandra's original calculations. A small payment made for each vote polled by a candidate radically alters the expected financial burdens on candidates. It makes it viable for a much larger number of people to participate. The field of candidates changes from less than one per cent of the eligible population at present to potentially the entire adult population. Here's how:

Let a payment of Rs X be made per vote polled, with $n = 6$ and $\theta = 0.02$, as before.[19] Mr Harishchandra expects 10 lakh voters to cast their vote at the election. His expected PV_{return} now becomes:

$$PV_{return} = \frac{10X}{6} + \frac{3.96}{n} + \frac{3.96}{n(1+\theta)} + \cdots + \frac{3.96}{n(1+\theta)^4} + \frac{0.96}{n(1+\theta)^5} + \cdots + \frac{0.96}{n(1+\theta)^{29}}$$

With a government payment (X) of only Rs 8.39 per vote cast in his favour, Mr Harishchandra can expect to break even after spending Rs 20 lakhs of his own money on the election. This still leaves him with no income after repaying his loan. A payment of around Rs 25 per vote will make it practicable for Mr Harishchandra to contest the election, even with six serious candidates flanked against him. He is empowered by this method to take a calculated risk. The electoral fray now becomes a genuine contest, not suicide.

Mr Harishchandra may, of course, still hesitate, since corrupt candidates will continue to spend huge amounts of black money without any accountability and threaten honest people should they attempt to contest. With strong auditing systems, anyone found using black money will be thrown behind bars. Further, over time, the new incentives created by state funding will allow many more honest and competent candidates to contest. There will finally come a turning point when morally challenged candidates will be shut out completely by the public which will only choose to vote for good candidates.

A ONE RUPEE FREEDOM MOVEMENT

The level of corruption in a society essentially depends on two factors: the opportunity available for corruption and incentive for corruption.

- While I haven't discussed the issue of opportunity in this chapter, our socialist regime – which empowers our governments to interfere virtually in each activity of ours – has clearly provided a wide range of opportunities for corruption in India to a wide range of political representatives and bureaucrats.

- On the second of these factors, this chapter confirms that Indian politicians have a great incentive to be corrupt.

This is also an apt place to inform the world that not all Indians are moral pygmies. We do continue to have a large number of honest people that the world never gets to see or hear of, because the combination of our socialism and shoddy electoral system prevents anyone but the corrupt from rising to the top. Our system also breaks the back of the honest; completely demoralizes them. The world will, of course, ask us: 'You've had 60 years of independence, so why can't you get your own house in order?' To which we must ask the world to be patient, for we have only recently started recognizing the causes of our problems. And we have hardly started our journey on the path to freedom. Our citizens are very sleepy headed and not yet awake either.

We, the sleeping citizens of India, must wake up and take responsibility for allowing these major flaws to develop in our democratic system of governance. We are also responsible for letting the weeds of socialist corruption overwhelm the fledgling tree of democracy and freedom in India. To scare the wits out of our corrupt representatives and to make them start paying attention, let us begin by going to our district officers today, and, for only one rupee each, get our own copy of a recent set of electoral accounts. Then, let us study these accounts and raise the issues we discover in our local press, and write to the Election Commission. That will be a very effective way to start a real freedom moment for India. We can call it the one rupee freedom movement.

Now we will, in the next chapter, find out why our bureaucracy is so inept and ineffective.

Chapter 5

Why is our Bureaucracy so Inept?

> The really basic thing in government is policy. Bad administration, to be sure, can destroy good policy, but good administration can never save bad policy.
>
> Adlai E Stevenson Jr[1]

We could, for convenience, visualize India as a large ship jointly owned by us, the citizens. Elected political representatives can then be likened to a captain hired to take this ship to a desired destination. Bureaucrats, the next layer of public managers, are its sailors. There is a wide range of bureaucrats including public servants, defence forces, police and the judiciary. Our political representatives constitute our government and the Bureaucracy (do note the capital B), the machinery of the government. It is our political representatives' task to design and use this machinery to deliver upon the agreed objectives for which we have hired them. Bureaucrats are directly accountable to our representatives and only indirectly to us.

This relationship between citizens, who are the sovereign principals in a free society, and their agents and sub-agents is depicted in the diagram below.

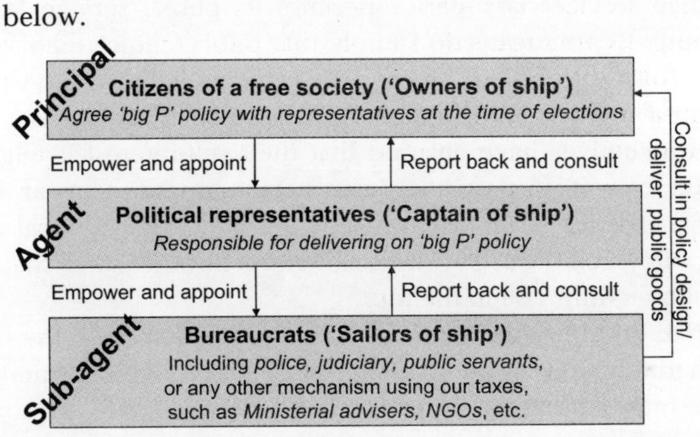

For a free society to have a good Bureaucracy is almost as important as having a good political leadership. But India's bureaucracy falls well short of international best practice. Indeed, to say that our Bureaucracy is sloppy, sluggish, inefficient and therefore ineffective is perhaps an understatement. It won't do us any good to get outstanding political leaders generated by the reforms outlined in the previous chapter and then force these leaders to use the shabby Indian bureaucracy to deliver results.

Having used the term Bureaucracy in an unusually broad sense so far, I'll now revert the use of this word to its more common meaning, namely, as the public services. Within the Indian public services, I'll focus almost entirely on public service leaders, primarily on the Indian Administrative Service (IAS). Pranab Bardhan, a well-known Indian economist, has rightly suggested that we should create a structural shift in the level of internal competition in the bureaucracy. 'It is anomalous to expect [economic] reform to be carried out by an administrative setup that for many years has functioned as an inert, arbitrary, heavy-handed, often corrupt, uncoordinated, monolith. Economic reform is about competition and incentives, and a governmental machinery that does not itself allow them in its own internal organization is an unconvincing proponent or carrier of that message.'[2] To advance Bardhan's perfect diagnosis, I will compare and contrast the Indian and Australian bureaucracies, having worked in them for a combined period of over 25 years.

The first thing to note is that the quality of personnel who hold leadership positions in Australia is significantly better than their Indian counterparts. This difference magnifies even further at the lower levels of the bureaucracy. Australian bureaucrats are significantly better in leadership skills and possess not only extensive specialist policy knowledge but also impeccable personal integrity. The Australian delivery of governance services is superior because its public service leaders are outstanding. By no means do I imply that public choice theory does not apply to Australia. Indeed, most civil servants here, as anywhere else, behave in a manner entirely consistent with such theory. But carefully designed incentives have ensured that their self-interest is aligned with the public interest. In particular, contractual appointments at the senior levels and absence of tenure ensures alignment with political representatives' policy goals. Further, internal competition ensures that only the best public servants rise to the top.

In India, on the other hand, while we pay attention to the principles of competition and merit in assembling our cricket team, which is therefore internationally competitive and can even beat Australia on a good day, we do not apply such principles to our bureaucracy. This has led to the vast chasm that I have noted above in the performances of these two bureaucracies.

ARE WE WEAK IN POLICY DESIGN OR IMPLEMENTATION?

While bureaucratic leadership is obviously an issue, how does it impact performance? Does the poor performance of the Indian bureaucracy lie in bad policy or in poor implementation? Some commentators such as Paul Appleby and Gurcharan Das have suggested that poor implementation is a problem peculiar to India, and has allegedly arisen from a uniquely Indian trait of lack of action-mindedness. This view believes poor project management is the primary weaknesses of the Indian bureaucracy.

However, I don't think there is some uniquely Indian trait we face. When Indians do decide upon something, they act effectively, as with India's independence movement. Indian private sector performance, which is world class in many ways, also leads us to discount such notions, as does the outstanding performance of Indians who settle abroad. When faced with an improved system, the same ineffective Indians respond well and perform brilliantly. I agree that Indians haven't displayed the action-mindedness needed in demanding freedom for their country and fixing the systemic problems discussed in this book, but that is because these issues have perhaps not been clearly explained to them earlier. Having said that, one can agree that poor project management is a major weakness in the Indian bureaucracy.

But the malaise starts elsewhere. I believe it stars with lack of systems thinking. Indians seem to be able to fit in beautifully into good systems designed by others, but rarely design good systems on their own. At least part of the blame for poor thinking skills must fall on our rote-based educational system which does not develop critical thinking. As a result the Indian bureaucracy fails most in policy conceptualization.

What kind of policy skills am I talking about? Both high level and operational. We elect our political representatives on the basis of their election commitments. These commitments, along with other policy choices that our political representatives make, can be said to constitute a nation's 'big P' policy. Given these policies, a bureaucrat's job is to design 'small p' policy, e.g. to:

- design the drafting instructions for relevant laws and regulations;
- examine the advantages and disadvantages of relevant options to implement the policies. This includes pointing out the risks of 'big P' policies. For instance, the design of import tariffs should specify the significant costs to the economy of having tariffs. The political representative is not obliged to agree with a bureaucrat's advice. If the political representative insists on continuing with bad policy, then the bureaucrat's task is to design the least cost method of implementing bad policy;
- translate policy innovatively into manageable strategic chunks (programmes), and design measurable deliverables and performance indicators; and
- design the actual process to deliver these programmes, including tactical management through policies for building leadership and tactical skills.

In doing this work, policy skills of a very high order are required. Good policy is seamlessly deliverable as it takes into account all aspects of the delivery process. Through it, political decision-making and bureaucratic management skills align the political or strategic intent with tactical expertise. Good policy design mitigates most potential problems with implementation. In the end we don't have bad implementation; we only have bad policy. Lack of project management is, in the end, merely a policy gap, needing appropriate policies to ensure such skills are properly developed and sourced.

We have seen how India's 'big P' socialist policy has been a total disaster. Since our socialist agenda was initiated by Nehru and his fellow-leaders, not by bureaucrats, we perhaps should not blame them for our bigger policy failures. In India's case, though, bureaucrats have played a much greater role in determining 'big P' policy than is played by bureaucrats in developed countries, given that most of our politicians barely have any interest in policy, or at most the haziest idea of what they want to achieve. Therefore the failures of India's socialism have been considerably magnified by bad policy input from inept bureaucrats. In the end, policy which rolls out from New Delhi or state headquarters is, as a rule, not implementable.

Bad policy is policy that is unable to pierce the veil of incentives and predict, and therefore control, what will happen during implementation. Similarly, policy that believes that issuing an order or issuing a manual will get the job done is simply bad policy. The design of good policy maximizes the freedom of citizens while overcoming all reasonably foreseeable barriers to implementation.

Our 'small p' policies also fail to anticipate that lurking below each public servant – the person who will finally deliver the policy – is a full-fledged human being with predictable self-interested behaviour. Most of these self-interested behaviours are not, by any means, unethical – merely different from the public interest. While the self-interest of private citizens in the market leads to the amazing outcomes of coordination and efficiency discussed in Chapter 2, bureaucratic self-interest leads to the opposite results, of blocking freedom, of ineffectiveness, of needless paper work. The following reasons show why there is no natural method available to ensure effective outcomes inside a bureaucracy:

- The market creates incentives for private manufactures to produce the greatest possible quantity of goods and services, of the highest possible quality, at the cheapest possible cost. This means, among other things, using the least number of people to get a job done. On the other hand, it is in a bureaucrat's interest to produce the least amount of products, of the lowest product quality, at the greatest possible cost. This generally means using the largest possible number of people.
- A producer makes the greatest profit by keeping his costs down, whereas the bureaucrat receives the most profit (salary) by increasing the number of people that report to him. Ineffective process design easily leads to more people being employed for each task, which, in turn, leads to a larger 'empire' for the bureaucrat, and to greater prestige.
- The bureaucrat faces almost no constraint of funds. A seemingly infinite pile of money is always to be found inside governments – money which is best attracted not by creating a small and efficient organization, but by creating a mammoth, inefficient one. It is in a bureaucrat's self-interest to complicate and confuse things so that more funds are always needed than are available. Bureaucrats complain, no matter how much money is poured into their organizations, that their ineffectiveness arises not from poor design but from inadequate funding; hence they need even more funding.
- The bottom-line (salary) of the bureaucrat does not depend on his performance being assessed by the 'market', in this case citizens. No matter how a bureaucrat performs, his salary is assured. A business will go bankrupt instantaneously if it fails to perform, but governments don't go bankrupt: they merely raise taxes or print more money. As a lifelong bureaucrat I know this

strange feeling of a huge amount of taxpayers' money waiting to be spent at the 'end of the year' without any direct feedback from the citizens on whether this money should be spent or returned to them. No producer can even dream of this strange feeling, because every rupee he spends returns with instantaneous feedback from the market.

- The producer's interest is to master his discipline and to keep acquiring knowledge, since that knowledge will convert into profits. The bureaucrat's interest, on the other hand, is to not undertake personal hard work or acquire knowledge. Instead, it in his interest to delegate every possible task to others, including to 'consultants'. A producer therefore becomes smarter over time while a bureaucrat becomes shrewd, but also very ignorant and arrogant.
- If we want a bureaucrat to remove a particular evil, such as poverty, the bureaucrat is reluctant to do so because if the problem is removed, then his job becomes redundant. So he creates complexities, writes abstruse papers for conferences and generally confounds matters.
- While we pay the bureaucrat to advance our interests, it is quite likely that he is advancing sectarian interests on the sly; for instance, by hiring people only from his community. The complexity of the Indian economic, social and political environment creates a particularly high risk of bureaucrats serving interests different from the public interest.
- A range of local factors also impinge on a bureaucrat's incentives. Public servants working in remote small towns, development blocks or villages in India face very strong local pressures; even risks to their life. Being generally ill-paid, their financial privations play into the hands of corrupt local politicians and feudal interests. The bureaucrat can be readily 'bought' or pressurized.

A bureaucrat's self-interest therefore sits in complete opposition to the public interest in most instances. This must be factored into good policy design. In particular, far greater effort must be put on systems of internal competition and accountability in India than is necessary in developed countries. Large private companies have similar problems in keeping their managers in check, but they have learnt to minimize this problem through the use of modern agency theory. Similar models must be applied to the design of our bureaucracy so that policy design becomes effective.

THE SHELTER TO INEPTITUDE PROVIDED BY THE CONSTITUTION

But aren't IAS officers some of the finest minds of India? Wouldn't they all know about these policy constraints and work diligently to anticipate and resolve them? Unfortunately, barring a few exceptions, this is not the case. The problem does not lie with the innate ability of IAS officers but with their professional competence and suitability for the jobs they perform. It lies in the end with their rigid, tenure-based incentives. These sluggish incentives quickly drain out any aspiration, or even scope, for world-class performance. There is no passion, no hunger in the IAS to adopt the world's best practice; there are no rewards for outstanding policy advice and innovation; and there is no punishment for failure to deliver even the most basic outcomes. Instead, there are massive rewards for corruption and sycophancy.

Advanced countries have taken on board the latest advances and learnings of the past 40 years – from the literature of agency theory, public choice, knowledge management, innovation, human resource management and leadership – to build competitive, merit-based public service systems which are closely aligned to political representatives' strategies and which reward policy expertise and leadership. In doing so, these countries have overcome most of the innate problems which all bureaucracies face and have transformed their public servants into dynamic agents of change and excellence.

India needs such outstanding agents of change, motivated from within themselves to deliver us the world's best practice. But we are saddled with the antiquated public service model that the British bequeathed to us. Even that model, for whatever it was worth at one time, has become fetid upon coming into contact with our sectarian, caste-based and geocentric passions. Our stagnant and rotting model now stinks for miles and compares badly with the clear and fast flowing spring of dynamism found in the West.

This putrid build-up of bureaucratic toxins in India can be attributed to the hothouse provided to the IAS by our Constitution. It was Sardar Patel's idea to keep the old British ICS structure almost entirely intact, without requiring any review. 'Remove them [the ICS]', Patel argued, 'and I see nothing but a picture of chaos all over the country'. Nehru, who was not a fan of the ICS, did not have an alternative plan in mind. The Constituent Assembly thus created a very powerful sanctuary for the ICS and its successor all-India services through Articles 308–23 of the Constitution. Thus we came to be saddled with a bureaucratic machinery fully sheltered by the Constitution from any review or improvements.

While India was one of the few developing countries in 1947 that had a well-established bureaucracy and there is no doubt that Patel and Nehru were right in 1949 to stick with this bureaucratic machinery, they made two key mistakes: (a) embedding outdated public service structures directly into the Constitution – which is very hard to change, and (b) making no provision for a full review of the bureaucratic machinery in a few years' time. Today our hands are largely tied behind our backs. Our Constitution defines the public services effectively as permanent and tenured through Article 312. Further, the process for removal from office of a member of the all-India services is so cumbersome that these positions have become sinecures. While tedious due process and inquiry may be fine where corruption is alleged, what about sheer incompetence? Why are citizens required by the Constitution to keep paying for officers who are ineffective? What about the rights of taxpayers to get value for the taxes?

A better way for Nehru and Patel to have resolved their dilemma was by including an enabling provision in the Constitution for the creation of relevant public service legislation from time to time. That would have left each generation free to create appropriate structures with relevant details, making the public services structures flexible and responsive. Changing the Constitution is always hard, but it is made even more so by the impregnable wall of self-defence now built up by vested interests in the IAS and other services. As a result, something that was a necessary evil in 1949 has become our bane. Our antiquated bureaucracy was designed for revenue collection and enforcement of law and order under a colonial administration. This so-called steel frame is ill-designed to deliver good governance in an environment marked by rapid change, dramatic gains in knowledge and specialization, and global competition. It is incapable of performing high level policy and project management roles since it is not a professional body but a feudal aristocracy.

Once the ICS (later IAS) became part of Nehru's socialist formula, boom times began for these services. The public sector grew rapidly and created many prized positions with perquisites which kept civil servants salivating in anticipation even as the buying power of their salaries dropped precipitously under socialist dispensation. The Fifth Pay Commission (1994–7) 'set right' some of this salary decline. However, Pay Commissions are not designed to deal with public service reforms. The real question before us should be: higher salaries for what? Higher salaries without systematic reform will add little value to the people of India. Nevertheless, low salaries, combined with tenure and poor incentives, are a recipe for disaster.

In the meanwhile, Britain and many other free countries have innovated extensively and moved far away from the static models of the 1850s. If you are interested, I have summarized the history of public services in India and England over the past 150 years in the *Online Notes,*[3] to show how, by the 1850s, the Indian civil service was perhaps at the cutting edge of public administration in the world. But also, very regrettably, India's public services have stagnated since then while the rest of the world has continued to evolve and reform. The most important public administration reforms in the world since then include the abolition of tenure in the top echelons of the public services and bringing about alignment with political strategy. Let's explore these changes.

THE AGILITY OF MODERN PUBLIC SERVICES

The more recent public service reforms originated in the UK and in Australia. The New Zealand reforms, which came in later, were more radical and influential internationally. Given my familiarity with Australian public services, I will focus primarily on Australian public administration reforms as an illustration of a modern public service. My exposition, based heavily on my experience, is biased towards issues which I believe are of particular relevance to India. The list I have drawn up below may therefore not match similar lists drawn up by academics.

At the outset we note that the Australian Constitution[4] has been the great enabler of reform in Australia, unlike its Indian counterpart. It is much shorter and non-prescriptive and allows Australian governments to legislate on matters of relevant detail. Australia has therefore innovated extensively by periodically reviewing its public service legislation. England retains even greater agility in its law making process, not having a Constitution in the first place. Australia has therefore remade its administrative framework three times in the twentieth century through its Public Service Acts of 1902, 1922 and 1999, unlike India which has not reviewed its bureaucracy since the 1850s or so. These Public Service Acts provide the framework for the Australian Public Service (APS) at the Australian Commonwealth (the Commonwealth is the counterpart of the Indian Central Government). Its states have also enacted their own public administration legislation, each reviewed and modernized independently. The other important high-level difference to note at the outset is that there is no 'sharing' of senior executives between the states and centre (Commonwealth). Each unit of administration in Australia recruits its public servants independently.

The Australian Public Service Act of 1902 required open competitive examinations to recruit public servants wherever practicable. It also laid down the primacy of merit in promotions. This sounds somewhat like the ICS of 1853. It created a Public Service Commissioner to inspect departments and promote efficiency. But over the years, the APS has diverged significantly from India's ICS-type system and has transformed itself 'from a centralised system with a complex classification structure based on permanent positions to a decentralised, simplified structure based on continuing employment and contracts' (Professor John Halligan).[5]

I have chosen to list nine key features of the APS below to contrast it with our fossilized IAS. These features show that flexibility and efficiency can be generated even within moribund public service institutions, and that we need not lose all hope for India! There does exist a better way to govern ourselves, if only we are willing to open our eyes.

MARKET COMPETITIVENESS OF REMUNERATION

In any free market (in this case we are talking of the labour market) we are likely to get what we pay for. The forces of competition invariably drive the price of each commodity down to the point which reflects its true underlying value. Not all people are equally capable; so the best indicator of their value is their price or salary. Private companies are aware that they have to pay a premium for high-quality talent. Similarly, to attract high quality talent, APS remuneration has always been based on 'market competitiveness'. Even at the senior levels, where it is not always practical to fully match private sector salaries, salaries are broadly comparable with the private sector. Senior public service managers in Australia are paid in the vicinity of Rs 1.5 crores per year in equivalent dollars.

Indeed, the Whitlam Government of the early 1970s (in Australia) raised salaries and other work conditions of public servants to a level slightly above what purely competitive analysis would call for, so as to set an example for the community on good working conditions. 'In some instances, employment conditions improved in advance of community standards, including paid maternity leave, increased annual leave, the extension of annual leave loading, flexible working hours, and changes to workers compensation and long service leave.'[6] Similarly, when pay competitiveness had eroded somewhat in the early 1980s, the Public Service Board reviewed salaries to ensure competitiveness with private sector salaries.

In the meanwhile, the discretion to offer different salaries to different public servants has increased significantly in the APS. In response to economic and technological change and the growth of specialization, the APS is now no longer treated as a single labour market with common employment standards. Each department and agency is empowered to develop its own remuneration policy within broad parameters. This means each department functions like an independent private sector company, attracting the best talent needed for its needs through flexible remuneration.

On the other hand, remuneration policy in India has been dictated like everything else not by common sense but by the ideology of Nehruvian socialism. Since equality is the be-all of the socialist model, the Cornwallis principle was reversed after independence and senior public service salaries were allowed to erode. This was done by fully compensating junior positions for inflation while senior executives were only partially compensated. According to the Fifth Pay Commission (1994–7) this 'erosion was a consequence of a deliberate policy followed for a long time under the mistaken impression that impoverishment of the higher bureaucracy was an essential ingredient of a socialist pattern of society'.

Second, in India, civil servants are always exhorted to sacrifice for the sake of the country. While it is true that good civil servants are not driven only by money, they do expect to be looked after reasonably well as acknowledgement of their contributions and for the management burden they shoulder. In any event, it is improper for civil servants (or anyone else for that matter) to be asked to sacrifice. Indeed, the concept of sacrifice is anathema to a free society. A free citizen never sacrifices and never asks anyone for a sacrifice. If I were to have the occasion to save the life of a drowning child at the cost of my own, that would not be a sacrifice. Having voluntarily chosen such a course of action, possibly in a split second, I would have gained by setting a clear example of ethical behaviour for my children. What may appear to be altruism on the surface is often enlightened and reasoned selfishness – the ultimate virtue. Enlightened selfishness and so-called altruism merge seamlessly into one.[7] As a general rule, each of us helps our society most by looking after ourselves and standing on our own feet. A free society is therefore only entitled to make an appeal to the self-interest of others.

NO TENURED SERVICE AT SENIOR LEVELS

For a while, higher positions in the civil services were drawn in Australia from the ranks of career officials with longer experience – similar to what happens in India today. But there is a huge difference between being competent and being experienced. Merely having worked for many years in government does not qualify a person to undertake all the senior roles that open up from time to time. In Australia, as with India, the principle of merit over seniority never worked as intended so long as people kept getting promoted in this manner. Therefore Australia identified tenure as a key barrier to merit.

Australia concluded in the main that senior managers, who have responsibility for large organizations or for large parts of their organizations, should not be tenured. Permanency dilutes responsiveness. It was decided that contractually hired senior managers must be paid very well but then held personally to account for their organization's performance, in the manner of private company chief executives. The Australian public service therefore has fixed term contractual appointments for its senior executives. Their continuation in their job is contingent on demonstrated value addition.

A digression to clarify two issues here.

- First, tenure may not always be a problem – particularly when appointments are made to specific positions at a professional level and these positions can be made redundant when necessary. Also, tenure is not inimical to merit up to a certain level. Tenured professors in USA are a world-class example of brilliance. Similarly, there are numerous tenured professional positions in Australia which do not suffer from the infirmities of tenure. For example, in the Victorian public services there are six tenured grades: VPS 1 to VPS 6. In these grades appointments are made to specific positions. There are no automatic rights to promotion merely because someone has put in a given number of years in a role. But importantly, tenure is notional, since redundancies are quite common. People can be asked to leave if their role changes or is no longer needed. Job security is not on offer even for such positions.
- Second, tenure seems to create the greatest problem when appointments are made to a 'service' and not to a specific position. In the IAS, people are appointed to a tenured service. Within this service they can be 'posted' to various roles, depending on their seniority. The key point is that they are not appointed to positions.

Their appointment remains to their service. Every member of a tenured service system naturally expects to be promoted irrespective of competence. Such civil servants strongly resist the promotion of a fellow-member over the shoulder of others; animosities and disquiet can spread very fast. To minimize such consequences, tenured civil services usually marginalize only the obviously depraved or insane, with all others being 'kicked up' the ladder at the predetermined chimes of the clock.

In Australia, on the other hand, the concept of a tenured service simply does not exist; it perhaps never did. Even though APS stands for Australian Public Service, it is not a service in the sense that the IAS is. It is best seen as a framework for appointments. To make these distinctions clear I have scanned relevant documents from my own life and placed them on the internet[8] to give real-life examples of:

- appointment to a tenured service (IAS);
- posting of officers of tenured services (IAS); and
- appointment to a non-tenured contractual public sector position (Australia).

Back to the APS reforms. Their reform started at the top, at the level of secretaries. The 1994 amendment of the Public Service Act 1922 provided for fixed-term appointments of secretaries. Most existing secretaries were then transitioned to five year contracts with performance measures and deliverables agreed to by the political executive. These secretaries were given a significant increase in salary in lieu of the loss of tenure. Since 1999, individual workplace agreements (contracts) using performance linked indicators have been widely used across the executive service, including a wide range of senior positions below those of secretary. A slight shift has recently occurred – from appointments to positions, to appointments to a 'level' – at the senior levels. This retains the advantage of the contractual appointment system while making it more convenient to respond to changes to the machinery of government, such as departmental reorganization.

It is true that not all senior positions in India have been taken from the IAS or other civil services. We have had 'outsiders' too, like Montek Singh Ahluwalia and Vijay Kelkar in the Finance Ministry. But these are exceptions to the rule. I am not aware, though, if these people were recruited through an open, contestable process. For most positions in India, though, the sheer number of years that a person warms a chair matters the most, not whether the person has produced anything world-class while occupying that chair. As a rule, senior positions in India are filled by drawing lots out of an 'empanelled' pool of officers – people deemed to be eligible on the basis primarily of seniority but also a few notional merit-related criteria.

OPEN MARKET RECRUITMENT BY APPLICATION FOR EACH POSITION

People don't get transferred from one post to another in the APS. 'Mobility is generally at the discretion of the individual officer: they choose whether or not to apply for promotion, and which agency and location.'[9] This feature is crucial in minimizing the potential damage caused by tenure, since tenured positions have no rights to move from post to post (except at the non-tenured senior executive levels where appointments are now to a 'level').

All public servants in Australia therefore have to market their skills by applying for each individual position they seek. Recruitments are made through a decentralized system, not a public service commission. Candidates have to address specific selection criteria based on that role's core competencies. Then they are interviewed (if short-listed) by a selection panel of about three people from the organization. The appointing manager chairs the panel and is the final authority to recruit. This is a very important point. As managers directly face the consequences of bad recruitment, they try their best to recruit the very best person they can. It is not worthwhile for them to let their personal biases intrude into the selection process; therefore the best candidate generally gets the job. On the other hand, recruitment is extremely problematic in India, particularly in the states. State public service commissions are renowned for corruption (this bleak situation does not apply to the Union Public Service Commission which recruits the IAS and central services).

A great advantage of open market entry to specific positions, when coupled with competitive salaries, is that the APS is open to talented private sector managers as well. High-quality consultants from large consulting companies are often recruited to top positions in the public services. The obverse holds true, as well. Many public sector managers switch in the middle of their career to private companies. This exchange of world's best management practices adds significantly to the efficiency of the government services.

This open method without any age limit or retirement age also means that new migrants are treated almost entirely on par with local candidates in the recruitment process. The best people among those who apply are recruited, irrespective of their age or where they come from. Yes, there are periodic reports in the press in Australia about stereotyping of new immigrants based on misconceptions or generalizations about their language skills. It is said that some highly qualified candidates do not always get a foothold. Another problem is when potential employers do not care to contact referees from other countries. But in the same vein, elderly Australians and women also find it harder to get jobs in this system. Making detailed applications for tens of positions, including addressing selection criteria in great detail, can also be a very painful process for migrants and older candidates. But if one prepares well for a well-selected role, there is a good chance of being successful.

Let me give my own example. Had I migrated to India as an Australian citizen at age 41 (the age at which I came to Australia), I could never have entered government service at all for two reasons:

- no open recruitment is undertaken in India at that age; and
- non-citizens are not allowed to work in government in India anyway (in Australia, non-citizens are able to work in state government departments).

However, not only did I get a research job based on my technical statistical skills (nobody would consider me at the management level at that point!), but I was able to move into a management role after about three years. While this highly decentralized system can neglect the best candidate in some cases, on balance it seems to perform very well. At least until a demonstrably better system of recruitment and promotion by merit can be found, I believe India will do well to adopt this system entirely for its public services. Of course, numerous changes will have to be made before such a system can be implemented.

FLEXIBLE ARRANGEMENTS FOR RETIREMENT SAVINGS

One of the less widely known but extremely powerful drivers of the exchange of managerial talent between the public and private sectors in Australia is the system to save for retirement.

Indian retirement system

In the Indian public services, eligibility for pensions begins only after a person completes 20 years of (qualifying) service. Thereafter, the government pays a certain proportion of the last salary drawn as a pension for life, as well as a lump-sum gratuity. In addition, there is a General Provident Fund (GPF) to which an IAS officer must mandatorily contribute at least six per cent of his salary at a fixed rate of interest. This fund can be used for contingencies leading up to retirement.

The key problem with this system is its great rigidity. It blocks the free flow of managerial and professional talent across the public and private sectors. For instance, most IAS officers who would have liked to gain private sector experience have no choice but to wait to complete 20 years and take voluntary retirement. On the one hand, they can't return to public services if they resign prior to that, since no new recruitment takes place after the initial examinations. On the other hand, they cannot leave before 20 years without losing considerable benefits (as I have lost, for instance). These principles completely prevent the intermingling of experience between the public and private sectors in India. And after working exclusively in a tenured, low-performance public service for 20 years, even the high quality talent that is recruited into the IAS becomes valueless to the private sector. So if they were not 'brave' enough to get out by after seven to ten years, they are essentially stuck to perpetual mediocrity for life – and they can become very cynical about life. Very sour.

Australian retirement system

On the other hand, in Australia, public servants do not get any pension.[10] Instead, everyone in Australia, irrespective of the sector in which they work, can draw annuities upon retirement from their privately managed superannuation fund, based on the actual contributions made to this fund during their lifetime. Two types of contributions can be made to this fund:

- *Employer contributions*: Since 1992 employers are compulsorily required to contribute (a minimum of) 9 per cent of the wages of an employee into a fund selected by the employee. This is treated as an employee contribution for tax purposes.
- *Employee contributions*: Both the employee and employer can contribute beyond the mandated minimum; there are tax benefits for such contributions.

This forms a system of compulsory employee saving. Here we could well ask: why can't people be left free to save for themselves in a free society for their own retirement needs? (noting that GPF also acts as a compulsory saving). Such coercive savings seem to violate the principles of freedom. And yet, if we add the argument of equality of opportunity, things become clearer. A free society's government necessarily has to pick up the tab for any employee who falls below the poverty line after retirement; at least to bring that person above the poverty line. That creates a situation of moral hazard whereby some people may intentionally save insufficient amounts given that the government will always pick up the tab if they become poor. By forcing people to save at least a minimum amount through the superannuation system, a reasonable compromise is achieved. But leaving aside the question of whether this system of forced savings can be justified in a free society, it also has great practical merit. It enables people to move freely between the private and public sectors without any loss of retirement benefits. That is a great boon to the Australian economy.

GRADUATE INTAKE INTO SPECIFIC POSITIONS, NOT INTO A 'SERVICE'

Similar on the surface to recruitment into the IAS, graduate recruitment programmes in the Australian public services take in some of the best graduates available in the country or state after a gruelling system of tests and interviews (noting that there is no minimum or maximum age requirement, and final selection decision rests with the relevant departmental manager). Recruits are provided an on-the-job training for one year through job rotation in different roles in different departments, as well as induction which is provided by professional trainers hired by the public service authorities.[11] But the system diverges radically after that from the Indian one.

After the 12 months, those who meet requirements are confirmed into a junior professional (tenured) position in their recruiting department. Alternatively, the better ones are 'bid' up, i.e. paid more, and picked up by competing departments. At that stage they earn approximately what a new school teacher gets. Many of these recruits choose not to continue with the government and move permanently into the private sector. Others try out the private sector a few years later and then possibly return again to the public sector, later; given the complete flexibility of the labour market.

Most relevant to India, this system does not guarantee promotions to the freshly appointed recruits. As appointments are made to particular positions, not to a service, these recruits cannot move into senior executive positions as a matter of right like in the IAS. On the other hand, those who are ambitious and competent advance very rapidly into senior executive roles even within ten years, unlike in India where it could take up to 20 years to reach similar levels of responsibility. In that sense there is no 'ladder' to climb here, rung by rung; only a rope that anyone can scramble up as quickly as their competence and ambition lets them. Some secretaries to the government here, with responsibilities equivalent to that of as many as five secretaries to the Government of India, combined, could be as young as 38 or less, while Deputy Secretaries, with responsibilities comparable to those of five Joint Secretaries in the Government of India, combined could be as young as 35. From day one, it is clear to everyone that their future in the public services is determined exclusively by their own effort and merit, not by any automatic chain of progression of every 'batch'.

EXTENSIVE DELEGATION OF RESPONSIBILITY

Australian governments have very few departments. Each of them is extremely large and managed by a single secretary. The Australian Government has 18 departments. The Victorian Government has only 10. These extremely few departments are based on the concept of span of control, which makes for a more coherent and functional government. The Australian cabinet also comprises 18–20 ministers only.

In comparison, the Indian Government has over 50 ministries/ departments, and even the tiny state of Meghalaya maintains about 50 departments! More problematically, there is more than one secretary in many ministries or departments in various governments in India, thus creating more than 100 secretaries per government. If, to this large number we add the rigmarole of principal secretaries, commissioners and secretaries, additional secretaries, joint secretaries, directors, deputy secretaries and under secretaries, then the number of senior executives in India quickly multiplies into the tens of thousands across the country. (Fortunately, the number of secretaries in small states like Meghalaya is fewer, since many hold charge of more than one department.)

The reason why Australia is able to manage with so few departments and senior executives is that, first, these senior executives are far more competent and productive than their Indian counterparts and, second, because they are able to delegate extensively within their departments. This delegation is made possible because secretaries directly recruit individuals who report to them. This first-hand knowledge of the calibre of their direct reports gives them the confidence to leave them alone to perform their jobs; micro-management is not needed. The secretary is able to devote time to strategic thinking and people development since everyone is competent for his or her level.

At professional levels below the executive, there is a solid base of analytical and writing skills in each Australian department. Policy specialists are hired in far greater proportions in Australia than in India. For example, there are over 100 high quality economists in the Victorian Department of Treasury and Finance, apart from nearly 100 finance professionals like chartered accountants. Other departments also hire high calibre economists and policy specialists. Each Victorian policy is thus carefully reviewed for compatibility with the principles of the relevant specialization as well as economic principles to ensure the best outcome for the state. In comparison, the state of Assam, where I have also worked, has probably ten modestly skilled economists between its two main Departments of Finance and Planning & Development. A strong base of highly skilled policy specialists gives senior executives in Australia the confidence to delegate far down the chain.

As a result, Australian departments are middle-heavy, unlike in India where they are top-heavy. Most senior executive positions in Australia are clustered at the Director level or lower, i.e. at the operational end. (By no means is a Director a junior position; their responsibility and pay is comparable to that of general managers in large private sector firms). This extensive delegation of responsibility also leads to great agility. Directors, or even Assistant Directors, advised by knowledgeable professionals, are empowered to directly brief ministers on matters of relatively small policy impact without having to 'go through' the secretary. It can therefore take only five to ten minutes for a completed policy briefing that may have taken ten days to prepare, to be delivered to the minister's office electronically, followed by the hand delivery of the hard copy with signatures from a couple of relevant officials. And of course there is no peon here! Officers take the signed policy briefings directly to ministers' offices. As a result, no paperwork sits for weeks or even months on any officer's desk as it does in India.

CONTESTABILITY OF POLICY ADVICE TO POLITICAL LEADERS

By the 1970s, the bureaucracy in Australia was being seen as being 'too elitist, too independent, too unrepresentative and insufficiently responsive'.[12] It was the sole provider of 'small p' policy advice to ministers and much of that advice was precedent-based which merely helped to reinforce entrenched bureaucratic practice. The world-leading reforms of the 1970s and 1980s in Australia marked a move away from bureaucratic monopoly over policy advice. As John Halligan notes:

> The reaction of Labour governments, in particular, Whitlam's (1972–75), and Hawke's (1983–92), was to challenge the public servants' monopoly over advice to ministers and to question their indispensability to the processes of government. The direction was made explicit in the White Paper Reforming the Australian Public Service (1983): 'the balance of power and influence has tipped too far in favour of permanent rather than elected office holders'.[13]

A moment's reflection will show us that the delivery of a government's policy or election commitments does not require a permanent civil service, or even a civil service at all. Anyone, and any organizational form that can best deliver results, will do. After all, as Alexander Pope said:

> For forms of government let fools contest;
> Whate'er is best administer'd is best:

The diagram in the beginning of this chapter shows that public services are, in the theoretical sense, merely one of the many alternative vehicles for the delivery of policy. Reverting to the metaphor of a ship and ship's captain, we – the country's (ship's) owners – first hire a government (i.e. the ship's captain). The captain should then be completely free to hire whomsoever he wishes to advise him and manage the ship's day-to-day logistics. After all, the agreement is with the captain. We don't care whom a captain hires so long as he gets us to the destination.

And so, there is no inherent virtue in policy neutrality at the senior levels in a civil service. A political party elected to government needs specialist leadership best suited to delivering its election commitments. If that means finding people with a strong understanding of the theory and practice of freedom, as would be the case if a liberal political party were to get elected in India, so be it. Bureaucrats or advisers who can best operationalize the delivery of freedom to us must then be found. In any event, no political leadership, even socialist, should be constrained in selecting its managers only from among a tenured service like the IAS comprising largely fumbling socialist die-hards who have never opened a book on policy after their initial training at the Academy.

Further, the proponents of an 'impartial' public service presume, rather disingenuously – even dangerously – an independent role for the unelected bureaucracy in determining the public interest. Bureaucrats are at best our sub-agents, only indirectly accountable to us through our political representatives. We must therefore leave it to our agents to decide whether they want to use them or hire alternative sub-agents. In any event, they can't be given any independence. We need to monitor bureaucrats closely, not flatter them by saying they should be independent. We must ensure a clear line of sight for accountability in a democratic political system. It is only by handing over the full control over bureaucrats to our chosen political representatives that we can precisely attribute the success or failure of policy outcomes to our representatives. If a ship hits an iceberg and sinks, we clearly know whom to blame – the captain of the ship. Sailors are mere tools of the captain. Politicians should not be in a position to excuse themselves from responsibility by taking the plea that they were 'saddled with' an unresponsive bureaucracy. Hey! Change it anyway you like and make it work! We only care for results and nothing else!

The modern governance system therefore empowers politicians to undertake radical surgery, if necessary, to fix bureaucratic incompetence, sluggishness or policy incompatibility. (If you are interested, I have provided a further discussion of this issue in the *Online Notes.*[14])

ACCESS TO THE LATEST TECHNOLOGY, INFORMATION AND TRAINING

The strategies in place to build capability in the public services in Australia leave the Indian public service system in the dust and adds to the vast gap between the performance of the two services. Australian bureaucrats are provided with the latest information and high quality training, even coaching. No matter how good individual players in a cricket team might be, and no matter how good their captain, we can't expect them to go very far – unless we choose to live in the Bollywood fictional world of *Lagaan* – without the best quality cricketing equipment and coaching. When a matter as important as delivering outstanding governance is at stake, there should be no compromise. The following points need to be noted:

- Access to up-to-date *electronic* databases is crucial for the development of competent policy advice. I have listed some of the databases available to Australian public servants in Appendix 5 of the *Online Notes.*

- Constant efforts are made to *upgrade* the skills and capability of public servants. Literally hundreds of specialized training courses are on offer to choose from. I am particularly impressed by the continuous improvement network[15] that brings in people like Edward de Bono, the well-known teacher of creative thinking, to talk to groups of public servants. Participation in the network is voluntary.
- Partial funding as well as leave from work for pursing higher degrees from outstanding Australian universities is also available, depending on the organization's needs, to public servants who display ambition, competence and commitment. Each public servant is enabled to go as far as he or she wishes to go, or can.
- Not only are the *departmental* libraries well stocked, but are managed by expert Reference Librarians, who are able to obtain a copy of practically any book published anywhere in the world within a week or two.

This phenomenal access to knowledge contrasts sadly with the information vacuum experienced by public servants in India. Exceptions notwithstanding, access to knowledge is neither sought, nor expected, nor therefore made available to Indian bureaucrats. The following are two illustrative examples:

a) In 1999 and 2000 I was responsible for the oversight of the government's library services for the state of Meghalaya. Not to talk of district or departmental libraries, even the State Library was in shambles, despite its grandiose building. Similarly, even though I headed the newly created Information Technology Department in Meghalaya in 2000, I could not get e-mail on my office computer, not to speak of the internet. Did I do anything to rectify these problems? Yes, I did,[16] but that is not the point here.

b) India does have a relatively well-equipped National Academy of Administration in Mussoorie, where I taught in 1994. But what it provides can at best be called induction training. Professional training is quite a different kettle of fish, well beyond its capacity. The Academy doesn't even teach the basics of economics and public administration properly, leaving a great muddle in the minds of its young officers.

If India wishes to become a great country (recall the '*mahaan*' in '*Mera Bharat Mahaan*'?), then access to such information, knowledge and training is absolutely critical; not in a remote academy, but at each desk, in each office.

BUREAUCRATS CAN JOIN POLITICAL PARTIES AND CONTEST ELECTIONS

One more key feature that I strongly advocate for India is the mobility in Australia not only between the public and private sectors but between the public sector and politics. The Victorian Public Administration Act 2004[17] allows public servants to 'belong to, and hold office in, a political party'. They can also contest elections; but they must resign from the public service before doing that. However, they retain 'the right of re-appointment or re-employment if unsuccessful',[18] 'within two months after the declaration of the poll at that election'. Sitting MPs who lose their seats are also permitted to return to their original public service employment.

Relatively few public servants take this route to politics. The more common route is for public servants to resign and become ministerial advisers first, before advancing to senior political roles. As an illustration, the current Prime Minister of Australia, Kevin Rudd, worked in the Department of Foreign Affairs as a bureaucrat from 1981–8 before becoming a political adviser as Chief of Staff to the Labour Opposition Leader in Queensland. From 1992–5, he reverted to public service, this time as the senior most secretary to the Government of Queensland (he was only 35 then!). Either way, whether people go straight into politics or through the ministerial adviser route, Australian public life is enriched with a continuous supply of very high quality and experienced talent at the political level.

* * *

In addition to these dramatically powerful reforms found in the Australian public services, enormous efforts are constantly underway to further improve governance and the public services. The aim in the West is to make public services an even more useful instrument to protect the freedoms of citizens. For those interested, I have outlined some key areas of reform underway in the West in the *Online Notes.*[19]

With this bird's eye view of modern reforms, it is time to understand the Indian situation in some detail.

INDIAN BUREAUCRACY TODAY

Unfortunately for India, its bureaucracy performs miserably on every possible indicator of governance. Everything we see in our daily lives is an indication of its poor performance. It may be hard to distinguish which portion of the blame for misgovernance should be attributed to the bureaucracy and which to the Nehruvian socialism, but given that the IAS is in many ways more powerful than political representatives because of its Constitutional sinecure, I am inclined to attribute to it at least half the blame for India's poor governance. In particular, inefficiencies at the operational level can almost entirely be attributed to it.

The situation is dire for India. In my 18 years in the IAS I did not come across a single officer who could compare, in policy leadership and quality of implementation, with an average senior manager in the public services of Australia. If there was to be a Public Service World Cup, even the F team of the Australia with its hands tied behind its back will defeat the IAS. The difference between these two is like an Argentinean football team versus a village football team from interior Bihar. Sure, there are some good natured and honest folk in the IAS; even individually brilliant ones who are particularly good at trivia – questions of the sort asked in *Kaun Banega Crorepati*[20] – but not one of them is equipped to be a thoughtful, analytical and delivery-oriented public service leader who can make entire organizations perform to world-class standards.

I will probably lose a few friends among my former IAS colleagues for making such statements. But this book is not about any individuals, and it is not about me. It is about India's system, and it is about India's future. Those of us who are part of this mess (or have been part of this mess) have very little ahead of us. It is the future we must look to. The key message of this chapter is that having outstanding raw talent like we have in the IAS is simply not enough. There has to be a constant struggle to excel and to 'over-achieve'. India cannot settle for anything less than the world's best.

POOR LEADERSHIP SKILLS

Generalist civil services like the IAS are often advocated on the ground that technical people are not good people managers and leaders of organizations. Generalists presumably can do such things well. The IAS are presumably good leaders, else the case for their existence would fall apart. They allegedly specialize in management skills and deliver better outcomes for organizations. Unfortunately, generalist IAS officers perform extremely poorly on this core function (not because of their innate lack of ability but because of lack of training and incentives).

Leading large organizations to not merely good, but great results calls for Level 5 leadership (*cf.* Jim Collins). However, India does not expect such excellence of its civil servants. Instead, low level authoritarian and arrogant styles are typical of the IAS. A few officers are genuinely humble, but that's perhaps the best that can be said of them. There is little strategic capacity and policy knowledge, no matter to who you look. The leadership I'm referring to has some of the following characteristics:

- self awareness and careful reflection, involving a deep understanding of one's strengths and weaknesses;
- keen awareness of what is going on around oneself;
- humility to acknowledge that one doesn't know most things and therefore it is better to ask;
- respect for others and looking beyond appearances;
- seeking new ideas and constantly innovating by giving new ideas a fair chance;
- determination to keep learning, particularly about how the rest of the world consistently outperforms India; and, finally,
- relentless will and determination to make India the world's greatest country, ever. This means never giving up this quest despite all obstacles.

This potent combination of skills, knowledge, and sensitivity is the kind of leadership that the IAS needs to display if it has to justify India's experiment to have generalists at the top of each government organization. But the IAS doesn't like to be told such things. Senior civil servants are seriously challenged by the very thought of innovation, or by suggestions for improvement. There is complete denial of need for a radical change in its culture to one that is focused on self-actualization. There is no considered reflection, and a strong distaste for debate. But level 5 leadership calls for vigorous debate on ways to increase its effectiveness.

Most IAS officers will confirm their very poor leadership ability by passing on the buck to politicians. They will claim that nothing can be done because of political pressures. But this excuse is not entirely valid (it does have partial merits). Despite politicians of the sort we have, there are a number of things which do not need the support, or even the awareness, of politicians to implement. These would include the following:

- Commit to a mission to always meet or exceed world-class standards in the provision of policy advice.
- Throw open internal debates for reform and cultural change. If the IAS can't do this systematically on its own, they can hire professionals to facilitate the debates.
- Hire experts to coach senior managers.
- Convert performance assessments into development conversations. Ministers write or comment only in a few of the annual performance assessments of IAS officers. What stops the rest of the performance reviews from becoming focused on development and capability building?
- Organize leadership development training for all its members as well as all other talented staff.
- Get 360° feedback regularly from all levels including from 'lowly' peons and drivers.

If the IAS does not want to be ousted, it must establish as its sole mission the delivery of world-class standards. If some officers brush aside this recommendation and claim they don't need such a mission, then they should prove that they are already the world's best by showing peer-reviewed international studies which cite the IAS as the world's best civil service. Else, they must start taking feedback from books such as this seriously and do something about it. Responsiveness to feedback may at least partially save it; else it is destined for the guillotine in the not too distant future. It is only a matter of time before a generation of clear-headed politicians will arise in India and sack this antiquated aristocracy that rules (not serves) India. When that happens, only those among its members who have risen to the personal leadership challenge will remain standing, the others being tossed out as weeds. The time for total mediocrity has surely passed now – six decades after independence!

NO EXPECTATION TO DELIVER RESULTS

So high is the raw talent of its recruits that the IAS could have been a world-beating Ferrari given some care and fine-tuning. Unfortunately, it has been used so long as a rundown *phat-phati* (auto-rickshaw) by politicians and senior officers within the service that it has begun to see itself as a smashed up auto-rickshaw. It has lost faith in itself, and lost sight of its original mission. Its members were among the brightest in India at one time, and they had great ideals upon joining the service. But that is all gone. They no longer have confidence in their ability to make a difference.

Before leaving the service I met a large number of senior civil servants across India in the year 2000 and approached many of them with different reform suggestions. I was appalled at the all-pervasive sense of helplessness even at the highest levels – a feeling that nothing could ever change. A good number of honest senior IAS officers were also desperate to get out but didn't know how to. And so these people plod on today, fulfilling the motions of work – things like filling out TA/DA forms, chasing after their 'pay slips' and car loans and other bits and pieces of paper in the Personnel Ministry, local Treasury and Accountant General's offices; aware that unless they spend their time in such trivial pursuits, even their future pensions won't be given to them, as their fellow-bureaucrats in the Accountant General's offices are renowned for losing all records of their very existence!

What happens is that from the first day of their working life, when they join as sub-divisional magistrates, there is no expectation placed upon them to perform outstandingly and to innovate. The main advice they get from their seniors is to 'be practical' and to 'manage'; which is the code for 'let the corrupt carry on with their work' and 'stay put'.

Now, people generally – and I'm not referring here to civil servants alone – learn either if they want to, or if they are likely to be kicked out for non-performance. Since Indian civil servants are promoted without any requirement to deliver any results at all, leave alone world-class results, there is no incentive for them to challenge themselves, having been recruited. Life in the IAS thus becomes a long and never-ending holiday. I remember organizing a two-week mid-career training programme for IAS officers in Mussoorie in mid-1994. Experts were invited from all over India to discuss their insights with these officers. One guest, the CEO of a major public sector IT company, spoke with a stammer. Upon hearing him speak, a number of IAS officers simply left the lecture mid-way – just walked out! More problematically, many participants repeatedly missed other lectures too; and used these two weeks as a holiday instead of as a learning experience. I don't blame them either since the heterogeneous mix was designed by young bureaucrats like me, a person completely ill-equipped at that stage to train others. In that way, India's civil servants fiddle away like Nero did while India's misgovernance burns out of control. They will never take responsibility for anything that has gone wrong with India – of that one thing I am sure.

And yet, there exist, even within this run-down service, a few exceptional people who have gone out of the way to educate and improve themselves. But after doing that, many have left the IAS or hope to leave as soon as they can. The service is unfortunately a complete dead end for such people. No one is ever going to let them apply their knowledge, anyway.

ARROGANT AND UNRESPONSIVE

While I have highlighted the leadership gaps already, arrogance is a particular feature worth looking at in detail. Professor R K Mishra, Director of the Institute of Public Enterprise, is right when he says:

> For the Indian civil service during the British period it was said that they were neither Indian, nor civil, nor public servants. It was expected that with independence they would be Indian in thinking and action. The general perception is that the Indian civil service has hardly changed [...] in terms of attitudes, mores and culture. A study of the overall perception of the officers of the IAS by members of the Indian Police Service, politicians, technocrats, and academicians points out that they project themselves as experts on everything. Their concern for, and focus on their own career is very high. They are self-opinionated, power-hungry, shrewd and manipulative, procedure and rule-focused, arrogant, inaccessible, judgemental and critical, and having concern for minor details. They have been rated very low on positive traits such as commitment to organization, trustworthiness, risk-taking, conscientiousness, innovativeness, and creativity. Most of the studies have rated them lowest as visionaries and transformational leaders. They are considered to be no-change agents.[21]

I fully and completely endorse this finding. Even the best civil servants in India create an impression of brusqueness, of being self-absorbed. They refuse to listen to what others try to tell them; their active listening skills are among the worst in the world, just a notch above Mugabe's. They are generally very demanding of their 'perquisites' and status symbols and do not hesitate to seek favours from businesses and subordinates. They stomp about with inflated egos like starlets in a small-time movie, and are therefore perceived as people who think that they exist at a level 'above' the rest of us. I was no exception to this; I too was one of them. My plea, in self-defence, is that I was not coached nor groomed by good role models. While that applies to the entire service, it is a very bad excuse; each of us is ultimately responsible to learn and improve.

In 2007 I wrote an article in *The Times of India*[22] on the Indian bureaucracy, summarizing this chapter. In response, a reader wrote: 'Regarding the IAS most of them have big egos but know nothing about their departments. [...] officers belonging to service should at least know their work, which they don't. Most of the time they do not go to office and those who do work cannot delegate'. Spot on! Therefore I would urge my former colleagues to try to listen to what the world is saying and reflect on it. The way to proceed would be to increase focus on leadership development of public servants as a high priority.

HUGE GAPS IN POLICY KNOWLEDGE

As already indicated, IAS officers are generally very poor at public policy analysis and design. Even if they do not have the time or expertise themselves to research each issue that they are faced with, they should be competent enough to know what to look for and how to acquire the relevant information. Unfortunately, most of them do not possess the basic skills to help them demand world-class policy briefings. Further, even though I know that things are changing fast, at least till seven years back most senior officers remained computer illiterate despite being offered many opportunities for training. Without having outstanding computer skills, the efficiency gains available to public servants today across the world simply cannot be tapped into.

NOT SUPPORTED WITH INFORMATION AND KNOWLEDGE SOURCES

IT infrastructure in the Indian Government is extremely weak. There is no access to international standards and to the latest academic literature. Today that can't be a major excuse, though. Simply having access to the internet should ease this problem considerably since policy documents of the developed countries are almost entirely available in the public domain. Indian civil servants can, if they so wish, literally cut and paste from the world's best policies and at least partly circumvent the extensive and expensive policy development route followed in free nations. But a person can only take a horse to the water; he can't make it drink. I suspect that even if this infrastructure is made available today, the vast majority of India's current crop of public servants won't open their minds and look for such things. I believe that for them to change, their incentives have to change; their sinecure has to be abolished.

CORRUPTION[23]

On a visit to Delhi from Assam in 1991, I was introduced to a young man in a restaurant by a friend. On finding out that I was originally allotted the Haryana 'cadre' but then moved to the Assam 'cadre', this young man asked me whether I changed cadres because there is more money to be made in Assam?[24] This shocking aspersion on my integrity was made because of the widespread feeling among the public that IAS officers are largely corrupt. By now that perception has become even more widespread, and we know that it is not without basis. Although it is difficult to estimate the magnitude of bureaucratic corruption, I have no doubt that at least some IAS officers are now corrupt to their very core – though these are fewer in number than Indian politicians who are almost all corrupt. Many other officers are either partially corrupt or on the way to becoming corrupt.

Let me talk about hard-core corruption first. These are officers who joined the IAS or civil services with the sole intent of 'making money'. The following are some examples:

- One of the persons who appeared in the civil services examination in 1981 along with me told me his aim was to join the Indian Revenue Service (i.e. the income tax service) because it is possible to make more money there than in the IAS. He was selected into a Group B Central Service in 1982. I don't know what has happened to him after that.
- An IAS colleague recruited along with me in 1982 said to me during our training days in the Academy about his objective of 'making money'. He had been a member of the Indian Revenue Service prior to joining the IAS and had already acquired a flat each in Mumbai and in Delhi. The damage this person has caused in the last 25 years can barely be imagined; unless, of course, he had a change of heart. In conversations I had with permanent teaching staff when I taught at the National Academy in 1994, I was told that the number of such IAS recruits who openly declare their corrupt intentions has been rising dramatically over the years.
- I know detailed stories about the exploits of some IAS officers from sources that have dealt closely with them (i.e. lower staff

who worked with them), to doubt that such 'hardcore' corruption is now endemic.

Apart from such hardcore corrupt IAS officers, who one hopes are still only a few, there are at least some who entered the service with the strong intention to remain honest but over the course of time may have become corrupt. It is important to consider what could cause such mid-career corruption.

Among the many problematic socialist policies in India, the absence of parity in salaries between executive positions in the public and private sectors has been a critical driver of such corruption. Recall that Lord Cornwallis had literally stamped out corruption from the ICS by paying its members handsomely. This principle worked well until its effect lasted into the 1960s. But as C P Srivastava showed, from Nehru's time itself the buying power of a secretary's salary started falling rapidly in comparison to its 1947 buying power.[25] By 1985, a secretary to the Indian Government could afford to buy only a quarter of what his predecessors in 1947 could afford. In the meanwhile the country's per capita income was growing, albeit slowly; and private-sector salaries were booming despite artificial checks imposed on them by the government. Today, the highest paid civil servant in India, the Cabinet Secretary, is paid less than what a fresh management trainee is paid by some multinational companies. The consequences of this dramatic disparity are predictable:

- First, there will a significant disincentive for high quality people with integrity to enter the civil services, thus restricting the pool of entrants to a much lower quality, or dramatically increasing the hardcore corrupt.
- Second, for those who have entered the service long ago and attained senior positions now, the continuous devaluation of their lifelong financial net worth – relative not only to their friends who joined the private sector, but relative to young children around them, who, fresh from college, earn far more than they do – can have serious consequences. Those who can, try hard to leave as soon as possible. Those who can't may well think of corruption.

As we would expect, officers who have upgraded their knowledge and capability over the years have started to resign en-masse, something that was unheard of in the past. Many have settled abroad, mostly in the USA. A few have joined the Indian private sector. As a result, the government is now being forced to increase its intake into the IAS due to the unexpected resignations of many senior officers. But such mid-career moves (generally made after 20 years so the officer can hold on to his or her voluntary retirement benefits) are not an option for everyone.

One can barely imagine the humiliation and pressures put on the vast majority of honest officers who are forced to continue at relatively poor pay, with forthcoming pressures to get their children educated abroad or to get their daughters married, and property prices shooting through the roof. The Indian society has always placed considerable value on material success. At such a late stage in their career they are cornered from all sides – the society lumps them together with the corrupt and doubts their integrity; their corrupt colleagues flourish in unprecedented ways; politicians scout only for officers who can assist them in their plunder. Under these circumstances one sadly wonders how many of these officers will be able to resist the temptations around them and emerge untarnished at the end of their careers.

By no means am I making an argument here for and across-the-board increase in civil services salaries through Pay Commissions. For the vast majority of civil servants, who have not opened a single book after entering the civil service (and who will definitely not read *this* book), higher salaries without a guarantee of radical improvement in productivity is not an option. The solution has to be found elsewhere; through a radical shift in incentives.

BUILDING A NEW BUREAUCRACY FOR INDIA

I must unfortunately conclude that our British India bureaucratic system is beyond resuscitation; it has terminal ailments and can't be resuscitated. It needs a total rebuild, from ground up. It has to be dismantled and a new public service system erected to replace it. With political commitment, such a reconstruction should be possible within five years as detailed in Chapter 6. I highlight the key changes needed at this stage.

The key principles behind the new system will be deceptively simple:

- Recruit the best people to leadership positions on salaries comparable with the private sector.
- Let these leaders then similarly recruit the best people they can find; and so on, down the chain.
- Spend all possible effort to develop these people into Level 5 leaders so they can become role models for others, and thus help to transform the competence and culture of the entire bureaucracy.

Recruit senior roles from the open market, and abolish tenure

A first step would be to hire extremely competent people as public service leaders – people with multifaceted leadership ability including high quality people-management skills, significant policy knowledge and demonstrated strategic thinking skills. Obviously, such people have to be paid well. The open market intake should apply in the first instance only to senior executive positions but in a phased manner to all positions. All senior appointments will have to be contractual, with the contracts permitting the government to let the executives seek better opportunities elsewhere (polite language for dismissal!) for underperformance without any rights created against such dismissals.

From what I know about the Indian system, it will be very hard, if not impossible, to find such people within the Indian civil services. Even IAS officers trained abroad are generally not in the league I am referring to. The hunt for talent would therefore have to focus on our private sector which has been developing an excellent reputation internationally. A few Indian academicians of international repute with extensive industry experience could also be potentially tapped. Such academicians will bring the latest policy knowledge and comparative understandings of the world, which are likely to prove crucial in designing strategic policy directions. The third category to look for would be Indians working in the private sector abroad in very senior positions.

Pay senior public servants salaries comparable to the private sector

It will be crucial that salaries between the private and public sectors are broadly equalized – no open market intake can succeed without this. Such parity would of course apply only to senior executives appointed on contracts. No Pay Commission-type across-the-board hike should be contemplated. People must always be paid in terms of their productivity; the salary must be deserved. This policy will also help reduce corruption (the elimination of corruption will depend on a much wider set of reforms, including the electoral reforms touched upon in the previous chapter).

Reduce the number of departments

Ahmed Shafiqul Huque, an Associate Professor in McMaster University in Canada, has identified an explosion in the number of departments in the Indian Government over the years:

> The number of departments in the central government of India grew from three (Public, Secret, and Revenue) in 1774 to eight in 1833, while the central secretariat was reorganised into four departments, namely, Home, Foreign, Finance, and Military in 1843. The number of departments rose to 10 in 1919, and 18 in 1947. These were subsequently re-designated as ministries. There were 20 ministries and departments in India in 1952, 54 in 1978, and 70 in 1993.[26]

Despite the great complexity of modern societies, increases in the complexity of the government machinery are not justifiable, as we saw in the Australian example. The disease of reckless expansion of the government machinery in India goes well beyond an increase in the number of departments. There has also been an exponential increase in the number of senior executive positions. Multiple departments with multiple secretaries exist today not to meet any genuine need but for the following two reasons:

- First, to accommodate the large number of IAS officers recruited from the mid-1960s onwards who have been promoted through the automation of seniority.
- There are also increasing pressures on Prime Ministers and Chief Ministers who often lead coalition governments today, to accommodate MPs and MLAs who want ministerial berths in return for support – leading to pressures to create even more departments.

The solution to this fungal growth of low performing departments and officers is to significantly reduce the number of departments as well as positions of secretaries and joint secretaries. This can happen only with outstanding leadership, which means that open market recruitment will have to come first. That will have to be followed by very careful restructuring of the machinery of the government including the professionalization of departments. Only after that can the much tighter new structures be put in place.

* * *

The problems of ineffectiveness, lack of innovation, and corruption in the Indian bureaucracy can be speedily reduced through reforms such as these. But many questions remain. A few people have written to me over the last year pointing out the Herculean difficulties involved in delivering such reforms. I have been told that these reforms are too radical for the Indian situation. I have been asked: who will select these high quality people; and can we trust our ministers to perform this task well enough? Then, what about the IAS itself – won't its enormously powerful lobby prevent such changes? And finally, there are the huge Constitutional barriers to reform.

These challenges cannot and should not be brushed aside. Reform is going to be a great challenge but I would suggest that we must make it a practice to deal with difficulties through an even greater application of our minds. Throwing up our hands in despair, a common response in India, is totally unacceptable. India can, for a start, readily seek assistance from countries which have taken such steps in the past. As Professor John Halligan explained in an email to me on 18 December 2007, 'The Australian reforms have been implemented over twenty-five years, and a number of the reforms that you propose were introduced over time. It is important to lay the foundations for reform and to build on them with various levels for change'.

The next chapter brings this book to a close by pulling together threads from across this book. The next chapter also includes issues that I could not find space to discuss earlier. What should emerge from the entire book, but particularly from the next chapter, is a far-reaching and ambitious plan for change – a plan to completely break free of Nehru's legacy of mediocrity. It is perhaps time for us to start thinking about India's tryst with greatness.

Chapter 6

Unleashing India – A Blueprint

As long as you're going to be thinking anyway, think BIG.
Donald Trump[1]

If we recast the above statement, we could also say, 'As long as you're going to be choosing anyway, choose to be the world's best'. I suggest that there is just no point in our aspiring for poverty alleviation. Let us aspire to be the world's richest country. That should fix the irritant of poverty. If we stretch our ambitions and work towards them, then even if we fail to get exactly what we want, we'll get close to our goal. This book stretches our arms towards greatness – not satisfied with mediocrity of any sort; let us aspire for freedom and wealth on a grand scale.

In the previous chapters we got a helicopter view of India's parched landscape which is pock-marked with gaping blackholes of socialist corruption. We found ministers and Prime Ministers sitting at the singularities of these blackholes, sucking public funds away from their intended use and generating vast deserts of poverty. We also upturned stinking, fungus-coated rocks such as our Parliament and found slothful socialist minions and communally inspired insects with bloodshot eyes swarming under them. It wasn't the most pleasant of journeys. We had to hold our nose in a few chapters. But by now we have all the information we need. We stand poised to pinpoint the precise locations in India's governance landscape where the clear springs of freedom are found; some springs waiting for thousands of years to be released; some springs that were visible at times in our ancient history but which were choked by Nehruvian socialism. In this manner we will harness the springs of freedom into a great River of Freedom to purify the heart and soul of India. This River of Freedom that we release will irrigate India with honesty, justice and equality of opportunity, dispelling gloom and misery from our land forever. Then, and only then, we will declare India to be truly *mahaan*; in fact, others will say that about us.

I use a rather unconventional style of exposition in this chapter. I am going to think really big here; no hiding behind the bush of academic niceties, no 'ifs and buts'. What I will advocate is a bold and clear path to freedom. The other day, a globally admired Indian business personality came to Melbourne. I knew this person had expressed considerable frustration with the Indian political and bureaucratic system. I asked this person after his speech whether he had any plan for India to move in the direction he visualized. On his replying he had one, I asked him to outline it for the benefit of the audience but he parried my request. I later wrote to him but got no response. Either there was no plan, or if there was one, it was a well-guarded secret.

I mention this incident to suggest that we need to get out of our chronic habit of criticizing without taking action. We need to outline our preferred methods which will bring about the change we want. We need to spell out our proposals in sufficient detail and share them with everyone else. Then we must engage in an open discussion; there is not much point in marking our proposals 'top-secret' and locking them up in a safe. This chapter is my blueprint to unleash India. It is my resistance to the cult of mediocrity and corruption foisted on us by Nehruvian socialism. Contrary to all appearances, I do not claim special wisdom. All I ask is that my plan be considered with an open and critical mind, just as I would examine similar plans from you and others. While examining our plans in this manner, we could ask questions, such as the following, to ensure that we are on the right track; in particular that we are all aspiring for freedom and not some dangerous thing like equality:

- Will the implementation of our plans enhance the levels of freedom and its obverse, justice, in India?
- Will our plans help us in creating a government that is not only efficient and effective but also fully accountable?
- Will our plans encourage us, the *citizens*, to take responsibility for ourselves and to stop depending for everything on the government?

My blueprint requires 70 per cent of the reform to be led by high-quality political representatives and the remaining 30 per cent by a dramatically improved bureaucracy. Of course, nothing will happen without people like *you* getting actively involved and providing the mandate as well as the leadership India needs. The immediate purpose of this book is therefore to make *you* a leader; nothing less than that can work. If *you too* hide behind the bush, as have millions of others before you since 1947, then India isn't going anywhere far – I can assure you of that!

This chapter is structured around a super-sized thought experiment which asks: *what would I do if I became India's Prime Minister?* Such a thought-experiment is familiar to many of us from school days when we wrote essays on such grandiose themes. But adults don't write essays of this sort, wary of being perceived as arrogant. This hesitation to start from the top, by looking at the big picture and working one's way down to the detail, is unfortunate. Anyway, for whatever it is worth, here is my plan.

WHAT WOULD I DO IF I BECAME INDIA'S PRIME MINISTER?

At the outset, let me confirm, as an aspiring politician must always do, that if I ever become Prime Minister of India, I would deliver a set of policies and programmes that would shift it entirely out of its current orbit of mediocrity, corruption and filth. My blueprint will return to us our innate freedoms taken away by our tribes, our kings and by Nehruvian socialists. These policies would take India into the spaces of the mind never before visualized in India, where each Indian could aspire to become dramatically better off and the country made anew and entirely corruption-free. Indeed, free.

But let me rewind! How would I become a Prime Minister in the first place? I could attempt to become one by joining an existing populist party and work my way up the chain of grubby politics. But as the tenor of this book shows, I will never join parties which I see as India's enemies. Corruption and freedom never go hand in hand. Equally, no existing political party will have me as its member for I do not meet the minimum qualification of having well known ancestors, lots of black money and links to the mafia. It appears that my grand thought-experiment is likely to prove abortive!

PEOPLE I AM WILLING TO WORK WITH

All this posturing doesn't mean I am a reluctant politician who believes that writing a book will solve India's problems. At the same time, I can't enter politics if the very purpose of achieving ethical liberalism is defeated at the first step. So, if not these political parties, whom could I work with? There are essentially two options: (1) I could start my own party and have good people join me; or (2) I could join a small, existing party which is broadly aligned with my views, and tweak its policies and character to meet my standards. Either way, the conditions for my participation in political processes will be the same. So let me record them. I hope you will agree with these conditions, in which case we will be two of us. Even if two of us out of a billion is not a big number, two is more than one, and the trend will be in the right direction! Freedom can do with two people in place of one.

The people with whom I would be willing to work with must have impeccable ethical standards, grounded in freedom. That is the bare minimum. They must be wholly committed to the advancement of freedom and fully understand the philosophy and logic of freedom. The group or party would follow the highest standards of internal democratic decision-making and public disclosure of all sources of its funding and expenditures. In addition, the leaders of the group would need to meet the following criteria:

- They must be extremely competent and able to formulate clear headed policy on complex issues, consistent with the logic of freedom.
- They must be capable of dealing with challenging problems were they to become future ministers, without panicking and running for shortcuts or politically expedient solutions.
- They must be at least Level 4, if not Level 5, leaders – people who are very superior[2] and therefore humble enough to listen to others and assimilate and build on the feedback they receive from others. They must be willing to admit mistakes, and willing to change their mind on the basis of new evidence.
- They must be team players, willing to work in any capacity that the party asks them to, recognizing that groups or teams comprising expert individuals are generally wiser than isolated geniuses no matter how brilliant.
- They must be willing to consult with citizens widely on all policy issues.
- They need not be perfect (no one is), but they must be transparent about themselves and willing to expose their lives and minds for public scrutiny.
- Over and above these qualities, these people will need to have lion hearts and an unwavering determination to overcome the greatest adversity in order to achieve their goal.[3]

I have no doubt that thousands of such outstanding people exist in India. You are perhaps one of them; so I could potentially work with you. But why would any such person join me, given that I have not a spare paisa in my pocket, and political parties need thousand crores of rupees to succeed? I believe that good people will join me because of my clarity of vision and strategy that will help to deliver much better lives for them and for their children. It is in the self-interest of Indians to embrace my ideas, particularly if they do not want to be:

- known as the *third* generation in independent India that stood by, doing nothing to fight the plague of corruption that racks the vitals of this country;
- left alone in India in their old age with their children having abandoned the country; or
- killed prematurely by pollution, poverty, ignorance, disease or potholes.

People would join me because they agree with me. For instance, I am not asking anyone to be corrupt, or to do any wrong thing. Instead, I am asking people to become the leader they want India to have and in doing so, make India, their *own* country, into the greatest country on earth. Surely, that is something worth doing?

THE FREEDOM TEAM OF 1,500 PEOPLE

In the end, everything great must begin with the right people. As Jim Collins noted, *First Who, Then What.*[4] It also matters a great deal *what* these people believe in. They must stand for freedom, else there is no point in coming together. Now, why 1,500? This is the number of leaders India needs to kick-start a freedom movement. This number is roughly equal to three outstanding leaders for 550 constituencies. That way, if one of them can't contest the elections at the last minute, two others will be ready to stand up. And if that second one is killed by the mafia, then the third will rise. Whoever is left will contest the assembly elections. In this manner a good prime minister can be found for India and the message of freedom also taken to the state assemblies. So initially we have the simple task of finding only 1,500 exceptionally good and competent people to form the Freedom Team of India.[5]

No one has to find 1,500 people at one go. Just finding one more leader will do. There is great power in civil society. If you think you meet the criteria specified above, then your next job is to find one more person like you. When only good people are allowed to join and to continue, the Freedom Team will strengthen quickly. No person of poor moral character should be allowed to join; or if selected by accident, allowed to continue. Hopefully, among a billion people, 1,500 good people (50 per cent of them being women) should be easy to find. This group can then formulate a blueprint which they can take to the people of India and finally, after contesting elections, get the mandate to implement. I have suggested a process by which this can be done in the *Online Notes*,[6] but I will now skip straight to my blueprint.

THE FREEDOM AGENDA FOR INDIA

First of all, we should be very reluctant to dismantle anything related to governance without fully understanding its impacts. For example, we should be extremely loathe to jeopardize our already weak justice and police systems. Being therefore wary of reducing any of the strengths we have built so far, my objective in this blueprint is to develop a constructive story which incrementally, but systematically, rebuilds, and then strengthens, the pillars of liberty in India. It is like re-building a road in small sections without disturbing the flow of the usual traffic.

To begin with, each of 'my' ministers would be required to sign and publish a Ministerial Portfolio Contract with India upon being sworn in. These contracts, based on the party's blueprint, would have been designed prior to the elections. The contracts would list the deliverables for which the minister would be responsible in the first year. At the end of each year, ministers would report publicly on their achievements. If a minister fails to deliver upon significant commitments, he or she would relinquish his or her position and hand over to a second-in-command who would have been groomed for the job as part of the contract.

RAISING RESOURCES

Advancing freedom calls for a strong government capable of providing us with security, justice, law and order, and requisite social and physical infrastructure, to be paid for collectively by citizens through taxes. We also need our government to be efficient, i.e. to be able to maximize the benefits from each rupee it spends. Finally, we need the government to be effective, i.e. the products and services it delivers should be first-rate and achieve their intended objectives.

These three requirements for a government are very stringent and need appropriate resourcing and expertise. Meeting these won't come cheaply. A cheap government is guaranteed to be ineffective since quality will become its first casualty. But today India has a cheap government.

Only a little over one-sixth of our GDP[7] is spent on services provided by government, with at least a quarter of this being sucked out by corruption; so Indian governance runs on one-eighth of our GDP. This share of GDP is less than one-third of what most free countries spend. In this manner, by spreading thinly a very small amount of money over a very large number of public servants and a vast array of services, the quality of each service provided by our government is mediocre, even discounting corruption. There is no point in delivering services in a mediocre manner. Mediocre delivery also fails to include adequate checks on accountability. As a result, the tentacles of corruption are able to slither into every nook and crevice of the government.

We need the effective and high quality delivery of a few, well chosen services. My government will therefore not run thousands of socialist services and low performing welfare 'programmes'. What it does choose to provide, though, will be of a first-rate, world-class standard. My government will provide the highest level of freedom practicable (justice, and law and order), and selected social and physical infrastructure, but only at market cost.

But even after cutting down frivolous socialist programmes, I expect that in the first two and a half years, when many such programmes will be phased out, and core focus rebuilt, my government's expenses will increase significantly. I also expect tax revenues to lag significantly since the revenue system will need a vast amount of restructuring. Therefore, innovative solutions, compatible with freedom, will be found to tide over the funds constraints of the first two to three years. For those interested I have detailed some solutions to overcome this funds shortfall in the *Online Notes.*

REFORMING PUBLIC FINANCE

Having set things in place to ensure that sufficient revenues are available for its first three years, public finance reforms will be given urgent attention. It is important to increase the tax base in India to a level that permits its governments to provide high-quality services. The basis of our taxes is our social contract, or Constitution, founded on an agreement between real people to pay taxes in lieu of services received. Public funds will therefore be raised by asking each real individual who is able to pay for the services the country provides that individual. Companies or associations of people will not be taxed in the longer term. Details of these reforms are provided in the *Online Notes.*

BUILDING CAPABILITY TO GOVERN

Most of this chapter deals with fixing our poor governance which is our Achilles' heel. The reforms under this section are intended to attract Level 4 or 5 leaders into the political and bureaucratic wings of the government, and to develop them from within.

Enabling public servants to represent people

Some honest members of India's civil services who have been seeking knowledge actively throughout their life are very well-placed to bridge the divide between socialism and capitalism in India and to become initiators of change. Their knowledge of our operating environment as well as policy options available under a regime of freedom could prove invaluable to India. Public servants will therefore be permitted to resign to contest elections and to return to their earlier positions within two months of the declaration of election results should they be unsuccessful. This reform will improve the quality of the candidate pool in subsequent elections; particularly at the state levels.

Appointments of Cabinet Secretary and ministerial staff

The ball of bureaucratic accountability will be set rolling by reducing the current exclusive reliance on the bureaucracy for policy advice and implementation. To signal this change the Cabinet Secretary will no longer be a public service position. This will mark the divide between political representatives and the bureaucracy, between the agent and sub-agent. This position will henceforth be held by an MP in the rank of Minister of State without voting rights in the Cabinet. The incumbent public service Cabinet Secretary will be offered a redundancy package; or, alternatively, reverted to his or her state cadre. Ministers will also be empowered to appoint a small team of political ministerial advisers on short-term contracts which will run concurrently to the ministers' appointments.

Compensation for peoples' representatives

Being committed to a squeaky clean government, I cannot afford the luxury of Cabinet colleagues being paid poorly. As an interim measure, my Cabinet will significantly increase the salary of members of Parliament. State Governments will also be funded for similar increases for their assemblies and councils. The monthly wage of MPs and MLAs would go up from the current Rs 33,000 to, say, Rs 3,50,000, with proportionate increases for ministers. There will also be an annual adjustment based on the cost of living. Simultaneously, all perquisites and indirect benefits will be abolished.

A system of performance bonuses for all MPs and MLAs will be introduced:

- For every one per cent increase in per capita GDP growth beyond five per cent per annum, all our representatives will get a one-off five per cent bonus.
- For every one per cent permanent reduction – defined as a reduction sustained for two years – in the number of people below the poverty line, MPs and MLAs will get a permanent one per cent increase in their base salary. Once the negative income tax system is fully established, the entire reduction in poverty will be incorporated permanently into the base salary.
- For every ten ranks that India rises on a sustained basis of two years in Transparency International rankings, there will be a five per cent one-off bonus.
- There will be a permanent 20 per cent increase on base salary upon India's becoming the world's least corrupt country for two years in a row.
- The sum of these bonuses will be limited to a total of 50 per cent of the base salary in any given year.

A virtuous cycle of morality will thus be established which will not only eliminate poverty but also overcome the vicious cycle of corruption established by Nehruvian socialism. Legislation will also be introduced to create a genuinely independent Political Representative Incentives Commission charged with research on, and making recommendations on the following:

- a compensation mechanism for peoples' representatives that will eliminate all reasonably foreseeable incentives for corruption, or will otherwise promote the freedom of citizens; and
- any matter related to the mechanisms of political representation, such as electoral laws.

The Commission would consult widely with the community and look at international best practice. The recommendations of the Commission, made at its sole discretion and whenever it considers fit, would bind the public exchequer, i.e. there will be no voting on its recommendations. This will eliminate the dilemma faced by political representatives who find the public or media unsupportive when they vote for an increase in their own salaries. Such lack of public support creates strong incentives for subterfuge through a host of 'perquisites' and underhand dealings. The independent commission will bring sanity into a matter as fundamental and important as this.

HIGH PRIORITY ELECTORAL REFORM

Interim electoral reforms, such as following, based on the arguments outlined in Chapter 4 would be introduced in Parliament:

- repeal of the requirement in the Representation of the People Act for Indian political parties to swear allegiance to socialism;
- removal of limits on political fund raising and expenditures subject to stringent disclosure. These disclosure requirements will include third party audits and audit by the Election Commission. There would be penalties of up to Rs 10 crores and jail terms of up to three year for failures to accurately report on and declare all receipts and expenditures related to political purposes. Penalties for making unauthorized political expenditures on behalf of another person would be increased to Rs 1 crore along with a jail term of up to one year;
- state funding of elections (being retrospective for the elections that would have led to the formation of my government) would be introduced. Candidates who secure more than one-twentieth of the valid votes polled will be reimbursed Rs 25 for each vote polled on a formula linked to the population and geographical extent of the constituency, normalized to an assumed 100 per cent voting rate. Surveillance will be strengthened through video cameras in polling booths and other security measures taken, as well as very significant penalties imposed, on people who engage in booth capturing; and
- the security deposit for elections would be increased to Rs 5 lakhs from the current Rs 10,000, and forfeited when less than one-twentieth of valid votes are polled by a candidate. This lower forfeiture limit will allow many more candidates to contest, while the much higher security deposit will deter non-serious candidates.

There is clearly some arbitrariness in these numbers which will need to be fine-tuned over time to ensure that the gate is kept open for serious candidates but shut out for frivolous ones.

FREEDOM MINISTRY AND A NEW CONSTITUTION

A new Freedom Ministry and Department will be created at once, charged with promoting our freedoms. It will be headed by a Minister for Freedom. The Prime Minister and the Minister of State for Cabinet would be served by this Department as well, which would deal with political affairs (excluding internal security) and advise Cabinet on the extent to which all new laws and regulations proposed are compatible with freedom. It will also deal with matters that fall across more than one department, such as general principles of recruitment to the public services and subjects not allocated to other departments.

- The Indian Policy Office (IPO) would form its core advisory area comprising policy professionals with demonstrated capability to analyse policy in relation to economic impacts and impacts on our freedom. The IPO will, by and large, hire new analysts through open competition, including Indians currently teaching economics and finance in the world's top universities – these people will be hired on short or medium term contracts and paid salaries comparable to what they are currently drawing abroad. The idea is to suck back top class policy talent of Indian origin currently sitting abroad. This office will function as a division of the Department but will retain significant independence in its advice. The Minister for Freedom would provide the Cabinet with the IPO's original advice, as well as his or her own comments and recommendations.
- A separate division of this department will review all existing laws to assess their compatibility with freedom.
- The department will coordinate all legislation required by this blueprint, particularly a new Public Administration Act and Superannuation Act by the ninth month.
- In Chapter 3, we saw how a new Indian Constitution can be fast-tracked. Processes to create a new Constitution will be put in place by the Department, such as convening a new Constituent Assembly with the approval of all the states within six months. The draft Constitution so prepared will be put to a referendum within six months of its completion. The task of translating the existing Constitution into relevant Acts would also be co-ordinated by the Freedom Department to ensure that, subject to the referendum being successful, the new Constitution would be able to take effect on or before the first day of the thirty-first month of my government.

- Surveys will be commissioned by the Freedom Minister through an independent organization to assess citizens' views on the level of corruption and service delivery in various departments. Results would be published quarterly and inform the public self-reviews of ministers as well as confidential performance reviews of secretaries.

Phase 1 – Build Up (first two and a half years)

Now to the bureaucracy. The first two and a half years of my government are being characterized here as *Phase 1 – Build up*, following Jim Collins. The second half of this five-year term is being characterized as *Phase 2 – Breakthrough.* Since much of the improvement in India's governance will depend on the active participation of states, they will be provided incentives to initiate similar reforms. I will immediately write to public service heads, asking that the bureaucracy start examining all its work in the light of freedom of the people, and explore constructive ways to systematically step aside from needlessly interventionist activities.

After the Phase 1 restructure the number of departments would be brought down to ten, with around 20 ministerial portfolios and 20 Ministers of State (the latter to ensure orderly succession). Each portfolio would be served by one of the ten departments with a total of ten secretaries in all. Apart from the Freedom Department, other departments will be: i) defence, ii) justice (including internal security, police, support to the judiciary and protection of consumers), iii) external affairs, iv) public finance, v) physical infrastructure, vi) social infrastructure (e.g. public health, poverty elimination through negative income tax, and the regulation, not direct management, of education and medical facilities), vii) commerce (including regulation of industry and agriculture), viii) social capital and community (fostering voluntarism and conducive social relations in the community), and ix) sustainability (managing the ecology – with a time horizon of 1,000 years).

Two principles will underpin the change programme in the *Build up* phase: (1) the need to move the structures from the current to the new in a systematic and effective manner, and (2) to do so in a manner by which everyone involved is enabled to understand the rationale for the change and through which no one becomes financially worse off, or experiences distress, for up to five years at the end of Phase 1. This commitment would be on a sliding scale, from one year for staff with less than five years service, up to five years for staff with greater than 15 years service.

The part relating to significant distress bears some elaboration. The idea behind it is that nobody should experience either financial or psychological distress in consequence to this change programme, for that would violate the principles of justice. These employees were not responsible for the policy mess and culture of incompetence created by politicians who adopted Nehruvian socialism. Therefore, my government owes them a duty of care to ensure that they are given a reasonable time to rebuild their life where their departure becomes necessary. The government must always be a model employer and set the highest standards of behaviour and people management. Ensuring the health and safety of employees will be a major duty of managers of this change programme. Managers will be empowered to make relatively small adjustments to the speed of the change to humanely manage employee well-being. Throughout this process, collective bargaining will also be encouraged, without sacrificing decisiveness. Collective representation is an opportunity to understand the concerns of employees and to engage them actively in the change process. We definitely don't want the current styles of authoritarian management to continue.

The timelines and deliverables for Phase 1 are outlined below. The month in the sub-headings refers to the time when an activity will be completed:

- **Month 1:** The Planning Commission will be shut down from day one. Its policy analysis functions will be transferred either to existing departments or to the IPO. All commitments made under the Five-Year or other Plans will be scrapped. All previously committed funding will be up for review at the time of renewal or extension of funding on a case-by-case basis. Files of the Planning Commission will be sent to the National Archives for recording and open access to researchers.
- **Month 2:** My government will not undertake a useless reshuffle of IAS officers. Instead, as a first step, all deputations and postings to and from the IAS, IPS and IFS state cadres to the Central Government will be frozen from the sixtieth day, after which the system of transfers and deputations at the level of joint secretary and above would be scrapped. All new appointments except new recruits to the civil services (and the IPO) will be frozen until Phase 2, urgent requirements being met by ad hoc contracting. The annual intake of new civil

service recruits by UPSC will continue till Phase 1 is completed to prevent shortages of trained personnel at the grassroots in the states. These recruits will be treated at par with other employees at the end of Phase 1, and will be able to apply for Phase 2 positions either in Central or State Governments, keeping in mind that traditional roles like sub-divisional magistrates and district magistrates would no longer exist in Phase 2 in states which participate in these reforms.

- **Month 2:** Secretaries of existing departments will be given two months to come up with a well-defined set of core competencies including knowledge and leadership standards, as reviewed by internationally reputed consultants, for each position in the rank of joint secretary (and above) to the Government of India.
- **Month 3:** Upon approval of these competencies by the relevant ministers – and the Freedom Minister, to ensure consistency in the standards – all civilian positions at senior executive levels will, without exception, be advertised publicly on the first day of the third month of my government assuming office. There will be no reduction in the number of senior positions in Phase 1. However, all such positions will henceforth be recruited entirely through the open market.
    - As most departments do not handle security matters, there is no reason why non-citizen permanent residents can't work in such ministries. Therefore, except for civilian positions in the defence and external affairs ministries, and some positions in the Freedom Department, senior positions in all other departments will be open to anyone with appropriate merit from practically anywhere in the world.[8] All they would need to do before appointment is to apply for permanent residency in India.
    - Compensation payable for these newly advertised positions would be at par with that of senior managers in multinational corporations in India, in the range of Rs 40–100 lakhs annually, to be individually negotiated – noting that a few senior policy analysts hired by the IPO from abroad will earn similar amounts as well.
    - Current civil service incumbents could apply to these positions along with others.
    - A series of interviews and presentations from shortlisted candidates on a range of complex policy matters would

be held by teams headed by the lead Cabinet Minister of the concerned department and another Cabinet Minister. Existing civil servants who are shortlisted would be encouraged to bring along with them a summary of their perspectives on the strategic plans for their departments (as outlined later). Strategic and persuasive discussion of such plans could help civil servants demonstrate their capability. The selected secretaries will be appointed first – under my signature – and given the option of forming a part of the interview team for joint secretaries. Each secretary would then formally appoint the joint secretaries and retain complete oversight of them, including the rights to dismissal.

  - All these appointments will be on 24-month contracts, extendable by three years if the incumbent is successful in obtaining the fewer Phase 2 positions.

- **Months 5 and 6:** Appointments will be completed in five months and appointees will start work at the commencement of the seventh month. Unsuccessful incumbents will relinquish their roles simultaneously.
  - Civil services incumbents appointed to these positions will have to resign from their civil service before taking up these appointments. They would also get the benefits admissible to them on voluntary retirement from their service, *over and above* their new contractual benefits. If they are not yet eligible for voluntary retirement, they would be deemed to have completed 20 years of service.
  - Unsuccessful civil service incumbents could either revert to the rank of a Director in the Central Government on their existing salary or revert to their state cadre. They could also select an individually negotiated redundancy package plus pensionary benefits under the relevant rules. No other government employee will be offered a redundancy package until the beginning of Phase 2.
  - If some of these positions cannot be filled because suitable candidates cannot be found, or if there are unforeseen delays in recruitment, experts of international or national stature may be tapped on the shoulder and offered short-term appointments on

mutually acceptable ad hoc terms at salaries potentially much higher than those indicated earlier.

- **Month 8:** *Departmental strategic plans:* The newly appointed secretaries would be given 60 days to prepare a 21-month strategic plan for their department to be delivered by the end of the eighth month to the Cabinet. They would work closely with their relevant ministers and the Freedom Department which would have already conducted background work through the IPO on each potential restructure. These plans will be published on the first working day of the ninth month, after Cabinet approval. These would specify the pathway to the restructure in sufficient detail to guide implementation. These plans will include, among other things, the deliverables and milestones listed below:
    - A high-level review of each major activity undertaken by each department to be completed by the end of the ninth month. A two to three page summary on each major activity would be presented to the Cabinet from the ninth to the twelfth months, and all reviews published on the internet after Cabinet endorsement. These reviews would provide the rationale for either continuing with an activity or reverting it to citizens (Box 13 in the *Online Notes*[9] outlines the principles that will guide these reviews[10]).
    - The strategic plans will specify the timelines for implementing organizational and structural change, even as there is no let-up in the delivery of core functions.
    - Regulation should not be directly implemented by departments. Regulatory enforcement and implementation will be de-linked from policy making to minimize capture of policy by regulators. Where such regulatory bodies do not already exist, the strategic plans will specify when a relevant independent regulatory will be established. As part of this process, the Reserve Bank would be made completely independent, tasked with focusing solely on inflation; in the longer term, the concept of central bank will be reviewed and most functions decentralized to the private banking system. To ensure independence of regulatory bodies, appointments of their chief executives would need to be endorsed by relevant Parliamentary Committees from

the beginning of Phase 2. This would eliminate perceptions of bias in the delivery of regulation. The delivery of laws will thus become independent of political considerations.

- The strategic plans will also specify when a separate strategic plan for each departmental public sector body, regulatory body, or undertaking dealt with by the department will be delivered – latest by the eleventh month. Without exception, all business undertakings including defence manufacturers will either be auctioned off in the international market or their shares sold to the people of India by the end of Phase 1. The government will stop being a businessman. Period. Not one business will remain in the government's hands. Buyers would need to protect the financial outcomes of staff of these undertakings for up to five years after Phase 1 on a sliding scale similar to that for public services. Defence undertakings will be sold only to companies fully owned by Indian citizens who live in India and employ Indian citizens; these companies will also provide periodic reports to the defence ministry and permit random inspections by authorized defence inspectors at any time of the day or night. Exports by such private defence companies would be vetted by the Defence Minister.
- A key element of the strategic plans will be the comprehensive modernization of the trappings of government administration. During Phase 2 there will be no concepts of clerks, peons, or drivers. Offices would be completely modernized and made 'open plan' with senior managers seated in the same work environment as their support staff, excluding joint secretaries and secretaries who could have their own rooms. There would be a number of small and large meeting rooms. State-of-the-art technology and facilities would be made available, including modern workstations with access to global databases and international standards, electronic document and records management; and more importantly, high quality toilets and kitchens for staff.
- The strategic plans will identify and deliver on the training needed to ensure that employees wanting to

work in Phase 2 possess relevant technical skills. The stringent competency requirements of Phase 2 will mean that those who don't shape up will have to be let go. In recruiting public service leaders for Phase 1, one of the important competencies will be their knowledge of the skill sets needed for modern governance. In particular, they must be capable of sourcing high quality trainers from across the world.

The Freedom Department will coordinate all departmental strategic plans and ensure that each major aspect is properly addressed. When these plans are added up it should become clear how the restructuring of the ten new departments will be completed.

- **Month 9:** *A new Public Administration Act:* The Freedom Minister would introduce a Public Administration Bill in the Parliament in the ninth month. This will essentially implement many of the suggestions already made in Chapter 5. For those interested I have provided details in the *Online Notes.* The Act would come into effect at the commencement of the thirty-first month.
- **Month 9:** *A new Superannuation Act:* As indicated in Chapter 5, one of the key barriers to occupational flexibility in India is the absence of a uniform superannuation scheme that applies both to the public and private sectors. A Superannuation Bill, upon the commencement of which the Central Provident Fund legislation and General Provident Funds would be disbanded, would be introduced in Parliament in the ninth month. This would require each employer, including the government, to transfer 10 per cent of an employee's gross salary, at a low rate of tax, into privately managed superannuation trusts that would invest these funds into risk categories selected by employees. This 10 per cent contribution would technically form part of the employee's contribution, and will be included explicitly in all salary packages. I have discussed further details of this important piece of reform in the *Online Notes.*[11]
- In this manner, by eliminating tenured appointments at senior levels, by introducing redundancy for all permanent positions and by enacting superannuation legislation, significant flexibility would be introduced into the Indian labour market. A number of other, more generic, labour market reforms will also be introduced which I do not touch upon here for want of space.

- **Month 9:** *Constitutional amendment to abolish the all-India services:* Also in the ninth month the Freedom Minister will introduce a Constitutional Amendment Bill to wind up existing civil services and repeal Articles 308 to 323. Approvals from states would be obtained and the Amendment enacted as soon as possible, to take effect from the thirty-first month at the latest. Through this process, there would no longer be any Constitutional barrier to the Phase 2 structures. Indeed, this amendment would be made effective as soon as the Public Administration Act is enacted.

  The amendment would automatically abolish the Union Public Service Commission (UPSC) in its current form. However, under the Public Administration Act, the UPSC will be reincarnated and headed by a Public Services Commissioner. It will shed its recruitment function except for the armed forces, for which a longer and different transition will be separately laid out. It will largely convert into a research organization on public administration and provide recommendations to government on world-best-practice for the bureaucracy. Its periodic recommendations could lead to further streamlining of the public services and help to further increase their agility, productivity and effectiveness. It would also establish newer, and usually better, working conditions every three years for the public services in consultation with employees and their representatives, subject to Cabinet approval. The practice of setting up ad hoc Pay Commissions would cease.
- **Month 22:** *Advertisement for Phase 2 positions:* Based on the details of the restructure, which should emerge clearly by the twentieth month, jobs for all individual Phase 2 positions will be advertised by the twenty-second month, eight months prior to the commencement of Phase 2. These will be open recruitments through the market using procedures prescribed in the Public Administration Act. Current employees of the government will be eligible (as will others) to apply for these, fewer, 'final' positions. All appointments made to these positions will be deemed appointments, effective only from the commencement of Phase 2.

  Advertisements for these positions will be staggered, the senior-most roles being recruited by the twenty-fifth month, well before the junior ones. Senior managers so appointed will chair the selection panels to recruit their future direct reports.

All appointments will be completed by the twenty-ninth month.

Phase 1 government employees not recruited to a Phase 2 position will be declared redundant with effect from the thirty-first month and suitably compensated. They would also be supported by the Freedom Department through training and guidance in setting up a business. It would be generally ensured that they do not become worse off for up to five years beyond the commencement of Phase 2 on the sliding scale mentioned earlier. It is expected that they will find something useful to do in the radically reformed economy of India. The Freedom Department will also monitor their health and well-being.

The performance indicators for Phase 2 secretaries will be significantly tougher than Phase 1 indicators. These will be linked closely to citizen perceptions of departmental performance and corruption. If an organization is perceived to be corrupt by more than a certain proportion of the public, this 'target' proportion being drastically reduced each year, Phase 2 secretaries will be dismissed automatically without recourse, despite not having been personally implicated in their department's corruption.

To ensure a fail-safe transition to Phase 2, suitable transitional arrangements and redundancies will be built into all systems for the first three months of Phase 2 to ensure that no core function is compromised even marginally.

Phase 2 – Breakthrough (second two and a half years)

The midnight of the first day of the thirty-first month of my government will be a momentous occasion. Major changes will take effect at that moment. The tryst with greatness would have begun. Among the changes, the new Constitution would become effective; tenured civil services will be disbanded; and all government functionaries who were successful in obtaining Phase 2 appointments transitioned to their new functions.

On the first working day after that most public sector employees will move into sparkling and well-equipped modern offices – offices which will have no resemblance to their smelly and file-infested socialist *avatars.* Most of the states will also transition in the same manner, or will do so a few months later. Public servants across India will thus move into a far more dynamic, flexible and challenging – as well as more remunerative and satisfying – work environment.

All roles transitioned to Phase 2 would be deemed to be new appointments, with the relevant secretary being the appointing authority. Fully computerized service records will be started afresh and earlier records archived while ensuring that the relevant leave records, records of disciplinary proceedings, and health and safety matters are adequately transferred to the new system. All underperformers would likely have been filtered out during selection processes for Phase 2, and so it is expected that the secretaries would start with a clean slate. But among other things, each secretary would put in place an effective performance management system in consultation with staff to proactively deal with underperformance. Secretaries will explicitly work towards the earliest possible termination of tenured underperforming employees subject to natural justice (except for executives where fewer requirements on natural justice would apply).

During Phase 2 many ministers appointed earlier to Phase 1 portfolios will no longer retain their roles due to a consolidation of portfolios. These MPs will be tasked with assisting the Freedom Minister to coordinate and complete a review of all existing policy and laws, supported by specialist teams from the IPO.

LOCAL GOVERNMENT REFORM

A major action for my government will be to initiate the reform of local governments in India with a special focus on urban governance. Urbanization is the natural consequence of the division of labour, specialization and innovation that arises from freedom. Free societies are urban societies. Given our model which opposed freedom and wealth, only 28 per cent of our population lives in urban areas, against 78 per cent in the USA, 84 per cent in South Korea, 86 per cent in Australia and 90 per cent in the UK. With the levels of freedom proposed in this book, India's urbanization should exceed 80 per cent by 2100 AD. This makes urban governance very important. Our cities are congested and polluted, with significant failures of infrastructure. They need to be managed by the people directly, and effectively.

An incentives-based governance model will be adopted, giving full control to elected representatives over the employment of bureaucrats working in local government bodies. This principle will also extend to rural local governments. Today, super-sized municipalities like the Municipal Corporation of Delhi[12] or the Calcutta Municipal Corporation manage, or rather, badly mismanage, our urban areas. The reason for this misgovernance is the absence of any accountability in the system. As a result, parallel 'governments' have started evolving everywhere, that require citizens to pay twice for the same service such as garbage collection – once to the municipality and the second time to local groups of residents who organize the garbage collection privately. This is anarchy. The solution is to have small local governments that are professionally run and directly supervised by citizens.

This supervision would not be toothless. Today, officials are appointed for life in municipalities and cannot be removed by elected citizens for non-performance. Elected citizens are decorative, an incidental add-on. In the reformed system, elected citizen supervisors would not only be able to veto decisions made about their local environment that they do not agree with, but they would also be fully empowered to dismiss their chief executives who would be hired on three year contracts. Consequently, complete control would be exercised on officials down the line. This is how the models of local government work in most parts of the free world.

Since the subject of local government falls within the purview of State Governments, this reform will have to be led by the states. Within three months of my government taking charge, it will frame a package of incentives for states to create fully elected local councils (*parishads*) of a manageable size. The ratio of elected local representatives to citizens would be brought in line with international best practice. For instance, Delhi will get around 300 elected councillors (including Mayors or *Pradhans*) in about 60 independent councils. These councils will be responsible for providing world-class civic amenities and managing local libraries and community halls. User charges such as land taxes and rates will form their primary source of revenue.

Land planning and zoning will be controlled by the councils with the help of professional land planners, environmental scientists and landscaping specialists. Some state inspectorates, such as the food inspectorate, will also be transferred to the councils. States will be provided incentives to modernize associated regulation, e.g. food regulation, to reflect risk-based approaches. These changes would lead to fewer but far more competent inspectors. All these staff will be fully accountable through the contractually appointed chief executives. Each council would be able to set its own rates independently and determine the level of amenities it will provide. Councils wishing to attract wealthier residents will therefore focus on better infrastructure such as parks, while also charging more money from residents. Citizens will therefore physically move to the better managed councils and vote with their feet. Because of the natural competition between a multiplicity of councils, the costs will be kept down. Through this process, world-class services will become the norm in India's cities.

Thereafter, districts and municipalities will be disbanded from the commencement of Phase 2. The 'imperial' Collectorates will be dismantled as well, and their land revenue staff transferred to these councils. India is not a colonial administration and does not need 'political' officers such as Divisional Commissioners and Deputy Commissioners. The concepts of administrative divisions and subdivisions will also be scrapped. Local governments will act as the eyes and ears of the State government. An overarching regulatory role will remain for State Governments in urban affairs, primarily in making enabling laws, in managing the ownership of land and in building geographical information systems to coordinate the records of land use. These local government reforms will be reviewed after five years to further refine governance at the local level.

SOME FIRST-ORDER CORE FUNCTIONS

A good government needs to deliver high quality outputs in at least three 'first-order' core areas – defence, police and justice. These functions must be carried out outstandingly well and, if necessary, to the detriment of all other functions. If funds run short, a government can always provide incentives to citizens to take up relatively secondary things like infrastructure through a range of innovative ways by transferring property rights over roads, airports, or railways. I have outlined key elements of reform in these first-order core functions in the *Online Notes.*[13]

SECOND-ORDER CORE FUNCTIONS: INFRASTRUCTURE AND EQUALITY OF OPPORTUNITY

After performing these first-order core functions outstandingly well, a government must focus on providing infrastructure and equality of opportunity. Appropriate funds need to be deployed to deliver second-order core functions well. Given space constraints, I do not discuss infrastructure provision here. All I note is that where goods are excludable, i.e. wherever boundaries can be drawn around an infrastructure and therefore user-pays ticketing is feasible, such infrastructure will be sold in a systematic manner to the private sector. Where partial ownership or property can be given to the private sector, such as through toll-based highways or other public–private partnerships, that option will be explored. Finally, where it is not feasible to privatize infrastructure because of non-excludability, the government will directly provide the service wherever possible, outsourcing it and acting as an auditor rather than manager.

But moving to the very important issue of equality of opportunity, four key aspects are involved in its provision: (a) elimination of poverty, (b) provision of school education, (c) higher education and (d) basic health.

Poverty elimination

India should be able to eliminate poverty even after spending far more money than before on core functions. Subsidies and poverty alleviation programmes today barely reach a small proportion of the poor each year, being almost entirely absorbed in administrative expenses and corruption. As such the poor can't be lifted above poverty. My preliminary estimates made in the year 2000 showed that if this money could be directly transferred to the poor, it would be almost exactly sufficient to pull all of the poor above the poverty line each year.[14] Funds are therefore not a major issue here; it is a matter of the way they are directed. Even if my preliminary research is wrong, i.e. even if, upon further analysis, it is found that the money needed to eliminate poverty is not cost-neutral and that it would need additional resources, banishing poverty is essential and must be done. The mind-numbing poverty experienced by millions of our citizens has to be abolished. A liberal government's key role is to ensure equal opportunity to each family.

As detailed in Chapter 2, a direct mechanism to transfer funds to millions of poor people in India will be put in place, based on annual income tax returns to be filed by each family. Instead of 1,000 government programmes that deploy 40 lakh bureaucrats in the name of helping the poor, we will only have *one* programme, called the negative income tax (NIT). India's largest IT companies will be invited to propose methodologies to implement this system. About half a dozen pilot projects will be rolled out by the end of the first year and the most effective (not cheapest) method will be selected for national implementation. These NIT payments will become fully operational in the fourth year across the country and, after a year of implementation and evaluation, all subsidies will be scrapped and the public distribution system shut down.

Over the subsequent years, the rapid growth of the market economy and improvements in education will make this policy mostly redundant as most people will rise beyond poverty on their own; indeed they would have become well-off. Nevertheless, *some* people would remain who can't cope with the demands of the market; so the NIT will be a continuing programme. The NIT will be linked to a *requirement to work* programme that will ensure that able-bodied people do not get paid if they are found to have avoided going to work. This programme will be managed through the private sector. The poverty line will also be kept low so that very few people will deliberately choose to be poor. Elimination of poverty will also include the payment of premium for private health insurance for each person. How major health care will be provided to all is outlined in the section titled *Health Care.*

School education

Twelve years of education is now a norm in most free nations. My government will guarantee support for the education of all permanent residents of the country who want to study up to standard 12 or age 18 (whichever comes first), noting that this does not amount to compulsory education. This would also include support for equivalent vocational training. Today, about 16 per cent of India's children in the age group 6–14 do not go to school at all, amounting to tens of millions of children. Most also drop out of school well before completing high school.

Getting every Indian to complete standard 12 may therefore sound like a pipe dream. But it will be achieved quickly with the policies outlined below. My government's solution will be to deliver high quality education to *all* children of India at the cheapest possible price. Since schooling is largely a state subject, therefore this policy will apply initially to Central Government schools only. However, states will be given incentives to move to this model.

My government will fund parents for their children's education, and not manage schools or appoint teachers. If we apply the criteria for the review of government activities (outlined in Box 13 in the *Online Notes*[15]) to the school sector, we find that the government does not need to build, own and maintain schools, or deal with lakhs of school teachers directly, in order to educate every child. The current approach is too centralized and bureaucratic. It leads to mediocrity since local information can never be factored into the equation. Having been a secretary of the Education Department in Assam, I have at least some knowledge of the extensive corruption in the education departments and directorates of India. I have also inspected *non-existent* primary school buildings which were shown as having been completed on paper. Our current socialist approaches are completely inappropriate, both theoretically and empirically.

Governments are also very soft on their own failures. A Director of Schools will generally demand stringent standards from private schools that want to be licensed but will be pathetically indifferent to the shoddiest quality of education provided by government schools themselves. However, if all education services are provided by the private sector (i.e. by private citizens themselves), a government regulator can become an effective judge of school quality. We also know that parents generally prefer to send their children to private schools because the standards of accountability of these schools are much higher. Parents get full value for the extra money they invest in their children's education. Privatizing all government schools will therefore ensure that all schools in India are fully accountable. Further, under the current system, the lands and buildings of government schools are not being used in the most efficient manner. Privatization will ensure much better resource utilization. By giving ownership – in most cases through educational consortiums – to teachers, the commitment of private school owners towards the maintenance of buildings and school infrastructure will also be enormously strengthened. As a rule, whatever exists without a specific owner is destined to be neglected. Finally, we know that managing a school is a hands-on exercise like managing a business. Governments are very inefficient in doing hands-on things and running businesses. The average government bureaucrat or teacher has good intentions but no incentive to deliver world-class educational services at the lowest possible cost. The private sector, on the other hand, can only make a living if it delivers high quality services in a cheaper and better way than its competition.

It will not be of concern to my government whether the privatized schools are run as 'for-profit' or 'not-for-profit' institutions. If, at the end of the process of maintaining a school and providing high quality educational services, a school can make a profit, this will only help, not hinder, the supply of *more* good schools. Profitability is the finest signal of quality in a marketplace. There is no reason why it should not be allowed to apply in the case of schools.

In this model, each child's school education will be funded, individually, up to year (commonly known as 'standard' in India) 12, as follows:

- Schooling will cost child 'A' *nothing* if parents choose a school which charges their 'A' a fee equal to or less than what the government is prepared to fund that particular child.
- Schooling will be *partially subsidized* where parents choose a school which charges a fee for 'A' over and above what the government is prepared to fund that particular child.

Schools will bill the government for each child *individually*. Schools will not receive funding as a lump-sum which is unrelated to the size and nature of their enrolments; they will get a specific amount for each *specific* child they enrol. Schools will therefore have the incentive to go out and literally beg parents – such as parents of child labourers – to send their children to school. The more the children that these schools can enrol and pass out at an agreed, independently tested standard, the greater the money they will receive.

This method of private sector provision of education is *as* guaranteed to succeed *as* India's current method is guaranteed to fail. This method will also ensure that the choices made by parents are honoured. Honouring parents' choices can only be a good thing. No one could be a greater well-wisher of a child than his or her own parents. A government should never interfere with a parent's choices without very good reason – only if both parents have a conclusive record of neglecting their children can a government make better decisions on behalf of the child. Let me now outline the model in detail.

School privatization

- As a first step, my government will get completely out of school ownership and management. Over the course of the first 30 months, all government schools will be privatized. Their land,[16] buildings and equipment will be sold at market rates through an open tender in which educationists working in these schools will be encouraged, through a (small) preference in the conditions of the sale, to form consortiums which can be registered as companies or societies, and make a bid. It is expected that such consortiums can create a persuasive business case to raise bank loans and buy the schools with repayments to be made from earnings made over the years.[17]

- Funds raised from the sale of schools will form part of a one-off increase in government revenues to be used to offset the initial increase in core function expenditures.
- The following conditions would apply to the sale:
  - The school's land cannot be sold for 50 years. The government would retain the right to acquire land from school owners for other public purposes where it becomes necessary to do so, upon payment of slightly greater than market value, after making suitable arrangements for the children affected.
  - The school's land or buildings cannot be used for any primary purpose other than school education. School owners will be allowed to operate business activities approved by the (local government) council from the school campus after school hours. There is no incompatibility between having temporary shops or a small gym as a side-business operating in the school building after school hours so long as the funds raised from these activities by the school help to keep it solvent and keep its fees low, while also meeting the quality standards prescribed by the education regulator.
  - The consortium which buys the school will not disadvantage existing staff for up to five years from the time of purchase of the school on a similar sliding scale referred to earlier.
- Schools will not be protected from competition in any way. Practically anyone could set up a school anywhere, charge any fee and try to attract students. There will be no quotas or limits on the number of schools in an area, even if this may make it harder to raise loans. This openness is necessary to prevent monopolies of any sort arising in what should be a completely free market. So long as a school complies with quality requirements, through 'deemed licensing', it could be launched. Schools would self-assess against standards established by an independent association of educators nominated by the education industry, and notify the education regulator of their existence – that would amount to becoming a licensee. Stiff penalties would apply if a school was later found to have violated the standards. Schools would be permitted to enrol children *only* at the beginning of a school year and parents will not be able to change their children's schools during the year unless there are exceptional circumstances.

- To prevent the financial collapse of schools through mismanagement, each school will be compulsorily required to purchase bankruptcy, fire, workers' compensation and public liability insurance from the market, to be reinsured initially by the education regulator until the rates of school collapse are better assessed and private market premiums fine-tuned. If the buyers of a school turn out to be bad managers, or worse, this insurance will prevent the school from going belly-up and children from suffering.
- This model will create a competitive market for high quality schooling. Only the most efficient schools, fully accountable to the parents for the quality of education they provide, will survive. Poorly managed schools will be bought out by more efficient schools. There will be no barrier to the potential size of a consortium. An efficient consortium could potentially buy out *all* schools in the country. So long as even one other efficient competitor could set up a school in any place in the country, the size of the consortium would not matter.

Child-based funding

- School will bill the government each month (or quarter), seeking reimbursement against *eligible vouchers* (eligibility below) for each child, *by name.*
- By the thirtieth month, my government would have allotted a unique identification number to each child in India between the ages of four and eighteen, in preparation for this programme. This number would be linked to a database which records key biological features[18] of the child and photographs of his/her parents, to prevent potential falsification of records commonly done by illegal immigrants to India.[19] A new identification number would thereafter be allotted to each child who subsequently reaches the age of four. This database will be linked to the previous year's income tax return of the child's parents, and would generate a voucher of a *specific value*, linked to that income and to the expected educational costs for a child of that age. Vouchers will therefore differ in value. Children of poor parents will get vouchers of a much higher value than children of wealthy parents.
- Children would go to a school selected by their parents. Parents would pay an amount over and above what the government

voucher reimburses the school for each of their children separately. Poor parents would of course not pay anything since they would have high-value vouchers. Richer parents will pay a top-up amount.

- This higher allocation for poorer parents is a crucial part of the model. The system today does not provide genuine equal opportunity even though it is based on the socialist ideology of equality. The quality difference between government and private schools is therefore quite vast, and does not allow children from rural areas or slums to prosper. My government's policy would make schools in rural areas or slums extremely attractive to potential school owners, since children with predominantly high-value vouchers will attend such schools. Therefore schools in economically backward areas will be able to afford much higher salaries for teachers, and potentially attract even better teachers than schools in urban areas. In this manner, all schools will be able to provide a robust quality education at the minimum.
- An annual adjustment would be applied to the value of a child's voucher after the income of the child's parents is declared to the tax office. Excess payments made for the child to the school would be recouped through the parent's future taxes.
- The voucher system will be managed by a range of private service providers under strict conditions of accountability. The independent education regulator will monitor the quality of these providers and ensure the overall integrity of the voucher system. Stiff penalties will apply if preventable fraud is detected at any level.
- Schools would be required to report a child's death or transfer from the school within one month to the voucher service provider. Should it be found that a school has charged the government for a child who was no longer studying there, the school will face financial penalties including potential withdrawal of the school's license and criminal prosecution of the school owners.
- Education departments and directorates, as well as inspectorates of schools, would be mostly disbanded by the end of the thirtieth month; many of their teaching and non-teaching staff would have been, by then, employed by the larger consortiums. The social infrastructure department, which will manage the overall budget for school education, will work with the independent education

regulator to ensure that minimum outcome standards of educational attainment are met by each school, and that vouchers are administered properly.

Higher education

Higher education, on the other hand, is quite different from school education. There are no entitlements to this level of education.

No one can demand that every tennis player should be allowed to play in the Wimbledon tournament. It is one thing to provide a level playing field for people to develop their talent and quite another to demand entry to the highest levels of human activity. There is a thing called justice, by which only the best person, who not only has the talent but who has put in the necessary hard work, must win entry to the portals of higher competition. Entry into a portal of higher education is similarly a privilege, contingent upon significant hard work. It has nothing to do with providing anyone a level playing field.

Another reason why my government will not fund anyone's higher education is because it would mean the poor would subsidize the rich. Tertiary institutions are 'fishing nets' to catch the society's most talented people. Those who successfully complete tertiary education earn, on average, significantly more than those who are unable to gain admission to these institutions. The benefits of higher education are captured almost entirely by these people in exchange for services they provide when they join the workforce. Students going to tertiary institutes therefore will become much richer, on average, than the average taxpayer. If the average taxpayer were to subsidize their education it would amount to the poor subsidizing the (future) rich. There does remain the question of ensuring that all those who obtain admission to institutions of higher education are able to raise sufficient money to attend the courses. That can be easily resolved. In doing so, the policy outlined below will deliver the world's best tertiary education system to India. The objective is to create a hundred Harvard Universities in India, each a centre of excellence operating only on student fees and alumni donations.

Low interest loans to tertiary sector students

- Tertiary institutions will charge full fee virtually from everyone barring the few to whom they give scholarships. By the government not funding tertiary institutions, significant tax revenues currently allocated to higher education will be released for more essential purposes, even as the quality of university education and infrastructure is significantly boosted by the open market fee charged by universities.

- Those admitted to a course by any recognized tertiary education provider will be loaned money for 15 years at a low rate of interest by the government to attend that course:
    - An Indian citizen (not overseas citizen of India or permanent resident), who gains admission into an approved tertiary institution in India will be eligible to borrow from the government all fees charged by that institution, as well as the cost of necessary books and equipment and modest living costs.
    - These loans will bear a low interest – around one per cent more than the (variable) Reserve Bank rate. The repayment would be through the income tax system after the student gets a job and starts earning above three times the level of the poverty line. This loan will enable all meritorious persons in India to pursue higher education.
    - Even after India becomes completely free there will remain some tendency on the part of some students to leave the country after being educated at the taxpayers' expense. Such students may not return the loan and also pay taxes to other countries which did not invest a rupee in their education, but potentially not repay their loans to India. Where similar schemes operate elsewhere, as in Australia, an international agreement will be sought by those countries to ensure these loans are refunded to India. Either way, a system to monitor departing students will be established. Passports and immigration officials will be given access to the database of student loans. Students who leave India – even on a temporary visit – will need to furnish a bank guarantee equivalent to the amount of their currently outstanding loan plus the present value of all costs incurred by taxpayers on their school education. This guarantee would be forfeited should they fail to return within the stipulated time. Those without proof of this guarantee will be turned back at the immigration check and not permitted to leave India.

  - How will these student loans be funded? The basis of this loan model is that income streams from university students are far more secure than houses or land. Almost all university graduates will earn well, making it a trivial task to recover their loans through the tax system. Therefore, a rolling debt model will be used. From the thirty-first month, ten-year bonds will be issued equal in today's real value to the student loans expected to be issued (not repaid) that year. Prudent investors in India, including banks, will buy these bonds.
  - The bonds will be retired after ten years using multiple-year recoveries from students who would by then be in the workforce, noting that not all bond repayments will be met from student loan recoveries in a particular year. Apart from mismatches of timing between student earnings and the face value of the bonds, the residual costs of administering this programme will have to be paid by the taxpayer as well, plus the difference in interest costs between the effective rate of the bonds and the Bank rate and a write-off for defaults. This amount will form a subsidy for higher education. The justification for this small subsidy is that it provides an equal opportunity – to those selected for higher education – to complete their courses. With efficient management, the subsidy will be reduced considerably.

Tertiary sector privatization

- As with schools, there is no reason for the government to manage the delivery of tertiary education. Indeed, there is even less reason, since no bureaucrat can teach an Einstein or tell him how to manage his discipline. Let experts manage their own institutions. All government universities, technical colleges and the like will be sold off by the thirtieth month on the same pattern as schools, and accredited by imposing on them a few conditions necessary to demarcate them as institutions of tertiary education. These institutions will become *for-profit* corporations with shares traded on the stock market. Their sole business objective would be to provide tertiary education and they would use their lands for the primary purpose of higher education for 999 years.

- They will have operational independence. They would set their own salary structures to attract distinguished academic professionals and, consequently, bright students. They would determine the type and quality of tertiary education services they wish to deliver, the mix of courses to offer and other things that universities do. The competitive market will then deliver the best mix of options for students. Not one rupee will be spent on any 'educational planner' to predict the demand for graduates in specific areas. Only that much higher education will be provided as the market needs and will bear.
- The reason why universities won't jack up their fees to astronomical levels upon privatization is because of their critical need to attract customers – in this case, high quality students. High quality students, like any other self-interested person, will look for good quality but *low cost* education and force the fees down to competitive levels.
- Will some academic disciplines be ousted from the teaching agenda by this model? Doubting Thomases will argue that privatization will affect the supply of courses in arts and philosophy. But this argument is without basis. Modern private sector corporations recognize the great value of liberal education in broadening the perspectives of managers. Indeed, arts graduates do better in modern businesses than technical graduates because innovation, entrepreneurship, leadership, people management and strategic thinking have little to do with technical skills.
- In this manner, the freely operating tertiary education market will decide what courses are needed for India. I imagine we would get a hundred Indian Harvard Universities in a few decades through this model.

Health care

Health care can be split into two elements – basic health and hospitalization. Unlike higher education, basic health does form part of the requirements of equality of opportunity. However, to the extent that people should meet the costs of their visits to doctors and medication from their own savings or through insurance, this is a usual part of living and no extra effort is called for to equalize the playing field. The poverty line for purposes of NIT would include a buffer to allow for such routine costs to be incurred by the poor.

However, for major medical matters, things can become complex. Ideally, each free citizen should take private insurance or self-insure. However, people who have not self-insured but land up on the doorsteps of a hospital once they fall badly sick or get badly injured cannot be turned away in a free society, just as no one can be allowed to starve. Therefore the concept of voluntary insurance or self-insurance breaks down for hospitalization and emergency care. Major health care therefore becomes a public, not a private, good, being non-excludable. It calls for compulsory insurance. In the manner we pay for roads, defence and police, i.e. in proportion to our incomes and not in proportion to our use, hospitalization and emergency care will be provided by the government to every citizen by charging taxes which will form a compulsory insurance premium. People will be free to take private insurance at levels beyond this coverage for ambulance services, designer spectacles, a private hospital room, treatment at a hospital of choice or by a doctor of choice, use of experimental medicines or medical techniques not available for general use, early booking of elective surgery, or cosmetic surgery.

Having collected the hospitalization premium, the government will not directly deliver the service, but get it delivered. The country's geographical area will be carved into reasonably sized zones which will then be put out for tender. Private health consortiums wanting to provide prescribed health services of a prescribed standard, to all people living in these areas, will quote a single, flat price on a per-person basis. This quote would take into account the local costs of living including the difficulty of appointing doctors to remote areas. The lowest (or fittest) bidders would be awarded 30-year exclusive contracts for these geographical areas and paid the agreed amount each year for all people living in that area (the amount would change as population changes). This money would enable these consortiums to establish hospitals or to otherwise negotiate with private hospitals in that geographical area to ensure that appropriate services are provided to all people in that geographical area. Further, except for emergencies, people would be allocated specific hospitals for treatment in their living zones.

The health regulator will monitor the delivery of services. Stiff penalties for non-compliance with agreed standards will be imposed. By the end of the third year, when this system would have been fully implemented, the system of government primary health centres and hospitals will be shut down. Where possible, the lands and assets of these facilities will be sold to relevant private health consortiums which will also be required to take responsibility for the public health and hospital staff for up to five years.

SOME IMPORTANT NON-CORE FUNCTIONS

There are some non-core functions that a government can also perform, if funds so permit. I am focusing only on environmental sustainability here. Many aspects of environmental sustainability are core functions, being a part of justice.

Environmental sustainability

We have seen that the fundamental cause of poverty in a society is the lack of freedom. The size of a country's population has absolutely nothing to do with it. Free countries are rich no matter if they have a high population density (31 countries have a higher population density than India's, including countries like Hong Kong, Singapore, Taiwan, South Korea, Netherlands, Belgium and Japan) or low (such as with Ireland, United States, Sweden, New Zealand, Canada, Australia). On the other hand, low levels of freedom invariably lead to a large, poor and illiterate population. I have explained why India's large, illiterate population can be directly attributed to Nehruvian socialism in the *Online Notes.*[20] The explanation uses a conceptual model which formed the basis of my doctoral research. Therefore, had India not followed Nehru's socialism, its population would have been much smaller and significantly richer today. The diagram below summarizes the reasons and shows how freedom keeps the population size low and motivates parents to send their children to school.

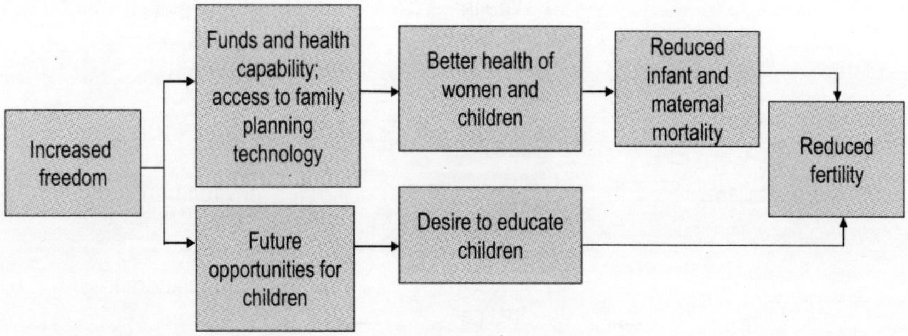

But while population size does not cause wealth or poverty, it impacts the environment significantly. India's large population has without doubt had an adverse impact on the environment, such as on our wildlife. In addition to creating a large population, Nehruvian socialism has also added to the depredations on India's environment. Our socialist pirates – ministers and officers charged with the responsibility of protecting forests and the environment – have personally looted our forests and connived with polluting industries to damage our environment.

- One of my earliest battles against corruption, in 1985–6, was an attempt to stop illegal felling in beautiful dense forests found in the Hojai subdivision of Assam. Trees were being cut illegally with the connivance of forest department officers, and possibly (almost certainly) of the minister.
- One of my friend's wealthy acquaintances in Delhi confided to me in the early 1990s how he made his wealth by illegal harvesting of native timber from Nagaland. The method he used was that of paying off Nagaland Ministers.

Socialism has also meant that we are a very poor country without the money to clean up our rivers and lakes, or to rehabilitate our denuded forests. Finally, the justice system in socialist India does not hold people to account for the pollution they cause. Under today's socialist dispensation, polluters invariably pass on the costs of their pollution to the society without any recourse available to citizens. Our environmental situation is very precarious as a result.

On the other hand, freedom leads to a good and sustainable environment. The relationship is depicted in the diagram below. There are three pathways to a good environment: (a) building greater awareness of environmental problems, (b) greater technological capability to deal with pollution, and (c) enforcing accountability firmly – a free society holds polluters to account.

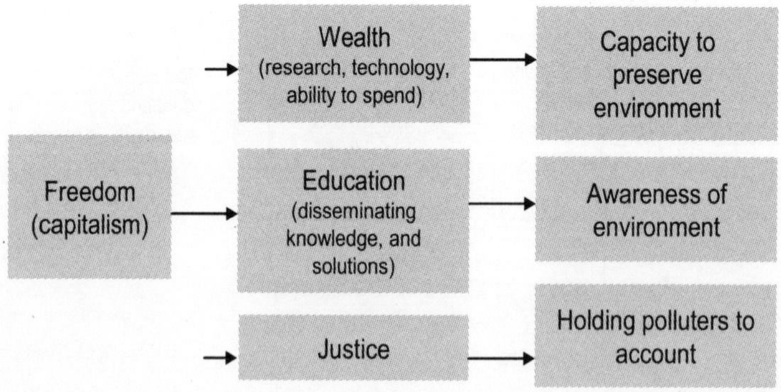

Unfortunately, the transition to freedom is always a time of great pollution. With even a slight increase in income arising from greater freedom, the use of energy, transportation and chemicals tends to rise steeply. Given our large population, things are therefore likely to get very bad before they start getting better. We have to brace ourselves for environmental disasters as the economy opens up.

To avert such disasters, my government will face this challenge head on and put in place the mechanisms of accountability and justice necessary for a clean environment. While wealth and the consequent capability to deal with pollution will take time to build, awareness building and enforcement of accountability will be the main pillars of my government's strategy to protect the environment. My government will also rapidly phase in, through regulation, the world's highest standards in the use of non-polluting technology wherever such technology exists. Without these steps, given the large population size bestowed by Nehruvians and the wealth generated by capitalism, the environment will be completely laid bare.

Accountability of polluters

Accountability or justice is the foremost value in a free society. Passing on costs to the rest of the society and the environment cannot be tolerated. Polluters *will* be made to pay, if necessary with deterrent levels of penalties. The following strategies, discussed in detail in Chapter 2, will be adopted:

- **Cost recovery**: To the extent that polluters can be individually identified, external costs will be recovered from them directly and polluters will be forced to repay the affected community. This can include mandatory requirements for polluters to clean up toxic spills, failure to do which would lead to imprisonment for extended periods.
- **Pigovian taxes**: To the extent that polluters cannot be individually identified, Pigovian taxes will be imposed on the activity that approximates most closely the activity undertaken by the polluters. A range of incentives-based solutions, such as trading of permits within limits to pollute, will also be used. In particular, carbon taxes will be imposed in a phased manner on electricity produced from coal. The revenue so collected will be used as follows:
    - o to provide (compensatory) subsidies to companies to increase plantations and forests. These subsidies will be

paid based on the actual growth of these forests confirmed through satellite imagery;
- o to fund Indian investors to build nuclear power stations while meeting the world's highest standards of safety and security under international supervision; and
- o if funds remain, to fund industry and universities, based on demonstrable results, to increase research in non-polluting technology.

In the *Online Notes*[21] I have also discussed the international ramifications of carbon pollution and how the West will be asked to deploy carbon taxes both to increase the developing world's forest cover through private plantations (see Chapter 2 on how this can be done) and also to significantly increase their own forests.

* * *

There are numerous other things that the blueprint would include, including things like enhancing innovation and increasing transparency which I have not included here for want of space.[22] By implementing this blueprint, each of our 113 crore people will be enabled to use their minds freely and innovatively for the first time ever in India's history. India will then be transported into the open spaces of endless beauty that Tagore spoke of in his *Heaven of Freedom* (see Chapter 1). I can visualize thereafter, not very far away, possibly in a few decades, the Indian economy becoming at least three times larger than that of USA, and its people being able to balance the needs of self-development, environment and the economy.

We cannot run after wealth as a nation, though, if we wish to be a great nation. We must only seek freedom. We must seek to live as individuals who are free to think for themselves. Wealth cannot be our objective; it will follow naturally from our freedom. In doing such things, these policies of freedom will make the India of tomorrow the world's greatest country in many more ways than the size of its economy. And wouldn't *that* be something that Gandhi, Tagore and Nehru would have been genuinely proud of?

FINAL COMMENTS

The capitalism advocated in this book is not about unfettered freedom, but about a system of freedom with accountability. I don't want to be told by anyone that I have been preaching unfettered, reckless freedom! Instead, this book has been clearly about self-discipline, moral responsibility, enlightened self-interest, even enlightened selfishness. There is a point where the philosophy of freedom merges seamlessly with the highest spiritual philosophies of mankind. However, ethical liberalism is a philosophy of action and does not tolerate corruption and decadence, unlike many spiritual perspectives which have no civic sense. Capitalism is a system of freedom with accountability. It is a delicate balance between competing needs.

I do not ask people to sit on their haunches like spiritualists do, watching their country go to the dogs even as their soul apparently achieves salvation. I do not believe that such methods will lead anyone to salvation, either. Inner peace, surely, but not salvation. There has to be a careful balance wrought between self-development and social development. The world we live in is the real test for what we stand for. Do we stand for humanity, for reason and for compassion? Or do we stand for extreme selfishness, so immersed in our soul that we lose all sense of our civic duties and responsibilities? No society will become free or remain free if its citizens are focused only on their own souls, to the neglect of vigilance over their temporal governments. Let us look after ourselves and our souls, but in doing so also discharge our duties and responsibilities as citizens. That will achieve the fine balance of enlightened selfishness, the greatest virtue of all.

And so stop just sitting there! Let us raise a commotion about corruption! Let us organize! I ask you to wake up. Freedom demands civil society; it demands voluntarism; it demands vigilance. This book can be summarized in the following scorecard:

Outcome for the Country and Society	Nehruvian Socialism (Equality)	Capitalism (Freedom, Equality of Opportunity)
Is the country a great place to raise our children?	×	✓
Are its people *independent*, i.e. they do not ask the government to do everything for them?	×	✓
Is justice delivered effectively and quickly?	×	✓
Are the people largely ethical? Is the society a moral society?	×	✓

Outcome for the Country and Society	Nehruvian Socialism (Equality)	Capitalism (Freedom, Equality of Opportunity)
Are the people secure? Is there law and order?	×	✓
Is the government free of corruption?	×	✓
Has poverty been banished?	×	✓
Are many of its people *deservingly* rich? Is inequality encouraged and charity to able-bodied people discouraged?	×	✓
Are religious and other discriminations severely punished?	×	✓
Are all children well educated, at least to standard 12?	×	✓
Is the country's infrastructure *world class*?	×	✓
Is the country's environment sustainable, and is its wildlife thriving?	×	✓
Do citizens *always* seek to *exceed* the world's highest standard in everything they do?	×	✓

Vladimir Putin, the President of Russia, recently said in an interview in the *Time* magazine[23] that 'One doesn't have to be a particularly bright highbrow to see the obvious, that the market economy has major advantages over an administrative system'. Even though Putin's Russia is nowhere as free as this book intends India to become, it now sees a clear advantage in moving towards freedom. The poisonous ideas of Marx have been trashed in Russia, the land which espoused them so vehemently for 70 years. But Indian socialists and communists continue to thrive in their Marxian world as never before. So if Putin's Russia can 'get it' why can't we – are we to conclude that we do not have sufficient people even as *bright* as ordinary Russians?

I trust that you are by now one with me on the virtues of freedom, capitalism, ethical liberalism, enlightened self-interest, enlightened selfishness ... whatever you call it. And yet, I am keenly aware that I have made recommendations in this book some of which you may not agree with. Indeed, I have not only received many positive comments on this book but also some objections. So I would like to discuss some of these objections here. A few general comments before I do so:

- Some readers pointed out that many good things are already happening in India. In accepting that, I would like to remind them that such good things have been motivated entirely by the initial burst of capitalism forced onto India by the IMF. We have still no internalized full-fledged capitalism, which is primarily about justice and good governance. We should not be content with morsels of capitalism when we can but should have it *fully*. There are still millions of poor and illiterate people in India. The task has barely begun, and good governance is not even on the horizon.
- Some readers said they agreed with parts of this book but not with other parts. I suggest that such an approach is not logically consistent. I see this entire book as one piece. People have only one real choice: to either agree *entirely* with this book, or to disagree with it *completely*. While this may sound like the height of arrogance, the problem is that my recommendations have been derived exclusively from the principles of freedom and the value of life. The recommendations of this book flow as a mathematical proof would, being either completely right or completely wrong. There are no grey areas in this book; people can't pick and choose. If you do, you will end up with a logically inconsistent model.
- The claim of impracticability doesn't hold water at all, either. For example, it could be claimed that we simply won't find enough high quality economists today to recruit into each State Government in India. But such an objection is a matter of detail. It may mean that we need to get there slowly, or it may mean that we need to bring back our economists who are forced to teach in Western countries today (or like me, help Western governments to even further improve their countries) instead of teaching (or working) in India. But it doesn't change our destination. Matters of practicality can always be worked out if there is a will.

Having said that, I can understand partial disagreements (a) where it can be shown that one of my particular recommendations is erroneous because it does not derive from freedom, or (b) if a better solution than the one I have suggested can be found, being equally or more compatible with freedom. As to the first of these, there is only one Truth, so please write to me at sabhlok@yahoo.com with your better arguments and evidence. I will discuss these suggestions on the blog I have created for this book. And I promise to change my mind wherever

I am conclusively shown to be wrong. The second of these disagreements is quite possible. Interplays of technology and incentives could mean that I may have missed out a better solution. I would be pleased to incorporate good solutions into potential future versions of this blueprint. Do write to me. Let us interact! Let this not be a passive book or a one-sided monologue but the beginning of a conversation leading to clarification of thought and then to action. One way would be for people to consider joining the Freedom Team and working on improved solutions together. Now to a discussion of the detailed objections I have received, in Box 4.

Box 4: Some objections to views expressed in this book

'Nehru did the right thing for his time'

A reader, commenting on a draft wrote, 'after independence, industrialists were not willing to invest in industries requiring larger gestation period'. Therefore, 'opening our economy to the world would have led to many a *devastating effect*'. The implication is that Nehru was right in taking upon himself the task of baking bread, making steel and stitching shirts for us instead of ensuring justice. The real point is not whether industry did or did not want to invest. It would be presumptuous for us to judge a particular investor's constraints. In a free market, where people put their own money on the line, each investor must decide for himself. The question is whether Nehru focused his efforts exclusively on promoting our freedoms or not. And the answer is, he did *not*. That is the real concern raised by this book. A government must give us freedom of choice. We can then decide if we want to invest our money or not.

But for argument's sake, let us examine the investment issue. Many Asian countries had opened up their economy well before India did in 1991. Japan opened up in the late nineteenth century, South Korea in the 1960s, China in 1979. *None of these countries was 'devastated' when they increased the levels of economic freedom.* They only became rich. There is no shred of evidence to indicate that our industrialists in 1947 were a bunch of fools who wouldn't have invested even when opportunities arose. These people had invested even under British rule and created large steel and cotton mills under harsh conditions. Reading the Tata story (*Creation of Wealth* by Russi M Lala) shows that we had world class industrialists who fought and worked hard to produce wealth. But Nehru never bothered to give us the rule of law, justice and infrastructure and let these people make the investment. Instead, he blocked investments through quotas and licensing. The public sector became the 'dog in the manger', destroying our wealth even as it prevented citizens from investing. How can we possibly blame our industry to justify Nehru's mindless attempts to become a government businessman?

'Reservations and the uniform civil code are necessary'

A reader has indicated that reservations and the uniform civil code must continue. However, based on the principles of freedom I am clear that there is no place in India for such things (see Chapter 3). At the same time, we must create uniform prohibitions on certain actions, minimum standards of accountability in social matters, but most important of all, equality of opportunity through elimination of poverty and provision of school education for all children. Enforcing equal opportunity and taking action against discrimination will also help. Such policies will yield a far superior outcome to the unjust and anti-freedom strategies found in our Constitution.

Capitalism leads to exploitation and guilt

An interesting objection I received against capitalism was that people are advocating corporate social responsibility (CSR) nowadays because of all the guilt that capitalism creates in the minds of chief executives (CEOs) of large companies who draw very large salaries. Apparently such people are exploitative and feel guilty. So they need to undertake CSR programmes. Two things: first, CEOs don't steal their salaries; they are *given* this money by the *owners* of the company (shareholders) because the CEOs provide much greater value to the shareholders. There is no exploitation involved here. It is a pure negotiation, a trade. Second, an industrialist can't ever feel guilty if he has produced wealth the right way. He has already contributed by providing employment to thousands of people; that is the biggest 'CSR'.

The modern idea of CSR is often just a clever marketing strategy, and I don't believe that such CSR programmes contributes one bit to a country. Countries don't become great on the basis of charity *of any sort.* They become great by competition and by creating wealth. Let Indian companies focus exclusively on generating profits and not distract their attention from wealth creation. Let India become a thousand times richer first. That will be the greatest CSR.

These solutions are too ambitious and too radical

According to this view, we have to be 'realistic' about India. Its problems are too deep-rooted to allow changes of the sort I have proposed – particularly in the short time span of five years. But the rate of change I have proposed is neither too fast nor too slow. I would like to suggest that wherever successful change has been made, it has been made fairly quickly. Change requires *will power*, and if momentum is not maintained, vested interests will gain strength and block the change. They will sap the will of the change leaders. The real blocker to such change is the availability of the *right people* to lead India to freedom. This exercise could take many years just to start. That is India's greatest challenge for the future, not the ambition or speed of these solutions, which can always be refined.

* * *

The observant reader would have noted that there is a deeper layer or message in this book. It is about becoming seekers of the Truth; about critical thinking. Tagore's *Heaven of Freedom* is, after all, a state of mind that each of us can aspire for, irrespective of whether our entire society is free. The government or a society can block our body but it can never chain our mind. To that extent we can be free irrespective of the society in which we live. A key message of this book is therefore about free thought and reason, about finding out the best way we can to live. This book seeks a cultural shift in India from blind acceptance of what our seniors or leaders tell us to asking probing questions and personally examining the facts. It is crucial for everyone to discover the truth about capitalism or socialism or whatever the 'ism' is, for themselves. As Sri Aurobindo (1872–1950) wrote: 'We must begin by accepting nothing on trust from any source whatsoever, by questioning everything and forming our own conclusions'.[24] That was also the message of Socrates and Buddha 2,500 years ago. I'm adding my squeaky voice to that hoary message.

And therefore the way to proceed would be to question *all* my assumptions and *all* my conclusions – if you have not already done so. It is possible that I have been *entirely* wrong! The free man doesn't claim, can never claim, complete knowledge and understanding. Also knock off all the dross and exaggeration you find in this book. Knock off anything that doesn't ring true or make sense to you. I will have achieved my purpose only if the *critical thinking process* behind the conclusions drawn in this book becomes *your own*. It is, of course, my hope that this thinking process will lead you to the *same or similar* conclusions as I have come to. If, after you have turned this book upside down and smacked it hard with a stick, it still manages to survive in one piece, then we can proceed to the next, last, steps of this journey – towards a new journey that you will need to create for yourself.

* * *

Once you have crossed that point, there is no time to look backward for even *one more second*! It is then time to face the future; time to *make* the future. What has happened is history – water under the bridge. Let's forget it. There is absolutely no point in regretting Nehru's misjudgements. We must follow Martin Luther King, Jr.'s counsel: 'Let us not seek to satisfy our thirst for freedom by drinking from the cup of bitterness [...] We must forever conduct our struggle on the high plane of dignity and discipline'.[25] And so with sprightly steps we now turn towards the next journey.

We have many urgent tasks before us. We need to ponder carefully over how each of us can become, or help inspire, 'leaders of ability, vision, and moral character'[26] to represent the citizens of free India. That India desperately needs good political representation is not in doubt. But the problem is it won't happen on its own. On the other hand, merely jumping into politics with brash fervour will not solve any of India's problems, either. There has to be a systematic effort. This is my suggested outline of the systematic effort India needs now to initiate its real freedom movement:

- Let any two believers in freedom come together with the aim of building a Freedom Team of India to an initial size of 1,500 persons. I am happy to coordinate an electronic platform for this if it will help anyone.[27] Using this platform is purely optional – any platform will do.
- The Freedom Team of India (or whatever else it is called) will then need to agree on what the new India will look like and

how its members will deliver the reforms if they were to ever come to power. I'll be pleased if Chapters 2 and 6 inform the answers to some of these questions. But of course, the blueprint would entirely be the work of the Freedom Team.

- After that will come the question of *who*. Once ready, this group of 1,500 should select outstanding leaders from among itself and form a new, ethics- and freedom-based political platform.
- Its leaders and supporters should then go from village to village, explaining the proposed policies to people.
- Finally, about 550 outstanding leaders should contest elections. With the right effort and good luck, a majority of them will hopefully get elected.
- After that it would be a matter of disciplined implementation of the planned reforms.
- It going to be that simple to change India!

Till now I have largely continued with the expositional tone of an Indian citizen because this book was started to support my political efforts of 2004–5 while I was still a citizen. After three failed attempts to establish a platform to reform India's governance, I forfeited my Indian citizenship on 17 November 2005 upon acquiring Australian citizenship. I am now an overseas Indian citizen. I can therefore play only a limited role in India's future unless India agrees to full dual citizenship in the future. However, the task I had started upon is still incomplete. Indeed, it has not even been started.

I have taken you along with me on a short journey, but the much longer journey lies ahead. The ball is in *your* court. You should carefully consider whether you wish to take up the personal challenge to lead India to greatness and the world to the new era of harmony, peace and freedom. If you are willing to give it a go, and keep learning on the way, then I applaud and welcome your initiative and appeal to India to join you in working for true freedom and greatness. I don't often pray, for I don't know if it works, but in this case I wish you Godspeed!

* * *

> The final end of the State consists not in dominating over men, restraining them by fear, subjecting them to the will of others. Rather, it has for its end so to act that its citizens shall in security develop soul and body and make free use of their reason. For the true end of the State is Liberty.
>
> Baruch Spinoza (1632–77)

Appendix 1

Our Accountability

Justice is the end of government. It is the end of society.

James Madison[1]

Freedom becomes relevant only in the presence of more than one thinking, and hence responsible, human being. Responsibility is the key to freedom. Persons or animals that exhibit purely instinctive behaviour cannot be free since they cannot carefully consider and evaluate the options available to them at each step, and choose, after due deliberation and planning, a course of action that they believe is appropriate. If a person with a chemical imbalance in his brain assaults another person, that person may not be acting freely. Similarly, psychiatrically unstable or intellectually challenged people may not be legally liable for their actions and hence cannot be deemed to be free.

The challenge for two or more of such thinking and responsible people cohabiting the universe is for each of them to do what they want to do, while being mindful of the mirror need of others to do what they want to do. The only sustainable way to ensure a reasonable balance among such conflicting demands on freedom is for citizens of a free society to mutually agree to rules for joint living. These rules amount to a 'Nash equilibrium',[2] under which everyone's liberty is balanced either by arbitrary rules of thumb such as traffic rules, or by precise conditions of justice and accountability. This principle is actually very simple and very ancient: 'Do unto others as you would have them do unto you'.

As free people we are required to balance the forces of our physical and emotional energy in our interactions with others to make sure that no one else is made worse off by our actions (or inaction). Nothing requires us to go out of the way to help others. We may, of course, choose to do so, but that is not an obligation on us. All freedom calls for is that we must not ever make others worse off – for that would diminish their life, even if by a tiny amount. This accountability exists whether it is enforced by a nominated third party or not. And yes, when we are called upon to rise and receive the just deserts of our actions, we cannot plead ignorance of the 'law' or of our mutually agreed rules as an excuse.

The exercise of our freedom thus requires us to carefully consider the consequences of our actions on others. At most times our actions are likely to be perceived differently by different observers, and therefore they will have differential impacts or consequences. We are obliged to be aware of these differential impacts, and to take steps to minimize potential misunderstandings arising from our actions. There is a natural limit or check in place, of course. Were we to hurt others, we know that a retributory cycle could be precipitated, for then these others may attempt to diminish our life similarly. So we are naturally careful not to hurt others even if there is no external government to enforce such accountability.

Accountability implicitly includes attribution, which is the recognition or acknowledgement of the ownership of consequences. Attribution is the arrow that unerringly points to the relevant actor. For example, who is it that is responsible for a particular consequence? Who is it that has won a race? Who is it that owns this piece of land or that, or this piece of bread? We have a firm belief that the runner that runs the fastest should be declared its winner. When the deserts of our actions are not attributed precisely, and outcomes are determined by bias or by chance, we have a sense of disquiet; we object to the diminution of justice that it entails. Such simple and obvious things constitute the net import of freedom, which is, in the end, a very trivial and ordinary concept. But nothing is more important than this simple concept.

I am calling this package, namely, the combination of our free choice and its natural accountability, including its matching attribution, the *loop of accountability*. I have also used this phrase in a few places in this book. This concept is best illustrated in the diagram that follows. Further, the Yin-Yang symbol in the beginning of this book can also represent the same concept.

Accountability is the detailed and precise account of our actions. The word 'accounts' is used here in its most generic sense, including:

- whether an action was called for and appropriate, namely, the existence and level of responsibility;
- whether the action was duly carried out, i.e. the level of an action or inaction;
- what were its consequences; and
- to whom did the consequences apply, namely, the attribution and precise debiting or crediting of outcomes.

The keeping and settling of accounts is also known as justice.

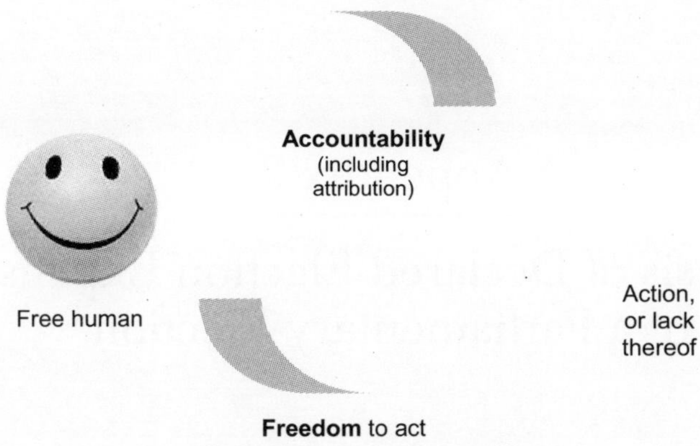

The loop of accountability

Let me illustrate with a very simple example. Let's assume that I walk into a grocery shop and ask for bread from the grocer. The grocer hands me a loaf of bread. I pay the grocer and take the bread. That marks the end of a transaction where the loop of accountability has 'closed'. There is no outstanding 'residue' left.

What has happened here? We observe that, being responsible for myself and my family's sustenance, I have freely, and of my own volition, stepped into the shop that belongs to someone else. I have then chosen to perform two further actions – first, to ask for bread, and, second, to receive the bread. Having done that, I have become instantaneously accountable for these actions. I must therefore necessarily perform the next action, namely, to settle the account and pay for the bread. I therefore pay for the bread. Note that exactly at the moment when I finish handing over the money, the ownership of the bread has changed. The bread as well as what I do with it is now attributed to me. The use of the bread is now in my sole discretion. This attribution applies even though the grocer did not write my name on the bread, nor did I register my ownership of the bread with the government.

This simple transaction illustrates the concept of freedom in its entirety. Our free actions are always accompanied by an expectation that we close the loop of accountability which is immediately and always generated. No residue should remain. This accounting is as precise as a mathematical equality. Indeed, most of our transactions in a free society are seamless, and the loop of accountability is duly closed. We note that if no one ever violated the loop of accountability, we would never need a government. That would be paradise.

Appendix 2

Analysis of Declared Election Expenses of a Parliamentary Election

The table below, relating to the electoral accounts of the 1999 Parliamentary hill constituency of Shillong, is self-explanatory. It relates to the text in the section on accounting of political party funds and election expenditure in Chapter 4. It may be noted that in 1999 the permissible expenditure limit for elections in this constituency was Rs 13 lakhs, not the usual Rs 15 lakhs admissible in larger constituencies at that time.

Name of Candidate	Party	Funds from Party	Funds from other Organization/s	Funds from other Individual	Funds from Candidate	Total Expenses	My Findings
S S Cajee	People's Democratic Movement	3.0	2.0	1.0	3.35	9.35	Part III, IV (I) not filled properly
S D Khongwir	United Democratic Party	0	0	1.38	4.58	5.96	Part IV(IV) filled improperly
P R Kyndiah	Indian National Congress	1.0	–	0.51	3.03	4.54	–
H S Lyngdoh	Hill State People's Democratic Party	N.A.	N.A.	N.A.	N.A.	N.A.	Part III, IV and V improper and unacceptable
K S Lyngdoh	Ajeya Bharat Party	0.34	–	–	0.12	0.46	Part IV (I) not properly filled out
T H Rangad	Bharatiya Janata Party	6.05	0	0.77	0	6.82	Part III not filled out

Name of Candidate	Party	Funds* from Party	Funds* from other Organization/s	Funds* from other Individual	Funds* from Candidate	Total Expenses	My Findings
D Saioo	Independent	–	–	–	–		Returns not filed by 7/11/99 as required in s.78 of R.O.P. Act, 1951
D Dympep	Independent	–	–	–	–		
A Lanong	Independent	–	–	–	–		

*Funds in Rs lakhs.

Notes

Acknowledgements

1. Vivekananda, cited in *Modern India*, NCERT, 1986, p.219.
2. [http://www.indiapolicy.sabhlokcity.com/debate/Notes/hayek_jstor.pdf].
3. PhD in Economics (University of Southern California) and a former member of the Indian Administrative Service (September 1982 – January 2001). If you'd like to know more about me please visit my website [http://www.sanjeev.sabhlokcity.com/], bearing in mind that the material there has evolved over the years, much of it being outdated, and written for a range of different audiences.

Preface

1. 'In large parts of India sectarian interests are fishing in the troubled waters mainly caused by a failed state, when the state cannot deliver the essential services', in Pranab Bardhan's 2003 oration. See Jha, Raghbendra, ed, *The First Ten K R Narayanan Orations: Essays by Eminent Persons on the Rapidly Transforming Indian Economy*, ANU E Press, The Australian National University, 2006. Available for downloading from [http://epress.anu.edu.au/narayanan_citation.htm].
2. For the younger generation who don't know about that movie, I am referring to Amitabh Bacchan.
3. [http://sanjeev.sabhlokcity.com/book1/BFN-Notes.doc].
4. That painting is reproduced on the internet at [http://www.sanjeev.sabhlokcity.com/indira-1975-small.jpg].
5. This (draft) book, *Becoming Rich and Powerful: A Primer for the Citizens of Pakistan, India and Bangladesh*, is available at [http://www.sanjeev.sabhlokcity.com/Bk/index.html].
6. My decision to leave the IAS was taken sometime then, eventuating in January 2001.
7. These writings are available today at [http://www.sanjeev.sabhlokcity.com/vip/].
8. [http://www.indiapolicy.sabhlokcity.com/].
9. My initial comments are available at [http://www.sanjeev.sabhlokcity.com/end-journey.html].

10. [http://www.liberalpartyofindia.sabhlokcity.com/].
11. *Patal*, or the Hindu Hell, is multi-storeyed; it has seven levels.
12. In *The Statesman*, 28 May 1984, cited in Rudolph, Lloyd I, and Rudolph, Susanne Hoeber, *In Pursuit of Lakshmi*, The University of Chicago Press, Chicago, 1987, p.83.
13. In the 2003 oration compiled in Jha, Raghbendra, op. cit.
14. *The Complete Works of Swami Vivekananda*, Vol. 4, Advaita Ashrama, Kolkata, February 1990, p.186.
15. Smith, Adam, *The Wealth of Nations* (1776), University of Chicago Press, Chicago, 1976.
16. I have explained this comment in Box 15 in the *Online Notes* at [http://sanjeev.sabhlokcity.com/book1/BFN-Notes.doc].
17. Our so-called 'mixed' economy had a destructive element that nullified the productive one. People working in areas not under government control, such as farmers, local shopkeepers and rickshaw pullers, worked unbearably hard to produce a little wealth. But then the government, with its slothful plunder, destroyed this little wealth they produced. The end result was a complete standstill in growth. The only saving grace is that the government could not banish the entrepreneurship of hundreds of millions of people merely by imposing its bureaucratic will, and therefore India still had a small, net positive growth rate. It is this entrepreneurship, which refused to be destroyed, that has now re-emerged and is driving India's growth after socialistic shackles have been partially removed.
18. Some more details in the *Online Notes* at [http://sanjeev.sabhlokcity.com/book1/BFN-Notes.doc].
19. Reported in the 9 January 2008 *Indian Express* [http://www.indianexpress.com/story/259361.html].
20. Socialist governments are among various statist forms of government; these are interventionist governments in which the state is elevated to a supreme status.

Chapter 1

1. Fisher, Louis, ed, *The Essential Gandhi*, Vintage Books, New York, 1962, p.196.
2. Although there were periods in British India such as in 1913–28 when 'Indian industrial growth was above world average', in Lal, Deepak, *The Hindu Equilibrium, Volume 1: Cultural Stability and Economic Stagnation*, Clarendon Press, Oxford, 1988.
3. There is an argument that a critical break in growth rates occurred in the 1980s and not in 1991. See Rodrik, Dani, and Subramanian, Arvind, 'From "Hindu Growth" to Productivity Surge: The Mystery of the Indian Growth Transition', IMF Working Paper, 2004. However, its basis has been questioned by T N Srinivasan in his 2004 comments on the Rodrik paper (also available at the IMF web site). I personally consider both the policy changes of the 1980s and 1990s as mere window-dressing in comparison to the spring cleaning or total reform that is needed, and so don't care much to classify either of them as 'reforms'.
4. In 'Understanding India's Reform Trajectory: Past Trends and Future Challenges', *India Review*, October 2004, p.269.

5. Smith, Vincent A, *The Oxford History of India*, Oxford University Press, London, 1958, p.7.
6. The 'reciprocal social and economic arrangements between families of different castes within a village community in India, by which one family exclusively performs certain services for the other, such as ministering to the ritual or providing agricultural labour, in return for pay, protection, and employment security', *Encyclopaedia Britannica Online.*
7. Obviously, some may, with reasonable cause, dispute this assessment. I have formed this judgement largely in comparison with what happened elsewhere in the world in those ancient times. It does appear to me that India was a far more civilized society in comparison with many Western ones of that time.
8. I will discuss, at some length, aspects of these advances in the Indian political philosophy of freedom in a separate volume. This book looks less at history and more into the future.
9. Khare, Harish, 'Restructuring of Values: Princes in 1971 Elections', *Comparative Studies in Society and History*, Vol. 15, No. 4, Cambridge University Press, Cambridge, 1973, pp.405–15.
10. From the Macaulay's Minute of Education, 2 February, 1835. [http://www.columbia.edu/itc/mealac/pritchett/00generallinks/macaulay/txt_minute_education_1835.html].
11. See [http://www.univ-lille1.fr/pfeda/Ngonut/2000/0003g.htm].
12. Fisher, Louis, op. cit.
13. From the *Harijan*, 3 June 1939, p.145 (or *Harijan*, 4 May 1947, p.134). See [http://www.gandhi-manibhavan.org/gandhiphilosophy/philosophy_trusteeship.htm].
14. *Harijan*, 31 March 1946, cited in Swarup, Devendra, ed, *Deendayal Upadhyaya's Integral Humanism*, Deendayal Research Institute, New Delhi, 1992, p.126.
15. *Harijan*, 3 June 1939, p.145.
16. In the chapter 'The Liberal Outlook', in Nehru, Jawaharlal, (1936), *Jawaharlal Nehru, An Autobiography*, Allied Publishers, Mumbai, 1962 edition.
17. Johari, J C, ed, *Voices of Indian Freedom Movement.* Vol. 9, Akshadeep Publishing House, New Delhi, 1993, p. 350.
18. *Ibid.*, p.361.
19. Hause, Malcolm E, 'India under the Impact of Western Political Ideas and Institutions', *The Western Political Quarterly*, Vol. 14, No. 4, University of Utah Press, Salt Lake City, 1961, p.883.
20. In its current avatar at [http://fabians.org.uk/], the Fabian Society provides ideological support to the Labour Party of UK, many of whose policies are, however, firmly grounded in capitalism.
21. E.g. in his 1931 *An Introduction to Politics* (George Allen & Unwin Ltd), Harold Laski says, 'The state […] is the crowning-point of the modern social edifice', p.15.
22. *Ibid.*, p.21.
23. In his *Capitalism and Freedom* (The University of Chicago Press, Chicago, 1982, p.45), Friedman summarizes his studies that show that the Great Depression was a consequence of the centralization and consequent bureaucratic 'acts of commission and omission' of the recently created central bank of USA, the

Federal Reserve, and that in the previous decentralized banking system, such a meltdown was 'highly unlikely' to have taken place.

24. *A Plan For The Economic Development of India (1944–45)*, also called the Bombay Plan, was authored by J R D Tata, G D Birla, Sir Shri Ram, Kasturbhai Lalbhai, A D Shroff, John Mathai, among others. Unfortunately, it affirmed 'that practically every aspect of economic life will have to be rigorously controlled by the Government'. There was little in it to distinguish it from the socialist planning approach adopted later by Nehru.
25. Political efforts in India to promote freedom have rarely been supported by big business. J R D Tata was an exception in his support for Swatantra Party, but he also contributed heavily to Nehru's Congress.
26. In a book entitled, *Soviet Russia: Some Random Sketches and Impressions* (1929), written after a visit to Stalin's Russia, Nehru showed how he was enchanted by Russia. Nehru wrote, 'No one can deny the fascination of this strange Eurasian country of the hammer and sickle, where workers and peasants sit on the thrones of the mighty and upset the best-laid schemes of mice and men', and 'Nothing is perhaps more confusing to the student of Russia than the conflicting reports that come of the treatment of prisoners [...] We are told of the Red Terror and ghastly and horrible details are provided for our consumption [...] Our own visit to the chief prison in Moscow created a most favourable impression on our minds'.
27. Cited in Hangen, Welles, *After Nehru, Who?* Rupert Hart-Davis, London, 1963, p.216.
28. Cited in Prabhu, R K, *An Anthology of Modern Indian Eloquence*, Bharatiya Vidya Bhavan, Mumbai, 1965, p.149.
29. Even today, you can be an ex-Prime Minister but if you are no longer in power, beware the 'humble' Patwari! The Deputy Commissioners' (DCs') powers remain all-pervasive, particularly if a young DC is friendly with the CM. MLAs and MPs from villages, particularly from minor parties and those in the opposition, approach the smartly dressed young DC like supplicants.
30. Pasricha, H R, *The Swatantra Party – Victory in Defeat*, The Rajaji Foundation, Mumbai, 2002.
31. Rudolph, Lloyd I, and Rudolph, Susanne Hoeber, *In Pursuit of Lakshmi*, The University of Chicago Press, Chicago, 1987, p.26.
32. Returns on investment were very significantly below that of the private sector. The ratio of after-tax profit to capital employed in non-oil public sector firms was only 0.7 per cent in comparison to the private sector return of 4.6 per cent (Source: *Ibid.*, p.24). Public funds were being dumped into the drain at an alarming rate! As Jagdish Bhagwati pointed out in his 1996 oration for the annual K R Narayanan lecture, 'the [...] policy adopted in the 1950s [...] spawned inefficient public sector enterprises [...] which [...] crippled the efficiency of the private sector [...] since the public sector enterprises supplied, or rather failed to adequately and efficiently supply, infrastructure inputs such as electricity and transportation over which they were granted monopoly of production'.
33. E.g. the 1948 Jeep scandal involving V K Krishna Menon. The 1951 Report on Public Administration (Planning Commission) said: 'quite a few of Nehru's ministers were corrupt and this was common knowledge'. The Santhanam

Committee Report of 1964 said: 'There is widespread impression that failure of integrity is not uncommon among ministers and that some ministers, who have held office during the last sixteen years have enriched themselves illegitimately, obtained good jobs for their sons and relations through nepotism and have reaped other advantages inconsistent with any notion of purity in public life'.

34. While I was part of the civil service I have seen this happen each time with new governments, and can recount at least a few true stories involving new ministers – indeed new chief ministers.
35. Where a *seer* (approximately a kilo) of *kaju* (cashew) costs one *taka* (one rupee), and so does one *seer* of *bhaja* (a rude mix of seeds and nuts).
36. According to Hindu mythology there are four cyclical ages, the *Krita Yuga*, the *Treta Yuga*, the *Dwapara Yuga* and the *Kali Yuga* (the age of evil). Some Hindus believe we are in the *Kali Yuga* now.
37. During my last few years as a government official, I had started avoiding government offices, partly because of the abominable filth and smells but more so because of the Kafkaesque process of negotiating the security maze into colleagues' offices.
38. The inverse relationship between expectations of economic growth and demand for children was explored and confirmed in my PhD research. A copy of my dissertation is available at [http://www.sanjeev.sabhlokcity.com/almaak/Dissertation/sabhlok-disstn-1999-web.pdf].
39. In 'Why Swatantra' see [http://www.liberalpartyofindia.sabhlokcity.com/writers/rajaji1.html].
40. Austin, Granville, *Working in a Democratic Constitution: A History of the Indian Experience*, Oxford University Press, Delhi, 1999, (2003 paperback edition), p.207.
41. For an account of its denouement, see Pasricha, H R, *The Swatantra Party – Victory in Defeat*, The Rajaji Foundation, Mumbai, 2002.
42. The specious arguments given by MPs in response to Sharad Joshi's attempt to implement this through his private members' Bill, *The Representation of the People (Amendment) Bill*, 2004, are available at [http://rajyasabha.nic.in/rsdebate/synopsis/206/s09122005.htm].
43. In his essay on 'The Concept of Liberalism and its Relevance for India', *Freedom and Dissent*, Democratic Research Service, Mumbai, 1985.

Chapter 2

1. Fisher, Louis, ed, *The Essential Gandhi*, Vintage Books, New York, 1962, p.221.
2. See the annual Index of Economic Freedom at [http://www.heritage.org/research/features/index/index.cfm].
3. [http://sanjeev.sabhlokcity.com/book1/BFN-Notes.doc].
4. [http://www.nriol.com/content/articles/article62.asp].
5. [http://www.indiatoday.com.au/coming_to_oz.php].
6. Prathap, Gangan, 'A Soft Mathematical Model for Brain Drain', *Current Science*, Vol. 85, No. 5, 2003, pp.593–6.
7. Kapur, Devesh, 'Ideas and Economic Reforms in India: The Role of International Migration and the Indian Diaspora', *India Review*, Vol. 3, No. 4, 2004, p.367.

8. A fringe of few home-grown criminals with pseudo-political agendas will probably always remain, e.g. even the relatively free USA couldn't avoid having its Oklahoma bomber.
9. This comment is perhaps no longer as true as it was till mid-2007, given the abortive UK suicide bomb attempt by an Indian.
10. [http://studyinaustralia.gov.au/Sia/en/WhyAustralia/NobelPrizes.htm].
11. 'Asia's Great Science Experiment', *Time*, 23 October 2006.
12. It is conceivable that some societies that are not free may also do relatively well on this variable while relatively more free ones may not do as well.
13. [http://sanjeev.sabhlokcity.com/book1/BFN-Notes.doc].
14. I must admit that there is a potential problem with this hypothesis, since China has had very low levels of freedom, still has a high average IQ but had very low levels of income till recently. There are clearly complex interrelationships between freedom, national income and IQ. I suspect the discriminatory Indian caste system explains most of the lower average Indian IQ.
15. Lynn, Richard, 'Race Differences in Intelligence: A Global Perspective', *Mankind Quarterly*, Vol. 31, Issue 3, Spring 1991.
16. There are many unresolved issues in relation to freedom of expression and excessive censorship by government which banned Salman Rushdie's *Satanic Verses*. There is also excessive self-censorship in our publishing industry which led to D N Jha publishing his *Myth of the Holy Cow* outside India. And then we have violent social boycotts that forced Deepa Mehta to produce *Water* not in India where its story is located, but in Sri Lanka.
17. In a written conversation on a day of silence in 1947 when he communicated through writing on slips of paper; cited in Fisher, Louis, op. cit., p.306.
18. Marketing and advertising is not coercion, no matter how 'distasteful' it may be. Nor do the so-called 'hard sell' tactics of a second hand car dealer or a 'cold call' from people who knock on our door, or ring our telephone, amount to coercion, for we can always choose our decisions.
19. E.g. when I work as a bureaucrat, hired on behalf of elected political representatives of India, I am renting my time, policy knowledge and skills to the government of the day. If I don't like what the government pays me, or the way it works, or the way it treats me, I can rent my services elsewhere, say to an Australian State Government. Of course, this particular instance is quite an extreme example, i.e. where labour moves across countries. But the voluntary nature of the employee relationship is to be clearly noted. And some labour markets are genuinely global today, for instance, the market for academic scholars. The best Indians professors always get picked up to teach in the USA, UK, or Australia. Indeed, about 80 per cent of our best economists now work abroad.
20. In almost all cases where a transaction is based on exchange of some service in lieu of money, we would be willing to pay a little bit more than what we usually end up paying. That extra bit that we would have paid but did not have to pay is the 'consumer surplus' of economics. The richer we get the greater the consumer surplus we receive, as we are asked to pay a 'market price' which is usually much less than what we would have been willing to pay.
21. This entire argument is called Pareto optimality.
22. The Edgeworth box, commonly found in elementary books of economics, is a beautiful illustration of this logical analysis.

23. In answering this question I would hark back to fundamentals of the theory of freedom – is there sufficient factual evidence that restrictions placed on people's freedom will, on balance, preserve or enhance life? Does the product hurt, poison, maim, or kill people? Is the restriction based on an individual's personal 'sense of morality' which is not related to its direct impacts on life?
24. In his *Omnipotent Government: The Rise of the Total State and Total War*, Yale University Press, New Haven, CT, 1944. Copy available at [http://www.mises.org/etexts/mises/og.asp].
25. Daniel B Klein shows how 'A habit of deceit is a mark of bad character, and bad character has a way of revealing itself no matter how cunning the individual. Deceit is both bad karma and bad business. I am inclined to agree with Montesquieu, Adam Smith, and Friedrich Hayek that commerce elevates manners and probity', in Klein's 'Trust for Hire: Voluntary Remedies for Quality and Safety', *Reputation: Studies in the Voluntary Elicitation of Good Conduct*, University of Michigan Press, Ann Arbor, 1997, pp.97–133. Information on an individual's character is spread through a range of modes of communication including gossip, newspapers and electronic media including chat groups and blogs on the internet, legal case law, or even information that we pay for such as the magazine *Consumer Reports* in the USA.
26. Economists generally assume that we all possess a mild version of this 'deceptiveness' or 'cleverness' 'opportunism'. They assume that we may short-circuit strictly ethical behaviour if there is no risk of detection. I cannot say that I have never pirated software, for example, or never used my official work hours for some personal business. The vast majority of us are not saints, but equally we're not rascals. We are what is called 'human'.
27. E.g. Standards Australia is a company limited by guarantee, with 72 members representing a range of industry groups, unions, professional associations and others.
28. Such as the obligation of the mine owner to spend time and resources to fully understand the risks to the safety of employees, and to exhaust all current knowledge on ways to prevent injury.
29. Traffic safety is not a market-related regulation generally, being a 'rule of thumb' of convenience, but there are elements in motor safety, such as seat belts, that may legitimately 'impinge' on our freedom (or more broadly, on markets) in the interest of safety.
30. I am compiling the science behind global warming at [http://www.sanjeev.sabhlokcity.com/co2/] for my personal knowledge.
31. In the *Journal of Law and Economics*, October 1960. Copy available at [http://www.sfu.ca/~allen/CoaseJLE1960.pdf].
32. [http://www.sanjeev.sabhlokcity.com/book1/BFN-Notes.doc].
33. I have put forth more arguments at [http://sabhlok.blogspot.com/2007_01_01_archive.html]. I will also discuss this issue in more detail in my forthcoming book on the history of freedom.
34. Peter Bauer's studies confirm that foreign aid exacerbates poverty.
35. In an article entitled, 'A Rich Harvest and No Handouts', John Dyson shows in the *Reader's Digest* of January 2008 how eliminating subsidies in New Zealand has made their farmers so much more productive and richer.

36. This area of economic study is well researched and documented with George Stigler, in 1971, leading the way. In his paper, 'The Theory of Economic Regulation', Stigler found that 'as a rule, regulation is acquired by the industry and is designed and operated primarily for its benefit'.
37. [http://sanjeev.sabhlokcity.com/book1/BFN-Notes.doc].
38. Governments like to interfere in many subtle ways; e.g. there was a rule in my time that required government officers to use Indian Airlines for official journeys, even as competition was officially allowed to sprout in the Indian market. Such rules clearly violate freedom and fail to provide a level-playing field for business.
39. For those not familiar with these terms, they are among the many mechanical ways of measuring the levels of inequality in a society.
40. John Ruskin, *Unto This Last*, 1862. Internet edition: [http://socserv.mcmaster.ca/econ/ugcm/3ll3/ruskin/ruskin].
41. On this specific matter of progressive taxes, I differ from Bastiat, as I see progressive taxes (as opposed to flat tax) as being compatible with bringing about equality of opportunity and the elimination of poverty.
42. Bastiat, Frédéric (1850), *The Law*, Liberty Institute, Delhi, 1998, p.41.
43. It is not merely India that has a fascination for creating enormous policy complexity based on equity concerns, reducing the economic potential of the society. An example of excessive equity-based policies in Australia can be found at [http://www.healthtranslations.vic.gov.au/] (search for 'welfare benefits and services').
44. This is to the best of my knowledge, being fully aware of other similar projects running at that time; e.g. the records database of completed surveys, the Computerized Rural Information System Project (CRISP).
45. See the web version of the book I wrote for my DRDA on that project at [http://www.sanjeev.sabhlokcity.com/Bk-daisy/Daisy.doc].
46. See the paper at [http://www.indiapolicy.sabhlokcity.com/debate/Notes/NIT-paper.PDF].
47. Smith, Adam, *The Wealth of Nations* (1776), University of Chicago Press, Chicago, 1976, p.9.
48. Published in the *American Economic Review*, Vol. 35, No. 4, September 1945. Freely available on the internet.
49. A representation of our preference to shift our purchases from an existing good to another.
50. [http://sanjeev.sabhlokcity.com/book1/BFN-Notes.doc].
51. That our politicians (and even the police) are often implicated in mob violence is by now well documented. See data from Judicial Commission reports and case studies of numerous communal riots distributed to IAS officers at LBS National Academy, at [http://www.indiapolicy.sabhlokcity.com/communal/lbs-comm-notes.doc], and various publications by Madhu Kishwar cited at [http://www.indiapolicy.sabhlokcity.com/communal/riots.html].
52. [http://sanjeev.sabhlokcity.com/book1/BFN-Notes.doc].
53. Marx, Karl and Engels, Frederick (1848; English edition of 1888, edited by Friedrich Engels; internet edition), *Manifesto of the Communist Party* [http://www.fullbooks.com/The-Communist-Manifesto.html].
54. *Ibid.*

55. Cameron, Rondo, *A Concise Economic History of the World*, Oxford University Press, New York, 1993, pp.187–9.
56. Cited in Hangen's book, *After Nehru, Who?*, Rupert Hart-Davis, London, 1963, p.43.
57. Madsen, Richard, Review of David E Apter and Tony Saich's book, *Revolutionary Discourse in Mao's Republic, Contemporary Sociology*, Vol. 25 No. 2, American Sociological Association, Washington DC, 1996, p.187.

Chapter 3

1. Fisher, Louis, ed, *The Essential Gandhi*, Vintage Books, New York, 1962, p.196.
2. The first constitutional amendment which implemented this change is discussed later in this chapter.
3. For a competent exposition of the working of our Constitution, albeit with a bias towards welfare socialism, see Austin, Granville, (1999), *Working in a Democratic Constitution: A History of the Indian Experience*, Oxford University Press, Delhi, 2003 paperback edition.
4. On the web at [http://parliamentofindia.nic.in/ls/debates/debates.htm].
5. This short Preamble to the US Constitution is said to have been written by Gouverneur Morris.
6. The Constituent Assembly had become the provisional Parliament until the General Elections of 1951–2, leading to the first Parliament of April 1952.
7. Nuclear plants and arms factories are perfectly capable of being run as private businesses, e.g. as in the USA.
8. This amendment was motivated by Nehru's desire that government should exclusively operate a bus business in UP.
9. See the 'statement of objects and reasons' signed by Nehru, at [http://indiacode.nic.in/coiweb/amend/amend1.htm].
10. In Singh, V B, ed, *Nehru on Socialism*, Government of India, Ministry of Information and Broadcasting, Publications Division, Delhi, 1977, pp.56–7, cited in Roy, Subroto, *Pricing, Planning and Politics*, The Institute of Economic Affairs, London, 1984, p.35.
11. Cited in a review by Arthur M Schlesinger, Jr of *Harold Laski: A Life on the Left* by Isaac Kramnick and Barry Sheerman in *Washington Monthly*, November 1993.
12. Laski, Harold J, (1960), *A Grammar of Politics*, cited in Austin, Granville, (1999), *Working in a Democratic Constitution: A History of the Indian Experience*, Oxford University Press, Delhi, 2003 paperback edition. Footnote at p.77.
13. –, *An Introduction to Politics*, Unwin Brothers, London, 1931, p.15.
14. In his 1961 inaugural address as President.
15. Ray's views cited in Austin, Granville, op. cit., p. 244.
16. *Ibid.*, p.205.
17. *Ibid.*, p.254.
18. *Ibid.*, p.253.
19. [http://indiacode.nic.in/coiweb/amend/amend44.htm].
20. Cited in Austin, Granville, op. cit., p.108.

21. Mitra, Subrata K, and Fischer, Alexander, 'Sacred Laws and the Secular State: An Analytical Narrative of the Controversy over Personal Laws in India', *India Review*, Vol. 1, No. 3, July 2002, pp.99–130.
22. Sikand, Yoginder, 'Hindutva and the Dalit-Bahujans: Dangerous Portents', 2004, [http://www.countercurrents.org/comm-sikand230204.htm].
23. [http://sanjeev.sabhlokcity.com/book1/BFN-Notes.doc].
24. The fact that a Muslim Women (Protection of Rights on Divorce) Act, 1986, had to be separately promulgated makes it clear that by interfering in one religious law – in this case Hindu law – the Pandora's Box of all religious laws gets opened up, each creating needless controversy. The good thing is that, now, given this 1986 Act, and the Hindu laws of the1950s, it should be possible for a minimum standard to be enacted for divorce (for instance), and the religious laws repealed.
25. These comprise the Hindu Marriage Act 1955, Hindu Succession Act 1956, Hindu Minority & Guardianship Act 1956, Hindu Adoptions & Maintenance Act 1956, Hindu Disposition of Property Act 1916, and perhaps the Dowry Prohibition Act 1961. These have a long history with previous Acts that interpreted various elements of Hinduism, e.g. Hindu Widows' Remarriage Act 1856, the prohibition on polygamy among Hindus, Parsis and Christians (not Muslims) in the Indian Penal Code 1860, Native Converts Marriage Dissolution Act 1866, the Brahmo Samaj Marriage Act 1872, the Child Marriage Act 1929, the Anand Marriage Act 1909 and the Arya Marriage Validation Act 1937, among others.
26. See [http://www.etirupati.com/services.htm].
27. E.g. see [http://www.bjp.org/manifes/chap10.htm].
28. Nehru, cited in Austin, Granville, op. cit., p.654.
29. One of the leaders of the BJP, K R Malkani, wrote, 'the BJP had already raised the Ayodhya issue. And it had done so early in 1989, not on the basis of any electoral calculation, but on ideological conviction. Historic wrongs had to be righted, however, symbolically' ('BJP HISTORY: It's Birth and Early Growth', at [http://www.bjp.org/history/history.html]). RSS said in the *Organiser* of 14 January 1990 that it 'was not a case about the title of a place but of undoing a historical wrong and for that matter no court could decide it'.
30. When the demonstrators had pulled down the outer wall of the mosque around 1:30 pm, one could hear the frenzied slogans of Uma Bharati, another Hindutva leader on the stage: '*Aur ek dhakka do.* Babri Masjid *thod do. Aur jor. Aur jor!*' (One more hard push. Break the Babri Masjid. Harder. Harder!) (*The Week*, 20 December 1992, p.42). See also Mark Tully's account at [http://news.bbc.co.uk/2/hi/south_asia/2528025.stm].
31. Nehru, cited in Austin, Granville, op. cit., p.655.
32. In a written conversation with some socialists on a day of silence in 1947 when he communicated through writing on slips of paper; cited in Fisher, Louis, op. cit., p.306.
33. I have nothing against capital punishment being awarded in deserving cases. Mercy is never a virtue when innocent lives have been taken away brutally; it amounts to cowardice. Accountability is not driven by mercy – which is purely a matter for God to decide – but by individual justice.

34. Technically speaking, Nehru did not directly run the state administrations, which were under the State Governments. It was mostly Congress Governments that he was able to influence directly. But even non-Congress State Governments could easily be influenced in many ways by the powerful Centre.
35. The pitiable condition of police stations, judicial courts, revenue offices and that of 'lower' staff who are responsible for crucial functions has meant that corruption has perhaps become the sole lingua franca of the police and the revenue systems. Anyone with a bit of money can almost readily buy freedom, even after murder.
36. Cited in Austin, Granville, op. cit., p.245.
37. Fisher, Louis, op. cit., p.204.
38. Article entitled 'A Rich Harvest and No Handouts', by John Dyson, *Reader's Digest* of January 2008.
39. This is a paraphrase of the objective of the Victorian Government's Equal Opportunity Act.
40. Note: I use the noun 'transition' as a verb consciously here and in a few other places in this book even though it may not represent the most chaste English.
41. [http://sanjeev.sabhlokcity.com/book1/BFN-Notes.doc].

Chapter 4

1. In a campaign speech at Wittenberg College, Springfield, Ohio, 17 October 1960.
2. [http://www.jimcollins.com/lab/level5/index.html].
3. In my extrapolation, negative levels of leadership are possible with deteriorating ethical standards.
4. [http://www.indiapolicy.sabhlokcity.com/debate/notes.html].
5. Using an estimated GDP of about $1,040 billion in 2008 and an exchange rate of about Rs 40 to the dollar.
6. See Appendix 4 in the *Online Notes* for an analysis.
7. Present value is a convenient method to value future costs or incomes (cash flows) as an equivalent value today. Future cash flows are 'discounted' by a term called the discount rate, which, in the calculation shown, is the theta (θ).
8. A low discount rate is assumed, being a 'real' discount rate, since inflation is not factored into the cash flows. This is for simplicity.
9. Source spreadsheet: [http://www.sanjeev.sabhlokcity.com/book1/chapter4-calculations.xls].
10. I have the option, as an overseas Indian citizen, of reverting to Indian citizenship after one year of living in India. I'd like to get full dual citizenship before I think of contesting elections, given that my superannuation payments, potential age pension and medical benefits – being my only means of survival in old age – are payable only if I continue in Australia, the IAS having given me absolutely no savings or pension after nearly two decades.
11. Kumar, Arun, *The Black Economy in India*, Penguin India, 1999, pp.272–82, 296–8.
12. *Ibid.*, p.272.
13. Rule 88 of the Conduct of Election Rules, 1961, states: 'Inspection of account and the obtaining of copies thereof. – Any person shall on payment of a fee of

one rupee be entitled to inspect any such account and on payment of such fee as may be fixed by the Election Commission in his behalf be entitled to obtain attested copies of such account or of any part thereof'.

14. Under s.78 of the Representation of People Act, 'Every contesting candidate at an election shall, within thirty days from the date of election of the returned candidate or, if there are more than one returned candidate at the election and the dates of their election are different, the later of those two dates, lodge with the district election officer an account of his election expenses which shall be a true copy of the account kept by him or by his election agent under section 77'.
15. *Hindustan Times*, 1 May 2008; [http://www.hindustantimes.com/storypage/storypage.aspx?id=c588cb0c-1450-43a8-8a3c-72f1c0972e8c&&Headline=Party+funds+details+now+available].
16. See the original paper I circulated at [http://www.indiapolicy.sabhlokcity.com/debate/Notes/pol-funding.doc].
17. See [http://www.aec.gov.au/Parties_and_Representatives/Political_Disclosures/Current_Funding_Rate.htm] and [http://theage.com.au/articles/2004/11/02/1099362144561.html?from=storylhs].
18. It is assumed as before that Mr Harishchandra expects to poll one vote more than one-sixth of the votes polled, and therefore will not forfeit the security deposit.

Chapter 5

1. Speech in Chicago, Illinois, 29 September 1952.
2. In his 2003 oration – see Jha, Raghbendra, ed, *The First Ten K R Narayanan Orations: Essays by Eminent Persons on the Rapidly Transforming Indian Economy*, ANU E Press, The Australian National University, 2006. Available for downloading from [http://epress.anu.edu.au/narayanan_citation.htm].
3. [http://sanjeev.sabhlokcity.com/book1/BFN-Notes.doc].
4. [http://www.aph.gov.au/Senate/general/constitution/constit.pdf].
5. John Halligan (University of Canberra) in 'The Australian Civil Service System', a paper prepared for presentation at Civil Service Systems in Comparative Perspective, School of Public and Environmental Affairs, Indiana University, 5–8 April 1997. See [http://www.indiana.edu/~csrc/hallig2.html]. This paper forms part of Tummala, Krishna K, *Comparative Bureaucratic Systems*, Lexington Books, Lanham, MD, 2003, and also in Halligan, John, ed, *Civil Service Systems in Anglo-American Countries*, Edward Elgar Publishing, London, 2004.
6. Public Service and Merit Protection Commission, *Serving the Nation: 100 Years of Public Service*, Commonwealth of Australia, Canberra, 2001, p.175.
7. As Charles Darwin noted, 'Although a high standard of morality gives but a slight or no advantage to each individual man and his children over the other men of the same tribe [...] an advancement in the standard of morality will certainly give an immense advantage to one tribe over another' – in *The Descent of Man*, published in 1871.
8. See [http://www.sanjeev.sabhlokcity.com/book1/appointment-comparison.doc] (1.5 MB).

9. Halligan, 1997, op. cit.
10. Civil servants who were recruited before compulsory superannuation was implemented were eligible for pensions but these have largely been transitioned to the new scheme and are expected to provide for their old-age themselves.
11. E.g. see the Victorian graduate recruitment scheme at [http://www.graduates.vic.gov.au/].
12. Halligan. 1997, op. cit.
13. *Ibid.*
14. [http://www.sanjeev.sabhlokcity.com/book1/BFN-Notes.doc].
15. See [http://www.vpscin.org/].
16. Very briefly, I did get the State Library's books repaired (most were falling apart) and tried to introduce a bar-coding system for books and membership cards. This system could also be used to prevent mis-filing of books on shelves and prevent the ongoing disappearance of books from the library. On the IT front, I managed to persuade the Government of India to spend Rs 50 lakhs on the Meghalaya Secretariat but before any of this could come to fruition, a senior bureaucrat was irked by my questioning an existing, unproductive effort and I was relieved of my role. You can't ask questions to politically well-connected and potentially corrupt seniors in India.
17. Available for download from [http://www.legislation.vic.gov.au/].
18. Halligan, 1997, op. cit.
19. [http://sanjeev.sabhlokcity.com/book1/BFN-Notes.doc].
20. The TV serial, 'Who wants to be a millionaire?'
21. R K Mishra in 'National Civil Service System in India: A Critical View', Paper prepared for presentation at Civil Service Systems in Comparative Perspective, School of Public and Environmental Affairs, Indiana University, Bloomington, Indiana, 5–8 April 1997. This paper now forms part of Burns, John P and Bowornwathana, Bidhya, eds, *Civil Service Systems in Asia*, Edward Elgar Publishing Inc., Cheltenham, UK, 2001.
22. [http://timesofindia.indiatimes.com/Editorial/Reform_the_bureaucracy/articleshow/2242779.cms].
23. See also a term paper I wrote some years ago during my studies at the University of Southern California, copy at [http://www.indiapolicy.sabhlokcity.com/debate/Notes/term537.PDF].
24. Well why did I go to Assam? I changed cadre from Haryana in 1984 after my marriage to a colleague from Assam, because I felt I would be more useful to the people in Assam which was economically more backward, than in Haryana which was much more advanced. It would also give me an opportunity to learn more about my wife's state and her language. Plus, I found the Assam countryside extremely beautiful.
25. Srivastava, C P, *Corruption: India's Enemy Within*, MacMillan, Delhi, 2001, p.121.
26. Huque, Ahmed Shafiqul, *Asian Journal of Public Administration*, Vol. 16, No. 2, 1994, pp.249–59.

Chapter 6

1. Trump, Donald J, and Zanker, Bill, *Think BIG and Kick Ass in Business and Life*, HarperCollins, New York, 2007.
2. I had outlined the 1970s state of knowledge on this subject in an article, 'Who is a Superior Person?' published by the *Maharashtra Herald* on 21 March 1982. The fundamentals haven't changed even with modern leadership theory.
3. Indian politics can be very frightening. My encounter with 'baby' politics was in a contest with a Congress-I supported candidate for the position of secretary to the student council of DAV College, Jullundur, in 1978–9. A well-known gangster called Jarnail Singh, who had reputedly murdered a few people, met me in a dhaba (a country restaurant) near the college and asked me to withdraw (a school friend of mine, who later joined the IAS a couple of years after me, was a middleman for this intimidation, and can vouch for this). I chose not to withdraw. My supporters also created a defence strategy. In the end, for various reasons including lavish parties thrown by the Congress-I supported candidate to the small group of students entitled to vote in the restricted elections, I lost.
4. Collins, Jim, *Good to Great*, Harper Business, New York, 2001.
5. If interested, please join the Google group called Freedom Team of India I have started, at [http://www.freedom.sabhlokcity.com/].
6. [http://sanjeev.sabhlokcity.com/book1/BFN-Notes.doc].
7. GDP = Gross Domestic Product. It represents the total value of production in a country.
8. Citizens of a few countries will be ineligible due to national security concerns.
9. [http://www.sanjeev.sabhlokcity.com/book1/BFN-Notes.doc].
10. These principles will be revised and re-designed in the form of a checklist or guide before being used for the action strategic plans. The body of literature that will be used for such a checklist includes *The Victorian Guide to Regulation* available at [http://www.vcec.vic.gov.au/].
11. [http://www.sanjeev.sabhlokcity.com/book1/BFN-Notes.doc].
12. Lutyens's Delhi comes under the New Delhi Municipal Corporation, the cantonment under the Delhi Cantonment Board and the rest of Delhi – a mind-bogglingly large area, under the Municipal Corporation of Delhi. This is extreme centralization, which is incompatible with freedom. Freedom requires people to be free to mould their local environment as they please, subject to their joint accountability.
13. [http://www.sanjeev.sabhlokcity.com/book1/BFN-Notes.doc].
14. See my paper at [http://www.indiapolicy.sabhlokcity.com/debate/Notes/NIT-paper.PDF].
15. [http://www.sanjeev.sabhlokcity.com/book1/BFN-Notes.doc].
16. Where the land (as in many villages) has been donated by the community to the school, the proceeds of the sale relating to land will revert back to the local community.
17. If there are no buyers for schools in particularly remote areas, the existing arrangements will continue for another year, when a similar sale is attempted again.
18. Such as the iris of the eye, thumb/finger prints; ideally, a DNA record.

19. I refer to the example of Assam which has been swamped by well over a million illegal immigrants from Bangladesh. These immigrants usually obtain fake school certificates which link the illegal migrant to a pre-1964 migrant who was legalized by the Assam accord. The genuineness of these school certificates cannot be verified without a biological-based database.
20. [http://sanjeev.sabhlokcity.com/book1/BFN-Notes.doc].
21. [http://www.sanjeev.sabhlokcity.com/book1/BFN-Notes.doc].
22. See *Online Notes* at [http://sanjeev.sabhlokcity.com/book1/BFN-Notes.doc].
23. *Time*, 31 December 2007 – 7 January 2008, p.31.
24. Published posthumously, written c.1912. See [http://sabda.sriaurobindoashram.org/catalog/show.php?id=eNews506].
25. In his 'I Have a Dream' speech.
26. Fears, J Rufus, *Lectures on History of Freedom*, The Teaching Company. Cited at [http://www.teach12.com/ttcx/coursedesclong2.aspx?cid=480&id=480].
27. The Freedom Team of India group at [http://www.freedom.sabhlokcity.com/].

Appendix 1

1. In *The Federalist*, 6 February 1788.
2. This is a well-understood concept in economics so the reader can refer to standard text books on what this means; I'll discuss this in more detail in the second volume I'm engaged in writing at present.

Index